BUILDING EQUALITY AND OPPORTUNITY THROUGH SOCIAL GUARANTEES

NEW FRONTIERS OF SOCIAL POLICY

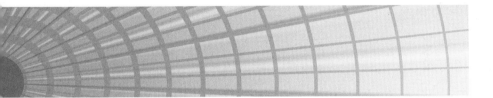

Building Equality and Opportunity through Social Guarantees

New Approaches to Public Policy and the Realization of Rights

Estanislao Gacitúa-Marió, Andrew Norton, and Sophia V. Georgieva, Editors

THE WORLD BANK
Washington, DC

ISBN: 978-0-8213-7883-0
eISBN: 978-0-8213-7963-9
DOI: 10.1596/978-0-8213-7883-0

Cover photo: © Edwin Huffman / World Bank Photo Library

Cover design: Naylor Design, Washington, DC

Library of Congress Cataloging-in-Publication Data
Building equality and opportunity through social guarantees: new approaches to public policy and the realization of rights / Estanislao Gacitúa-Marió, Andrew Norton, and Sophia V. Georgieva, editors.
    p. cm. — (New frontiers of social policy)
Includes bibliographical references and index.
ISBN 978-0-8213-7883-0 (pbk.)—ISBN 978-0-8213-7963-9 (electronic)
    1. Social policy. 2. Globalization—Social aspects. I. Gacitúa-Marió, Estanislao. II. Norton, Andrew, 1965- III. Georgieva, Sophia V.
HN18.3B85 2009
320.609172'4—dc22

                                                                    2009019925

NEW FRONTIERS OF SOCIAL POLICY

In many developing countries, the mixed record of state effectiveness, market imperfections, and persistent structural inequities has undermined the effectiveness of social policy. To overcome these constraints, social policy needs to move beyond conventional social service approaches toward development's goals of equitable opportunity and social justice. This series has been created to promote debate among the development community, policy makers, and academia, and to broaden understanding of social policy challenges in developing country contexts.

The books in the series are linked to the World Bank's Social Development Strategy. The strategy is aimed at empowering people by transforming institutions to make them more inclusive, responsive, and accountable. This involves the transformation of subjects and beneficiaries into citizens with rights and responsibilities. Themes in this series will include equity and development, assets and livelihoods, and citizenship and rights-based social policy, as well as the social dimensions of infrastructure and climate change.

Titles in the series:

- *Assets, Livelihoods, and Social Policy*
- *Building Equality and Opportunity through Social Guarantees: New Approaches to Public Policy and the Realization of Rights*
- *Inclusive States: Social Policy and Structural Inequalities*
- *Institutional Pathways to Equity: Addressing Inequality Traps*

Anis A. Dani
Series Editor
Adviser, Social Policy

CONTENTS

PART II. IMPLEMENTING SOCIAL POLICIES WITH A RIGHTS-BASED FOCUS: EXAMPLES FROM THE CARIBBEAN, LATIN AMERICA, AND SOUTH AFRICA

BOXES

This volume is the product of collaboration between the World Bank and a range of institutions—including the Organization of American States and the Chilean Foundation for Overcoming Poverty—who are cosponsors of the work presented here. Although this is not the place for detailed acknowledgment of all the people who have contributed, I would like to begin this foreword by stressing the collaborative character of this work and thanking our primary partners.

The book showcases an innovative approach to social policy that we believe can act to transform the capacity of states to implement policies to enhance equality of opportunity among citizens. The approach is built around the framework of social guarantees and emphasizes multiple dimensions in the delivery of services and the realization of rights. The social guarantees approach converts abstract rights into defined standards that can be used as a framework for making public policy accountable to citizens. It emphasizes that effective realization of social rights requires attention not just to dimensions of access, but also to elements of quality, financial protection, and the availability of mechanisms of redress. Social guarantees strengthen citizenship through an emphasis on the policy mechanisms and democratic processes needed to define and support such standards. Rigorous analysis of available public resources and of institutions, programmatic approaches, and legal frameworks is essential to underpin the provision of social guarantees and to ensure that the set standards can be delivered to all.

The volume examines both the *what* and the *how* questions with regard to improving service delivery—in other words, the politics for achieving policy change to the benefit of poor people. The experience of implementing health sector reforms with explicit guarantees in Chile is used to demonstrate the strong potential of a social guarantees policy framework to generate support across a wide spectrum of political and social groups. In a series of case studies, the volume demonstrates that the social guarantees approach can be applied across a range of other sectors, including housing and social protection. Most of the case studies are drawn from the Latin America and the Caribbean region. The case of South Africa has been included to illustrate novel ways through which the South African state has advanced its constitutionally mandated commitment to realize the right to housing.

In short, we present this material to suggest to policy communities a new and practical approach to promoting improved services, equality of opportunity, and citizens' rights through social policy. The social guarantees approach stimulates a clearer and stronger social contract between citizens and the state. In the long run, therefore, a more comprehensive approach to social policy—such as that advocated by the social guarantees framework—also may act to strengthen democratic governance.

José Miguel Insulza
Secretary General
Organization of American States

Estanislao Gacitúa-Marió is lead social development specialist with the Sustainable Development Department, Latin America and the Caribbean Region, at the World Bank. Dr. Gacitúa-Marió has a master of arts degree and a doctorate in sociology (international development). He has worked extensively on issues related to social analysis, community-driven development, poverty, exclusion, and social policy.

Andrew Norton is lead social scientist in the Social Development Department, Sustainable Development Network, at the World Bank. He has a doctorate in social anthropology, based on fieldwork in rural Mali, and previously held positions in the United Kingdom's Department for International Development and the Overseas Development Institute. He has worked extensively on a range of topics, including poverty analysis, social protection, social issues in climate change, human rights–based approaches to development, and the politics of the budget process.

Sophia V. Georgieva is a consultant with the World Bank's Social Development Department, working on issues of social analysis, social impacts of development projects, and rights-based approaches to social policy. She has a master's degree in Eurasian, Russian, and East European Studies from Georgetown University and bachelor's degrees in international relations and peace/conflict studies from Colgate University.

Gover Barja is director of the Master's in Public Policy and Management Program at the Catholic University of Bolivia. He received his doctorate and teaches classes in the macro- and microeconomics of development and in applied econometrics. Dr. Barja has conducted various research studies for the Bolivian Sectoral Regulation System, the World Bank, and the Inter-American Development Bank. He has published extensively on the topic of Bolivian structural reforms and their impact on policy performance, the economy, and welfare. His work has been published by international agencies, including the United Nations' Economic Commission for Latin America and the Caribbean, the Center for Global Development, the World Institute for Development Economics Research, and the North-South Institute.

Flávia Carbonari is a consultant with the Sustainable Development Department, Latin America and the Caribbean Region, at the World Bank. She joined the Bank in 2007 and holds a master's degree in Latin American studies from Georgetown University and bachelor's degrees in journalism and international relations from Pontifícia Universidade Católica de São Paulo, Brazil.

Fernando Filgueira has published extensively in academic reviews and in several books compiled and published in Europe, the United States, and various Latin American countries. His work is focused mainly on models of social economic development, evolution of welfare systems and social policies, poverty, family and social structure, and social policies evaluation. He has a doctorate in sociology from Northwestern University. Until December 2008, he served as director of the State Management and Evaluation Area, which reports to the Office of Budget and Planning of the Presidency of the Eastern Republic of Uruguay. In January 2009, he assumed a position as senior specialist at the Social

Development Division of the United Nations' Economic Commission for Latin America and the Caribbean.

Fernando García Serrano is a professor and researcher in anthropology at the Latin American Faculty for Social Sciences, Foreign Policy Research Institute, and at Pontificia Universidad Católica in Ecuador. He holds a master's degree in anthropology from Universidad Iberoamericana, Mexico, and has taught in universities in Bolivia, Mexico, Peru, and Spain. His areas of research include political anthropology, cultural and ethnic diversity, social identity and social movements, and legal anthropology. His most recent publications are *El Derecho a Ser: diversidad, identidad y cambio. Etnografía jurídica indígena y afroecuatoriana* (2004), and *Los Pueblos Indígenas del Ecuador: derecho y bienestar. Informe alternativo sobre el cumplimiento del Convenio 169 de la OIT* (2007).

Steen Lau Jorgensen is sector director of human development in the Middle East and North Africa Region at the World Bank. Prior to that, he served for seven years as director of the World Bank's Social Development Department. Mr. Jorgensen, a Danish national, has held various adviser and senior management positions at the Bank since he joined the institution in 1985, working on health, education, social development, and poverty issues in the Latin America and Africa regions. He holds a postgraduate degree in economics from the University of Aarhus, Denmark.

Sibonile Khoza is director for intergovernmental relations and constitutional roles and responsibilities in the Policy Development Unit of the Department of the Western Cape Premier, South Africa. Prior to this, he was senior researcher and coordinator of the Socio-Economic Rights Project of the Community Law Centre at the University of the Western Cape. In the latter capacity, he wrote, taught, lobbied, and presented worldwide on socioeconomic rights, particularly on the right to adequate food. He spearheaded and was involved in some of the important court cases on health care and housing rights that the Community Law Centre participated in as a friend of the court.

Ramiro Larrea Flores, a researcher in social development and social policy, has collaborated in various studies by the World Bank, the Inter-American Development Bank, and the United Nations Development Programme. He served as executive director of Ecuador's Center for Social Planning and Research from 1996 to 2002. Mr. Larrea holds a degree in agricultural economics from the Catholic University of Ecuador and a postgraduate degree in community empowerment and social inclusion from the World Bank Institute.

Sergio Lijtenstein has been executive director of the Research and Development Institute in Uruguay since November 2006. In September 2008, he took charge of the newly created Technical Secretariat on Mobility, Internal Migrations and Spatial Distribution of Population in the Office of Budget and Planning of the Presidency of the Eastern Republic of Uruguay. He is also a researcher at the Research Program on Integration, Poverty and Social Exclusion at Universidad Católica in Uruguay. Mr. Lijtenstein holds a degree in sociology from Universidad de la República, Uruguay, and a specialist certification in demographic methodologies and techniques from the Latin American and Caribbean Demographic Centre of the United Nations' Economic Commission for Latin America and the Caribbean. His main areas of work are social policy, social development, poverty, and education.

Lavern Louard-Greaves is an independent researcher and social development analyst. She served as the social policy analyst for the government of St. Kitts and Nevis from 1999 to 2007, holding responsibility for coordinating and conducting country poverty assessments. She has a master's degree in development studies and a bachelor's degree in sociology and psychology.

Leonardo Moreno is executive director of the Foundation for Overcoming Poverty in Santiago, Chile. Previously, he has served as legal adviser and department chief in Chile's Ministry of Housing and Urban Development (1990–94), Ministry of National Assets (1994–95), and Ministry of Planning and Cooperation (2001–02). Mr. Moreno has performed various consultancies for the World Bank and the United Nations, including participation in the elaboration of the Millennium Development Goals and of Chile's Human Rights Report for 1990–2002. He holds a degree in law and a master's degree in governance and human development from the Open University of Catalonia, Spain.

Rachel Hannah Nadelman is a social development analyst with the Sustainable Development Department, Latin America and the Caribbean Region, at the World Bank. She has a master of arts degree in international affairs from the New School and a bachelor of arts degree in comparative literature from Brown University. Prior to joining the Bank in 2007, Ms. Nadelman focused her fieldwork and research on community-based development and women's economic opportunities in East Africa, Latin America, and the United States.

Mauricio Rosenblüth is director of research at the Foundation for Overcoming Poverty in Chile. He has conducted and led various research studies, including the Proposal for Updating the Basic Needs Basket and the Voices of Poverty Study in Chile. Mr. Rosenblüth holds a degree in sociology from the University of Chile, and he has completed postgraduate studies in environmental impact evaluation at the Latin American Faculty for Social Sciences, Foreign Policy Research Institute, and in environmental economics at the Institute of Political Ecology in Chile. He teaches classes on social policy and poverty at Alberto Hurtado University and the University of Chile.

Rodrigo Serrano-Berthet is a senior social development specialist in the Latin America and the Caribbean Region at the World Bank. He holds a master's degree and a doctorate in public policy and international development from the Massachusetts Institute of Technology and a bachelor's degree in sociology from the University of Buenos Aires. His areas of research are participatory development and democratic governance, social capital and social cohesion, and crime and violence prevention. Dr. Serrano-Berthet joined the World Bank in 2003. Prior to that time, he worked as an international consultant for several development organizations.

Jorge E. Vargas studied both philosophy and sociology. He holds a master of science degree in economics and is a doctoral candidate in social sciences. He has served as vice-minister and minister of planning in Colombia. Since 1990, he has been a consultant to several multilateral agencies. He is an expert in human rights approaches to national development and in the design of economic policies that have high social impact.

Enrique Vásquez is a professor of economics at the University of the Pacific in Lima, Peru. He has served as adviser to the Office of the Prime Minister, the Ministry of Health, and the Presidency in Peru. He also has served as team leader of a number of international research studies in social policy for the World Bank, the United Nations Children's Fund, the Inter-American Development Bank, the U.S. Agency for International Development, Swiss Cooperation, and the government of Peru, among others. Dr. Vásquez holds a doctorate in politics and a master of science degree in public policy from Oxford University, England, as well as a bachelor's degree in economics from the University of the Pacific, Lima.

Carol Watson Williams is a social policy research consultant. She has worked extensively in social policy research and development in Jamaica and is a former manager of policy research at the Planning Institute of Jamaica, where she led the Jamaica Survey of Living Conditions. Her special area of interest is improving the educational performance of children, specifically concentrating on how issues of exclusion affect the social construction of a parental identity and the life chances of children.

ACKNOWLEDGMENTS

This volume is the product of extensive collaboration between the World Bank, the Department of Social Development and Employment of the Organization of American States (OAS), and the Chilean Foundation for Overcoming Poverty (FUNASUPO). It was based on a process that emphasized South-South learning, engaging academics, practitioners, and policy makers to assess multicountry experiences and approaches to building citizen rights through social policy. Crucial financial support from the United Kingdom's Department for International Development (DFID) enabled the study to have greater breadth and reach, expanding the number of countries that were included and enabling the results of this work to be presented and disseminated across the region. The United Nations' Economic Commission for Latin America and the Caribbean (ECLAC) and the Inter-American Development Bank (IADB) participated in formative discussions that helped shape the initial phases of the study.

In addition to the authors of this volume, many other individuals and institutions contributed to the development of this work. Local scholars from Latin American and Caribbean universities and research centers conducted the field research that informs most of the chapters in this book. These institutions include Universidad Alberto Hurtado, Chile; Universidad del Pacífico, Peru; Universidad Católica Damaso Larrañaga, Uruguay; the Faculty for Social Sciences, Foreign Policy Research Institute, Ecuador; Centro de Planificación y Estudios Sociales, Ecuador; the Planning Institute of Jamaica; Universidad Católica Boliviana Bolivia; and the Community Law Centre, University of the Western Cape, South Africa.

Francisco Pilotti, director of the Social Development and Employment Department of the OAS, was a steering force and provided valuable guidance throughout the drafting process. The peer reviewers of the initial concept note and preliminary reports—Caroline Moser (the University of Manchester/Brookings Institution), and Varun Gauri, Reider Kvam, and

Siobhan McInerney-Lankford (World Bank)—contributed significantly to sharpen and develop the focus of this book. Leonardo Moreno and Mauricio Rosenblüth (FUNASUPO) were instrumental in developing the conceptual framework presented here. Their advice to the in-country researchers who conducted the fieldwork and their engaging discussions with the editorial team greatly facilitated this research.

Many other individuals contributed to background papers and the development of the ideas articulated in this volume. Thelma Gómez and Tomás Rosada from the Rafael Landívar University in Guatemala prepared the Guatemala case. Sirley González and Francisco Palau from Paraguay contributed the Paraguay background paper. Louise Haagh (University of York) informed this work with a background report to the Technical Workshop on Challenges to Social Development Policy held in Asunción, Paraguay, in June 2008. Rosana Martinelli and Julie Nurse, from the Social Development and Employment Department of the OAS, provided valuable support. Jacqueline Mazza and Claudio Santibañez—from the IADB—and Carmen Artigas, Gabriela Salgado, and Ana Sojo—from ECLAC—participated in the discussion of earlier drafts and provided insightful comments. Gerard Howe, Jennie Richmond, and Kemi Williams of DFID were instrumental in arranging the partnerships that supported much of this work. We also are very grateful to Clare Ferguson of DFID for her insightful comments and input in the development of this work.

Within the World Bank, many colleagues supported us and helped us better define the concepts and further develop the ideas advanced in this book. Among them, we want to recognize Ramon Anría, Tomoko Kato, Lisandro Martín, Gracie Ochieng, William Reuben, Yoshinori Suzuki, and Nazumi Takeda, who worked with us at different stages in the development of this publication. Special thanks to Anis A. Dani, the editor of the series, who encouraged us to complete this work.

Throughout the process, the case studies and reports that evolved into this book were disseminated and discussed at local and regional events. These events included, but were not limited to, the Inter-Governmental Seminar on Cooperation and Development, sponsored by the Embassy of Chile in South Africa in January 2007; the Workshop on Explicit Guarantees in the Implementation of Economic, Social and Cultural Rights in Latin America and the Caribbean, hosted in Chile by ECLAC in April 2007; the Second Meeting of the Inter-American Committee on Social Development, hosted in Washington, DC, by the OAS in October 2007; the International Technical Consultation on the Challenges for Social Development Policies in Latin America and the Caribbean, sponsored by the World Bank and the OAS, in partnership with the Social Action Secretariat of the Government of Paraguay, held in Asunción, Paraguay, in June 2008; the First Meeting of Ministers and High Authorities of Social Development—Social Protection and Democratic Governance in the Americas, sponsored by the OAS and Chile's Ministry of Planning and held in Reñaca, Chile, in July 2008; and the Regional Conference on Horizontal Cooperation in Social Protection, organized by the OAS and held in Trinidad and Tobago in September 2008.

We are very grateful for all the support that we received from all these individuals and many others. Without the rich exchange of ideas that took place at all of these events, we would not have found the strength to develop this work.

BCLR	*Butterworths Constitutional Law Reports*
CARICOM	Caribbean Community
CSEC	Caribbean Secondary Education Certificate
FONASA	National Health Fund (Fondo Nacional de Salud) (Chile)
FUNASUPO	Foundation for Overcoming Poverty (Fundación para la Superación de la Pobreza) (Chile)
GDP	gross domestic product
HIV/AIDS	human immunodeficiency virus/acquired immuno-deficiency syndrome
IHI	Integral Health Insurance (Peru)
ISAPREs	private health insurance institutions (instituciones de salud previsional)
JSLC	Jamaica Survey of Living Conditions
KMA	Kingston Metropolitan Area
NGO	nongovernmental organization
OAS	Organization of American States
OECD	Organisation for Economic Co-operation and Development
OECS	Organization of Eastern Caribbean States
PANES	National Social Emergency Program (Plan de Atencíon Nacional a la Emergencia Social) (Uruguay)
PSIA	Poverty and Social Impact Analysis
REGH	Regime of Explicit Guarantees in Health (Chile)
SA	South African Law Reports
SD	Supreme Decree
SGSSS	General System of Social Security in Health (Sistema General de Seguridad Social en Salud) (Colombia)

SISBEN	Social Service Beneficiaries' Identification System (Sistema de Identificación de los Beneficiarios de los Servicios Sociales) (Colombia)
TAC	Treatment Action Campaign (South Africa)
UMCI	Universal Maternal and Child Insurance (Bolivia)
VAT	value added tax

All amounts are presented in U.S. dollars, unless otherwise indicated.

CHAPTER 1

Introduction: Social Policy, Citizenship, and the Realization of Rights

Andrew Norton, Estanislao Gacitúa-Marió, and Sophia V. Georgieva

The foundation of contemporary understanding of the link between social policy and the political realm is T. H. Marshall's insight that effective citizenship requires not only a political voice and a legally protected status, but also a certain level of socioeconomic security (Marshall 1965). This book explores and documents an approach that operates explicitly in the space Marshall identified. The framework of social guarantees sets out to build the dimension of citizenship that rests on the secure enjoyment of social and economic rights. The essence of a social guarantees approach is to take abstract notions of rights and convert them into concrete standards and entitlements against which citizens may make claims.

The notion of the social contract appears regularly in this discussion. We argue that the process of building and negotiating consensus between different social and political groups on the details of the guarantees can be used to rebuild or strengthen elements of the social contract. In effect, the idea of the social contract comprises two separate but closely connected ideas—a contract of government and a contract of society (Barker 1962). The contract of government theorizes that the state is based on a contract between rulers and the ruled. The concept of social guarantees can be seen as underpinning this element of the social contract because the understanding of what standards can be provided (and afforded) at any given time forms a central part of the contract of government. At some points in this volume, authors also refer to the "social-fiscal pact." This can be understood as an element of the contract of government that captures the mutual responsibilities of citizens and the state to collect and use revenues

1

for the delivery of any social policy program or service. Social guarantees therefore are seen here not primarily as a framework for technocratic decision making, but as an arena for social dialogue.

A further key dimension of social guarantees is the potential that defined standards provide to strengthen the agency of citizens by establishing a clear framework for claims on public policy. Van Gusteren (1978:29) has noted that the threat of legal redress always will be a partial answer to the attainment of social and economic rights, and argues that "what the clients of the welfare state also need in order to function as citizens are strategies to combat and cope with bureaucracy and professionalism." In addition to providing ways of prioritizing policy according to principles of equity, social guarantees also can give citizens such strategies by creating a common understanding of different actors' specific responsibilities for social provision.

The rest of this volume is divided into two parts. The first part explores a range of arguments that help formulate a rights-based approach to social policy (largely through the concept of social guarantees) and help situate that approach within a broader context in terms of contemporary trends in social policy. The second part of the book begins with the key case study that underpins our understanding of the nature and potential of the social guarantees approach as a practical methodology for policy implementation and design—the health sector reforms undertaken in Chile since 2001 through the Regime of Explicit Guarantees in Health (REGH). The second part then continues with a series of other case studies that explore the potential of using a social guarantees approach as a tool of assessment, analysis, and monitoring.

By way of introduction, this first chapter sets out to provide a basic outline of the key concepts that appear in the rest of the book; ground those concepts within the literature on social policy, human rights, and development; place the contributions of the various chapters within the overall argument; and offer some conclusions on the implications of this work for the development and implementation of social policy in developing countries.

Social Policy, Human Rights, and Development

In the past decade, there has been growing interest within the development community in the links between social policy and the building of social inclusion and citizenship. These concerns have been manifest in both a growing body of literature exploring the practical implications of these links (for example, see Kabeer [2005]; Dani and de Haan [2008]) and the engagement of major development institutions in exploring the significance of human rights for development dialogue (DFID 2000; Daniño 2006; OECD/DAC 2006).

This volume brings together a series of reflections and empirical investigations that address new approaches to social policy in developing countries explicitly pursuing the goal of building citizenship and rights. It has its origins in a collaborative work program between the Chilean Foundation for Overcoming Poverty, the Organization of American States, and the Social Development Department of the World Bank. As noted above, a major feature of this work has been the exploration of innovative approaches to promoting social inclusion through the development of policy approaches under a framework of "social guarantees" (World Bank 2008; World Bank/OAS 2008). The geographic focus of most of the material presented here is the Americas—specifically, Latin America and the Caribbean. Parts of the book, however, draw on comparative material from outside that region (chapter 4), and there is a case study of the South African experience (chapter 6).

The original departure point for this work was an explicit concern for rights-based approaches to social policy implementation. *Social policy* may have multiple definitions. The most significant distinction is between models that see social policy simply as "policies about the social sectors" and models that see it as an embodiment of cross-cutting concerns with equity, distribution, social justice, and social and livelihood security (Deacon et al. 2003; Moser and Dani 2008). In the latter model, social policy extends beyond the social sectors and has an extremely close relationship with economic policy. It is the latter interpretation that we follow here.

The rights approach to social policy is characterized in terms of three predominant features: [1] the definition and widespread communication of rights, entitlements, and standards that enable citizens to hold public policy makers and providers accountable for the delivery of social policy; [2] a commitment to the equitable delivery of the specified rights, entitlements, and standards; and [3] the availability of mechanisms of redress that citizens may use if they are unable to enjoy specified entitlements. Rights can be characterized as *legitimate claims that give rise to correlative obligations or duties*. Within this category we are concerned primarily with universal human rights—rights that apply equally to all human beings, irrespective of their membership in particular families, groups, religions, communities, or societies (Moser and Norton 2001). Most human rights apply to the individual, but sometimes the equal worth and dignity of all people can be ensured only through the recognition and protection of individuals' rights as members of a group (United Nations 2006). In practice, human rights are best seen as moral, political, or legal claims made on the basis of common humanity. The normative basis of the United Nations' system for promoting and protecting human rights comprises both international legal obligations and international ethical/political obligations.

This volume concentrates on principles that underlie a rights approach (equity, transparency, accountability, and redress) rather than on details of the legal and ethical instruments of the global human rights regime. In general, our focus is on policy and administrative systems rather than on legal systems—although some chapters (notably chapter 6 on South Africa) do address the role of the courts in relation to social and economic rights and the conditions under which the use of judicial channels for redress may become dynamic and effective. As van Gusteren (1978) notes, concepts of human rights are part of a family of concepts that has to do with the place of the individual in the political system and, therefore, are part of a language of citizenship.

The Social Guarantees Approach to the Negotiation of Policy Change

The social guarantees approach (outlined in chapter 2) brings a number of important features to the implementation of social policy efforts that seek to build citizenship through the realization of rights. First, the approach outlines the specific content of abstract rights in relation to characteristics of the delivery of services. The taxonomy of subguarantees offered in chapter 2 comprises the dimensions of access, quality, financial protection, revision and participation, and redress (see box 1.1). Thus, the framing of citizen expectations in relation to a right has a holistic character that militates against situations where the rapid expansion of the right of access can strain the capacity of delivery institutions to maintain provision quality.

The second major feature of a social guarantees approach is that it clarifies minimum standards and entitlements in relation to service delivery. The mechanisms for "continuous revision" of these standards and entitlements within a social guarantees framework are particularly

BOX 1.1

The Dimensions of a Social Guarantee: A Summary

Chapter 2 outlines in detail a taxonomy of the components of a social guarantee. There are two primary axes of this taxonomy—the breakdown into "subguarantees" and the analysis of policy domains (legal, institutional, instrumental, and financial) that back up their implementation. The framework of subguarantees adopted in this volume is as follows:

- *Subguarantee of access*: This subguarantee ensures that every eligible individual has timely access to the guaranteed services for as long as he or she needs them. It constitutes the core of a social guarantee and must be designed in a way that furthers equity and a better quality of life.
- *Subguarantee of quality*: This subguarantee ensures that entitlements and the procedures for delivering them are defined in line with established quality standards. Regular monitoring and evaluation procedures and mechanisms for publicly communicating the results of those evaluations are required.
- *Subguarantee of financial protection*: People who cannot afford the costs of accessing an entitlement (or receiving a guaranteed service) are ensured the ability to receive the entitlement. Financial commitments from either public or private sources make this possible. Expected contributions from the state, the beneficiaries, or other institutions are defined, preferably on the basis of beneficiaries' socioeconomic circumstances.
- *Subguarantee of continuous revision and participation*: This subguarantee ensures that the guarantee is revised periodically in alignment with resource availability, changing risks, political and social consensus, and relevant advances in science and technology. It also ensures that citizens have a voice in key elements of service delivery.
- *Subguarantee of redress*: This subguarantee ensures that individuals or groups may claim access to their entitlements according to the specified subguarantees. Redress mechanisms require definition of the situations in which citizens can claim access to services, and definition of the judicial and nonjudicial mechanisms by which those claims may be pursued and resolved.

Source: Authors' compilation.

important. The principle of "progressive realization" also is essential within the normative architecture for social and economic rights. According to this principle, governments should be proactive in strengthening the enjoyment of rights over time (or, in the words of the International Covenant on Economic, Social and Cultural Rights, should take steps in "achieving progressively the full realization of the rights recognized . . . to the maximum of available resources" [OHCHR 1976, art. 2]). Conversely, however, the principle of progressive realization can introduce an element of obscurity into the actual level of realization to be expected at any given time. The progressive realization may appear to be a "get-out clause" in relation to public obligations to support the realization of social and economic rights (Norton and Elson 2002). The concrete nature of the social guarantees framework addresses this problem in three important ways. First, it requires that immediate obligations be specified in relation to social and economic rights. Second, continuous revision requires a clearly defined process for ensuring that standards and entitlements can be delivered within available organizational and financial resources. Constantly testing the delivery of specific standards and entitlements against the institutional and fiscal environment gives concrete content to the principle of progressive realization. If this process works, it should prevent some of the well-documented perverse effects of entitlement-based systems of delivery—in particular, the tendency for provision set at a high standard to be rationed and made available only to those with the clout, contacts, and resources to make claims effectively. Finally, the process of arriving at agreement on the level of guarantees that can be supported at any given time creates a public space for deliberation on the social rights of citizens— a space that reinforces the democratic governance of social policy by offering an opportunity for individuals and groups to voice their concerns.

A third significant element of the social guarantees approach is its particular emphasis on values and systems of redress. This is well illustrated in the case of the REGH in Chile (chapter 5). This particular "policy ethnography" constitutes the only clear and explicit attempt to drive through policy and institutional change using the social guarantees model. Although a full evaluation of the impacts of this program is not yet possible, the authors document information to suggest that the program has reinforced efficiency, effectiveness, and equity in the delivery of health services. A key element of this experience was the role played by the Office of the Superintendent of Health—an office created with the legal power to enforce compliance in relation to social guarantees through both the private and the public service delivery sectors.

A fourth and final important dimension of the social guarantees approach is that it provides a unifying framework for addressing equity and fairness in service delivery across the different segments engaged in providing a service in a particular sector. These segments may include different levels of government (local and national) as well as the private and voluntary sectors. The specific context in which the REGH was introduced in Chile illustrates this very well: in 2001, policy makers there had to deal with a segmentation in health care delivery that produced great disparities in access and quality across different social groups. Low-income and high-risk populations were treated mainly by the public sector; high-income and low-risk groups were treated mostly by the private sector. The authors of chapter 5 describe the evolution of the social guarantees regime as a policy solution to impose some basic standards of equity and accountability across the whole system.

Politics of Social Guarantees

In chapter 3, the authors examine the interface between social policy and institutional and political processes. Social policy is seen as a key element of the social contract that underpins democratic governance and the state. The social guarantees framework builds on this understanding of social policy as a key element of the social contract and democratic governance by providing a structured forum for negotiating citizens' fundamental expectations of the state in the matter of social policy and service delivery. Again, the experience of the health sector reform in Chile is instructive. In the process of developing the social guarantees approach there, an interministerial committee led an extensive technical/political debate that involved actors from across the political spectrum, delegates from the health sector's professional associations and trade unions, and representatives of private sector interests. The committee, representing the executive branch of government, passed bills to the parliament before all details were defined, so space was opened for consensus to build between the ruling coalition and members of the opposition. Some of the crucial aspects of the political management of the process are outlined in chapter 5. Grasping the political potential of the social guarantees concept early in the process, the administration of President Ricardo Lagos was able to use it to develop such broad support (across the political spectrum, from the public, and from other significant stakeholders) that the fundamentals of the health care debate were redefined. The basics of the social guarantees approach effectively rose above the level of normal political competition to a consensus that reasonably can be seen as part of the social contract. Actors who otherwise might have contested the whole reform (private sector interests in the health system, for example) wound up negotiating details instead.

The example of the health reforms in Chile demonstrates how the social guarantees approach can be used as an explicit discourse for driving through policy change. A crucial element of this discourse is the way it can be used to move a technocratic discussion (for example, on the lists of illnesses that the program will cover) to a political and social arena. It is the quality of the social guarantees construct as a dimension of citizen rights that gives it this potential. But to realize the potential, it still is necessary to have skillful political management—and a structure of institutions that enables a broad multistakeholder dialogue. It is important to note the key role of a quasi-governmental, independent, social policy think tank in this process (namely, the Chilean Foundation for Overcoming Poverty). The capacity of such organizations to hold informal discussions across different technical and political communities is an interesting feature of the institutional architecture that made the Chilean reforms possible.

Social Guarantees as a Framework for Monitoring Policy Change

Another key element of the project we embarked on in developing this book was testing the extent to which the conceptual framework of social guarantees could be used as an assessment and monitoring tool specifically to learn how much any given policy system conforms to a set of legal, institutional, instrumental (programmatic), and fiscal arrangements that facilitate the realization of rights. Within this volume, studies reported in chapters 6 (South Africa), 7 (Bolivia, Ecuador, and Peru), 8 (the Caribbean region), 9 (Uruguay), and 10 (Colombia) were commissioned with the intention of assessing, through the lens of social guarantees, the extent to which rights were realized in whole or part. These studies were led by nationals of the countries concerned. The process of carrying them out involved discussions with key stakeholders in the public, private, and civil society/voluntary sectors, as well as in the research community. The basic framework for the assessments is outlined in chapter 2, and comprises the combination of subguarantees and institutional domains charted in table 1.1.

A major strength of this approach as a framework for comparative analysis is that it provides a means for assessing the robustness of the

Table 1.1. Matrix for the Domains and Dimensions of a Social Guarantee

Subguarantee Policy domain	Access	Quality	Financial protection	Continuous revision and participation	Redress
Legal					
Institutional					
Instrumental					
Financial					

Source: Authors' compilation.

social and institutional arrangements for realizing rights in a way that is sensitive to different fiscal capabilities of public bodies in different contexts. In this sense, it has a major advantage as a comparative framework to facilitate mutual exchange and learning over frameworks for assessing the delivery of social rights only through outcome data. The material presented in the following chapters supports the basic premise that the social guarantees framework is an effective tool for policy analysis. The cases examined include countries having common-law legal traditions (for example, Jamaica, South Africa, and St. Kitts and Nevis) as well as civil law traditions (Latin American countries studied) and a range of political circumstances.

The health sector was covered in all but the Uruguay case studies, and the education sector was covered in all but Chile, South Africa, and Uruguay. These sectors were considered suitable for comparison because of the frequency with which citizen rights are recognized explicitly.[1] In addition, the housing sector was examined in the South African and Jamaican cases, and social protection was analyzed in the Uruguay case study. The following general observations can be drawn from the case studies presented in subsequent chapters.

Access vs. Quality

Where entitlements and guarantees are built firmly into policy and legal frameworks, there is a tendency for the subguarantee of access to be predominant and that of quality to receive less attention. The disparity between access and quality is evident in a number of the case studies. The case of Peru, for example, shows a dramatic increase in the coverage of basic education, achieving the highest enrollment and completion rates for primary and secondary schools in the Andean region; yet only a small proportion of students has shown satisfactory learning results (see chapter 7). The case of Peru may be one of the most evident and well-researched examples of this discrepancy in the Latin American region, but the same trend can be observed in many other cases. The stark quality division between public and private education in Jamaica and the regrouping of students by academic performance after the primary grades in St. Kitts and Nevis contribute to perpetuating inequalities in schooling opportunities, especially in secondary school education (see chapter 8).

A common feature in these cases is the absence of well-defined quality standards and regular quality monitoring. In all of these states and sectors, an institution formally has been assigned the responsibility to monitor quality—a civil society organization such as a parent association, a respective ministry, or an agency. But the lack of clear and widely disseminated quality standards has limited the capacity of these institutions to keep providers accountable. In some cases, the guarantee of quality is addressed partially. For example, primary schools in St. Kitts and Nevis have instituted a common curriculum, annual evaluations and teacher trainings, and a curriculum development unit to control closely the fulfillment of their quality standards. The extension of quality guarantees into secondary schools is still pending.

A major potential of the social guarantees lens of analysis is to rebalance the understanding of obligation in service delivery so that issues of quality are given appropriate weight, compared with issues of access. In the analyzed case studies, some examples illustrate the potential of a more systematic approach to attention to quality for enhancing the realization of rights—Bolivia's educational quality measurement system, the curriculum development unit in St. Kitts and Nevis, and the Obligatory System of Health Quality Guarantee in Colombia. Nevertheless, in most of the countries and sectors discussed in this book, attention to quality is not yet systematic and lacks the degree of obligation to be considered a functioning "guarantee."

The case studies demonstrate that the ability to make claims against established norms of quality tends to follow already entrenched lines of social division. In the absence of a systematic and universal policy of control and accountability, the ability to make claims against quality standards remains a privilege of the higher-income and/or better-mobilized groups who naturally possess more means and information to demand accountability. If the policy goal is to fulfill basic entitlements for all, social guarantees analysis points to the need to disseminate and monitor universal quality standards far more widely in many cases.

Financial Protection

Financial protection, understood as concrete mechanisms to ensure the affordability of services that all citizens are entitled to receive, is another area to which the social guarantees analysis brings particular attention. In the education and health sectors discussed in the Andean and Caribbean cases in this volume, a number of public and private channels for financial assistance have been developed. This partial assistance, however, generally is not linked to a comprehensive system or calculation that aims to ensure universal affordability. For example, even though basic education is guaranteed as "free of charge" (except in Colombia), there are multiple related costs—clothing and uniforms, food, and transportation—that prevent many children who come from low-income families or reside in rural areas from attending school. Although various scholarships and assistance programs exist (for example, school feeding programs, free textbooks, and the like), they are not extended universally. Nor are students, parents, or communities sufficiently aware of available assistance options. The lack of a uniform system of financial protection has especially high consequences for rural residents, and even more dramatically so in states where students live in a high degree of geographic isolation (such as in Andean or Amazonian communities).

Thus, the analyses of basic education in the Andean and Caribbean cases shows that merely declaring a service "free and obligatory for all" does not guarantee it will be accessible and affordable for all. Only under a coordinated framework that guarantees assistance to all people who need it, and in which all citizens are aware of the available options, can the guarantee of financial protection be realized fully.

A workable financial protection framework for any given service would be constrained by available resources. Hence, establishing such a framework urges societies first to define feasible minimums on which a universal financial protection system can be based. Abolishing health care user fees in Jamaica, for example, was a universal and well-publicized measure of financial protection; yet it led to an overburdening of existing hospital capacity and generated quality concerns (see chapter 8). The REGH in Chile, with "financial protection" as one of its four explicit guarantees, is an example of a sophisticated model through which individuals of any income group can afford a set of specified services. The long-run adequacy of all details in this model may be questioned and reformed, but what matters from the perspective of rights is the will of policy makers in society as a whole to develop a system to ensure that entitlements are affordable to all people.

Redress Mechanisms

Provisions for redress are critical and are at the heart of the social guarantees approach. It is interesting to note that the strongest emphasis on this point comes from two societies that have experienced major political transformations—Chile and South Africa. The specific approaches are very different in the two cases. The South Africa case was included in this study to explore a situation in which the approach to realizing social and economic rights largely has been rooted in the legal system and the courts. That situation is in contrast to the Chile case in particular, where an expressed intention of the reforms was to provide quasi-legal forms of redress (for example, through the Office of the Superintendent of Health) that would be more accessible than the courts. The details of both cases, however, illustrate a deeper commonality. In each case, a problematic political history had left massive social dislocations and great inequality, and a new regime and political project was seeking mechanisms to transform highly unequal delivery of services and conditions on the ground.

In the South Africa case, the scale and form of the political transition allowed the legal system to play a genuinely transformational role. The radical rights-based Constitution (famously including strong provisions for social and economic rights) formed the basis of a culture of activism where civil society actors could back up marginalized groups in seeking redress through the courts. A fundamental feature was the appointment of a Constitutional Court with jurists who had been involved in drafting the social and economic rights provisions of the Constitution. The reforms in the Constitution and legal provisions on the role of the Constitutional Court created a situation whereby the court was positioned to play a transformational role in policy systems, with a commitment to distributional equity that is unlikely to be found in many other contexts. By contrast, the health reforms in Chile explicitly sought to create quasi-judicial and administrative forms of redress that would be more accessible than the courts to people without connections and resources—redress through health insurance agencies, the Office of the Superintendent of Health, and a system of mediation. Chile's attention to precisely defining the responsibilities of all actors and the time periods for claims resolution is also worth highlighting.

In most of our other case studies, systems of redress generally are weak and lack both specificity and outreach. Such conditions allow for weak delivery and, in some cases (such as in the housing sector in Jamaica), allow the persistence of political clientelism in the delivery of benefits. Even though administrative agents responsible for resolving citizen claims have been assigned formally for most of the social services discussed in this volume,[2] the lack of clearly defined standards for access, quality, or financial protection often inhibits the efficiency of those institutions in providing redress for service users.

Guarantees in the Legal, Institutional, and Financial Domains

Apart from focusing attention on areas that may be overlooked during policy design (such as quality, financial protection, and redress), the social guarantees approach highlights the importance of anchoring policy mechanisms in all four domains essential for the delivery of social policy: legal, institutional, instrumental, and fiscal. In other words, the approach makes it apparent that every policy or program established to guarantee given entitlements can be effective only if the roles and responsibilities of all key institutions are outlined clearly, the appropriate funding is secured, and all of these provisions have the proper legal backing to ensure that they cannot be modified or reversed easily.

The decree establishing Chile's REGH offers a good example of legislation, apart from the country's Constitution, that gives concrete meaning to health entitlements and outlines the responsibilities of all institutions involved. Such supporting legislation also has been developed successfully in other states (for example, for the National Social Emergency Program in Uruguay).

Even the best-formulated social service entitlements and frameworks for social equity would not have an impact without adequate financing. Thus, a fiscal agreement among state authorities and a funding plan for any guaranteed service or program are prerequisites for a functioning guarantee, along with its legal, institutional, and programmatic dimensions. In all of the Andean states, for instance, access to bilingual education is constitutionally guaranteed, and bilingual education programs have been established. However, the budgetary allocations that bilingual education programs receive from the state are minimal. The recent Plan for Social Equity in Uruguay, which reflects the government's commitment to a more integral social protection model, has considered a variety of funding sources, including tax reform, to secure the necessary budget for its multiple programs. The plan's viability thus depends on a fiscal pact yet to be consolidated among economic, financial, and social development authorities.

The Colombian case highlights the crucial role of civil society in implementing a social guarantees system. The 1991 Constitution created an environment for the recognition of fundamental economic and social rights and entitlements and for citizen participation. Even in a context of conflict and state fragility, this experience demonstrates that social policy can contribute to building citizenship and, more important, to building peace by providing accountability mechanisms that reinforce the fragile positions of civil society actors.

Components of a Comprehensive Approach to Social Policy

To set the debates outlined here in a broader context, the authors of chapter 4 focus on the transformations in social policy approaches needed to engage effectively with the benefits and downside risks of globalization. As they note, the enhanced flows of ideas, capital, and trade are likely to benefit people who are better connected, and poor people or those in less well-adapted productive sectors are likely to suffer more than others. It also is clear that the old welfare state model—where the state acts (or attempts to act) as the sole provider of services—is increasingly difficult to sustain as a framework for social policy delivery. To an ever-greater extent, the state must see its obligations as encompassing more than the role of service provider, particularly in regulating private and voluntary sector service provision and promoting community engagement in "coproducing" services. The analysis of a comprehensive approach to social policy (presented in chapter 4) indicates that the framework of social guarantees—with its explicit focus on enhancing equity across different segments of service delivery in any particular sector—will have increasing relevance for the design of pro-poor policies in a climate of globalization.

The authors of chapter 4 argue that a "comprehensive" approach to social policy can be discerned in a range of emerging and transitional economies. At the heart of this comprehensive approach is the transition from seeing social policy simply in terms of service delivery to beneficiaries (through state or market mechanisms) to seeing social policy as a key realm for creating and maintaining the social contract through a clearer definition of citizen and state rights and responsibilities. Tackling some of the standard objections to an enhanced focus on equity in public policy, the chapter demonstrates that greater social spending under some conditions can enhance, rather than constrain, economic growth. The authors also argue that rights-based approaches to delivery—with their emphasis on universal standards—do not lead necessarily to inefficient uses of public resources. Reviewing the literature on the targeting of service provision, they quote Skocpol's (1991) review of social programs in the United States to demonstrate that room exists within some kinds of universal policies for extra benefits and services that help less-privileged people without stigmatizing them—what can be termed "targeting within universalism." Finally, they echo chapter 3's conclusion in highlighting that such a comprehensive approach to social policy is more likely to emerge and be implemented effectively where there is a clear governmental authority structure to coordinate the social agenda within government and beyond. Approaches to the development of such a structure include creating a Ministry of Social Development or forming lead committees (sometimes termed "social cabinets") at a high level within the executive branch.

Conclusion

In their discussion of the targeting of social benefits, the authors of chapter 4 argue for "targeting that meets the citizenship test." By that wording, they mean using approaches to targeting that treat the recipients of social transfers as citizens with equal rights and obligations. On a broader front, the framework of social guarantees presented in this volume can be seen as an approach to developing "social policies that meet the citizenship test." The framework brings that focus, first, through clarifying the basis on which citizens can make claims on public policy by providing clear standards for realizing rights and, second, through offering an arena in which to negotiate the level of delivery possible at any given time across a wide range of social and political actors. The framework thus diminishes the space for bureaucratic discretion and creates a public space for determining what normally may be seen as technical issues (for example, the allocation of budget resources). The need to achieve a wide consensus on which services will be guaranteed and their level of protection enables society to exercise stronger control over policies, potentially raising the effectiveness of public spending (see chapter 5). The increased transparency and focus on equity also may strengthen democratic governance by reducing the space for political clientelism.

Within this volume, the case study of the health reforms in Chile is central because it demonstrates how a social guarantees framework may be used to generate enhanced political and social consensus around a progressive policy framework. Other studies presented here show how the framework can be used to analyze progress toward the realization of economic and social rights. With a few exceptions—in particular, Chile and South Africa—most social policies have not been designed with a rights perspective or merely have adopted rights-based principles without translating them into explicit policy provisions. The conditions under which a nascent guarantee (or a "preguarantee," a term suggested by FUNASUPO) may evolve into a full social guarantee will depend on the specific political and historical context. We hope that the case studies presented here can be of use to policy actors in thinking through how to reinforce this "direction of travel" in any given circumstances.

The material presented here also highlights the critical role played by systems of redress in making a rights-based approach to social policy effective in practice. Whereas the South Africa case demonstrates that under the right conditions the courts can play a major role in reinforcing claims and promoting distributive equity, it also suggests that the required conditions are demanding and will not be realized in many cases. Therefore, it also is crucial to design administrative and quasi-judicial forms of redress accessible to those without contacts or resources.

Finally, another key constitutive element of the rights-based approach is the strengthening of the delivery of social entitlements through public-private-civil society partnerships. Such alliances for social services provision can mitigate certain risks, such as the focus on short-term delivery for political payback, opposition from highly powerful stakeholders, or ineffective state delivery mechanisms. These partnerships also strengthen monitoring, and they can be used to evaluate and strengthen existing programs and to review the level of protection guaranteed. But the strong engagement of public policy in setting standards across the different sectors is a key feature in making such partnerships work to deliver equitable results and support the realization of social and economic rights for all citizens.

Notes

1. Gauri and Brinks (2008) note that the right to education has been featured in a majority of the world's constitutions since the beginning of the 20th century; and, that more than half of the constitutions have included the right to health care since about the middle of the 20th century.

2. For example, parent associations have the responsibility in Peru's education sector, and there is a special desk for social protection programs in Uruguay's Ministry of Social Development.

References

Barker, Ernest. 1962. "Introduction." In *Social Contract: Essays by Locke, Hume, and Rousseau,* v–lx. New York: Oxford University Press.

Dani, Anis A., and Arjan de Haan, eds. 2008. *Inclusive States: Social Policy and Structural Inequalities.* New Frontiers of Social Policy Series. Washington, DC: World Bank.

Daniño, Roberto. 2006. *The Legal Aspects of the World Bank's Work on Human Rights in Development Outreach.* Special Report on Human Rights and Development. Washington, DC: World Bank Institute.

Deacon, Bob, Eeva Ollila, Meri Koivusalo, and Paul Stubbs. 2003. *Global Social Governance: Themes and Prospects.* Helsinki, Finland: Ministry of Foreign Affairs.

DFID (U.K. Department for International Development). 2000. *Realizing Human Rights for Poor People: Strategies for Achieving the International Development Targets.* Target Strategy Paper. London: U.K. DFID.

Ferrajoli, Luigi. 2000. *El garantismo y la filosofía del derecho (The Guarantees Theory and the Philosophy of Law).* Translated by G. Pisarello, A. Estrada, and J. M. Díaz Martín. Bogotá: Universidad Externado de Colombia.

Gauri, Varun, and Daniel M. Brinks, eds. 2008. *Courting Social Justice: Judicial Enforcement of Social and Economic Rights in the Developing World.* Cambridge, U.K.: Cambridge University Press.

Kabeer, Naila, ed. 2005. *Inclusive Citizenship: Meanings and Expressions.* London: Zed Books.

Marshall, Thomas Humphrey. 1965. *Class, Citizenship and Social Development.* New York: Doubleday Anchor.

Moser, Caroline, and Anis A. Dani, eds. 2008. *Livelihoods, Assets and Social Policy.* Washington, DC: World Bank.

Moser, Caroline, and Andy Norton, with Tim Conway, Clare Ferguson, and Polly Vizard. 2001. *To Claim Our Rights: Livelihood Security, Human Rights and Sustainable Development.* London: Overseas Development Institute.

Norton, Andrew, and Diane Elson. 2002. *What's Behind the Budget? Politics, Rights and Accountability in the Budget Process.* London: Overseas Development Institute.

OECD/DAC (Organisation for Economic Co-operation and Development/ Development Assistance Committee). 2006. *The Development Dimension: Integrating Human Rights into Development: Donor Approaches, Experiences and Challenges.* Paris: OECD.

OHCHR (United Nations, Office of the High Commissioner for Human Rights). 1976. "International Covenant on Economic, Social and Cultural Rights." New York.

Skocpol, Theda. 1991. "Targeting within Universalism: Politically Viable Policies to Combat Poverty in the United States." In *The Urban Underclass,* ed.

Christopher Jenks and Paul E. Peterson, 411–36. Washington, DC: Brookings Institution Press.

United Nations. 2006. *Frequently Asked Questions on a Human Rights–Based Approach to Development Cooperation.* New York: United Nations.

van Gusteren, Herman. 1978. "Notes on the Theory of Citizenship." In *Democracy, Consensus and Social Contract,* ed. Pierre Birnbaum, Jack Lively, and Geraint Parry. Beverly Hills, CA: Sage Publications.

World Bank. 2008. *Realizing Rights through Social Guarantees: An Analysis of New Approaches to Social Policy in Latin America and South Africa.* Report 40047-GLB. Washington, DC: World Bank.

World Bank/OAS (Organization of American States). 2008. *Increasing Social Inclusion through Social Guarantees. A Policy Note.* Washington, DC: World Bank.

PART I

PERSPECTIVES ON RIGHTS-BASED

SOCIAL POLICY

CHAPTER 2

Increasing Social Inclusion through Social Guarantees

Estanislao Gacitúa-Marió and Andrew Norton

This chapter provides an overview of the conceptual framework leading to the social guarantees approach and its application as a tool for social policy design and service delivery. We start by tracing the philosophical underpinnings of a social guarantee, outlining the link and difference between rights and guarantees. We then examine the operational dimensions of social guarantees and challenges in their application to development policies and interventions. To conclude, we discuss domains of implementation, exploring the use of the social guarantees framework as a mechanism to coordinate, establish priorities in, and monitor social policy. We argue that the framework provides a means to translate a rights-based perspective on development into actionable social policy instruments that will strengthen democratic governance, thereby furthering inclusion and equal opportunity.

Based on a "system of guarantees" introduced by Ferrajoli (2001, 2004), social guarantees may be defined as sets of legal and administrative mechanisms that specify entitlements and obligations related to certain rights and that ensure the fulfillment of those obligations on the part of the state. The philosophical principles informing the notion of social guarantees draw heavily on John Rawls' (1971) theory of justice. These principles are based on the protection of basic liberties, and they emphasize that all policy changes and interventions should be judged first and foremost by how much they improve the well-being of society's least advantaged members.

Rawls' principles for achieving justice define the notion of primary social goods, which are necessary for the development and exercise of equal citizenship, including equality of opportunity. In essence, these primary goods are social goods that depend on social cooperation. Rawls understands basic needs to be the requisite conditions for moral autonomy, without which freedom is not possible.

Similarly, Doyal and Gough (1991) argue that basic needs are essential prerequisites for achieving any other goal, making informed choices, and participating in any society. Furthermore, those authors suggest that failing to meet these needs (fundamental rights) would lead to the lack of moral autonomy to define and pursue personal goals and achieve legitimate governance, or would lead to the lack of a political and economic system that can ensure equality of opportunities. In this context, Doyal and Gough argue that there is a societal need for a political and economic system that guarantees participation (as an institutional mechanism), which enables people to become self-aware of their societal needs and to develop the necessary consensus on which needs should be prioritized and equally recognized for all.

According to Abramovich (2006), the rights-based approach to development commonly is understood as a conceptual framework normatively based on international human rights standards and principles and operationally directed to promoting and protecting human rights. There are two main rationales for a human rights–based approach: (1) the intrinsic rationale, acknowledging that a human rights–based approach is the right thing to do, morally or legally; and (2) the instrumental rationale, recognizing that a human rights–based approach leads to better and more sustainable human development outcomes (United Nations 2006). In practice, the reason for pursuing a human rights–based approach is usually a blend of these two rationales.

A rights-based approach to social policy puts a focus on processes as well as outcomes. That is, the definition and realization of rights is a process that needs to be negotiated politically through a fair and fully inclusive dialogue. As a result of that dialogue, all people affected by the rights can agree freely and rationally that (1) the specified rights are in the mutual interest of everyone; (2) they reflect in-country conditions that are socially, technologically, and ecologically safeguarded; and (3) they allow for progressive fulfillment (Habermas 1996, 1998). The most difficult part of this process of defining, protecting, and realizing rights is defining the level of realization to be protected, because it involves building a new social contract that evolves from political consensus, social struggle, and structural transformations. This process implies thinking of individuals as holders of rights—not merely as beneficiaries of services—and defining norms and standards that enable citizens to be integrated into society (Habermas 1996, 1998). As a result, the claims emerging from these rights provide a path or framework for decision making that gives state, private, and civil society institutions a wide margin of discretion for selecting the specific measures they will use to realize these rights.

As described by Ferrajoli, a system of social guarantees comprises a "set of techniques that ensures the maximum fulfillment of constitutionally recognized rights" (2001:374). As such, social guarantees contribute to bridging the structural gap between declared norms and those norms' effective implementation.

Based on Ferrajoli (2000, 2001, 2004) and on further refinements of the conceptual framework done by the Chilean Foundation for Overcoming Poverty (FUNASUPO 2007), it is possible to identify five key characteristics that define a social guarantee: (1) it has a legal expression that results in an explicit state responsibility, (2) it is constructed in reference to a specific rightsholder, (3) it involves mechanisms of access and redress, (4) its mechanisms of access and redress are defined in a precise manner, and (5) it is flexible and revisable. As a result of these characteristics, a social guarantee helps reduce opportunity gaps across social groups.

Ferrajoli (2000, 2001, 2004) believes it is these characteristics that put a right into operation. Given that fundamental rights are abstract in form, they must be defined through other mechanisms so that their content can be made tangible. The notion of social guarantees resolves the issue of indeterminacy of the normative character of fundamental rights because it provides a minimum and standard content to a specific right (Alston 2003). Furthermore, Ferrajoli argues that these rights are held by all people, and it is that universality that is the defining quality of these basic rights (Rey Pérez 2002).

A rights approach contributes to sustainable development in two major ways. First, it reduces social and political risks by enhancing social justice and focusing on inclusion and nondiscrimination. Second, it creates stronger and more equitable institutions—not only state-owned but also civil and community ones (Moser and Norton 2001). Furthermore, the promotion and observance of human rights are considered core elements of the efforts to strengthen democracy and good governance. A rights perspective seeks to change the logic of the policy process so that the starting point is not the existence of people with needs that must be addressed, but the existence of people with rights to demand certain actions, services, and conduct (Theis 2003; Abramovich 2004).

A social guarantees approach to social policy can help protect a country's ability to meet citizens' needs and develop their capabilities. In other words, social guarantees give concrete operational meaning to economic and social rights. Policies that follow the social guarantees approach are the expression of a nondiscriminatory agreement based on the principles of equal opportunity and respect. In turn, those policies help elevate standards of social justice and reduce political and social risks that hamper democracy and growth. Social guarantees are safeguards that society provides to all its members, ensuring those members' access to essential opportunities and sources of well-being.

Throughout this book, authors will argue that a social guarantees approach is an innovative way to integrate a rights-based perspective into social policy. The approach moves beyond a purely normative framework to give concrete meaning to economic and social rights. Social guarantees can be used to strengthen the delivery and monitoring of social programs and to develop partnerships among public and private stakeholders that, in turn, can help develop a social contract to strengthen democratic governance.

Building of Social Guarantees

Social rights usually are defined in a general and abstract manner. To realize those rights effectively, policy makers need to determine the operational scope of each right and the actions necessary to fulfill it. The social guarantees approach is designed precisely to assist governments in this task. For example, to determine whether the population is exercising its right to education, a set of educational services needed to satisfy this right must be defined clearly, and society as a whole must commit to providing those services.

One difference between a right and a social guarantee lies in their relationship to one another: the former has an abstract and ethical content and the latter identifies specific mechanisms that a government can put in place to realize the right. Such mechanisms may vary across countries or historical periods. For instance, some countries have determined that the right to education involves primary education only; others have extended this right to secondary education. Recently, some countries also have incorporated preschool and/or university education in their definitions of an educational entitlement—for example, Article 28 of the 2008 National Constitution of Ecuador guarantees free public tertiary education in addition to the primary and secondary levels. Their doing so shows that the operational scope of the right to education may differ in various contexts. Another important difference between economic, social, and cultural rights and social guarantees is that rights are to be realized progressively, whereas guarantees imply immediate obligations. A social guarantee is effective only if the services associated with it are available in a nondiscriminatory manner to the groups or individuals to whom it applies.

At the same time, making rights operational through social guarantees gives those rights concrete meaning and contributes to their being realized. More important, countries executing social guarantees can define the entitlements in different manners to reflect the underlying political and social consensus achieved in society, the level of economic development, existing or future budgetary commitments, and the institutional landscape. Although guarantees are defined in a universal manner, actions taken by the state certainly should be more concentrated on issues concerning the most vulnerable groups—those who generally cannot obtain services by their own means. For instance, preventive nutritional programs that supply set food rations have emerged through just such government focus. Programs of that type constitute a social guarantee only if they stipulate the specific mechanisms for providing the service, if they are available to all people who are malnourished, and if they can be claimed by the entitled people. Complementary nutrition programs are just one of many mechanisms for guaranteeing services linked to the right to food; the same right can be supported through cash transfers or subsistence programs. There is a wide range of possible programs that relate to the realization of a right. The form a social guarantee takes varies according to the specific circumstances that affect or characterize rightsholders. Overall, social guarantees emphasize that the most efficient, effective, and culturally sensitive means for realizing the set of entitlements are undertaken.

Operational Dimensions of a Guarantee: Subguarantees

The general concept of the social guarantee can be disaggregated into more specific entities or subguarantees. These more focused mechanisms capture two types of citizen expectations with regard to the state: (1) expectations that guaranteed services will be available and (2) expectations that unavailable services can be redressed. The following five subguarantees present a way to disaggregate the broader concept of the social guarantee to clarify and make it useful in policy and program design, implementation, and evaluation. One of the key elements of the following typology is how it emphasizes a holistic perspective of service delivery in the realization of rights—a perspective that encompasses a range of important dimensions (including access, quality, financial protection participation, and redress) and one that can be applied across different segments of the delivery system (public, private, and voluntary).

1. *Subguarantee of access:* This is the technical provision ensuring that rightsholders are able to access a set of defined services. It ensures that every eligible person can obtain the guaranteed services in a timely manner and for the duration of need. Thus, the definition of an entitlement must contain a precise description of the guaranteed services, the minimum period during which the services should be provided, duties and obligations of the citizens to be eligible to receive the services, the maximum waiting period to receive the services, and the availability of information channels through which beneficiaries can be made aware of the above information. The subguarantee of access constitutes the core of a social guarantee, and it must be designed in a way that furthers equity and a better quality of life.

2. *Subguarantee of quality:* This refers to the technical procedures ensuring that the entitlements and the means for delivering them are defined clearly, according to established quality standards. To this effect, it requires that quality standards and the mechanisms for certifying and accrediting providers are well defined and followed. Thus, it demands regular monitoring and evaluation procedures and clear mechanisms for communicating to the public the results of those evaluations.

3. *Subguarantee of financial protection:* This refers to the mechanisms ensuring that people who cannot afford the costs of accessing the entitlements (or receiving the services) will be able to access them through financial commitments from either public or private sources. Formulating this subguarantee requires a clear definition of the financial contributions that the state, beneficiaries, or other institutions are expected to make. These contributions should be determined on the basis of the beneficiaries' socioeconomic situations. This subguarantee

captures the essence of the subsidiary state—that is, a state that intervenes to support the disbursement of basic services to those individuals or groups who otherwise would be unable to afford them.

4. *Subguarantee of continuous revision and participation:* This subguarantee has two dimensions. First, it refers to procedures ensuring that the guarantee is revised periodically according to the availability of resources, changing risks, political and social consensus, and the advances of science and technology. Formulating this subguarantee requires that the following elements be defined clearly: (1) the criteria for revision; (2) the period at which revisions should take place; (3) the mechanisms and procedures for reformulating and approving new services and provision channels; and (4) the actors who need to play roles in this process, including beneficiaries. It also requires defining the rights and duties linked to this participation, and identifying the stage(s) of the political or programming cycle in which civic participation will take place. The second dimension of this subguarantee captures provisions made to ensure that citizens have a voice in key elements of service delivery through their participation in making decisions on resource allocation or the details of service delivery. These provisions are particularly important at levels in the system where local officials have discretion that may advantage or disadvantage particular groups—perhaps where decisions concerning local-level budget processes or service delivery facilities are made (such as in committees or other participatory entities at the level of clinics, schools, and so forth).

5. *Subguarantee of redress:* This subguarantee ensures that individuals or groups can claim access to the guaranteed services, as well as claim the fulfillment of each subguarantee. The design of redress mechanisms requires an exact definition of the situations in which citizens may make claims or of the judicial and nonjudicial means through which those claims may be pursued and resolved. The maximum waiting periods for claim resolution and all restorative procedures, sanctions, and compensations should be defined clearly. This subguarantee might be exercised through administrative or judicial channels. Creating or appointing a responsible institution to deal with the overall claims process—including resolution of claims and enforcement of decisions and compensations—establishes a channel to resolve claims and leaves the use of courts as a citizen's last resort. Providing an alternative to the courts is important because courts

are expensive and hard for poor claimants to access. Furthermore, the alternative channel offers a way to strengthen social institutions, which are critical indicators of democratic governance and social stability.

Domains of Implementation

A system based on guarantees requires a normative (legal) framework that precisely defines the rights and their threshold of realization, including a commitment to the equitable delivery of the specified rights, entitlements, and standards to all people on a universal basis. This legal framework allows a clear definition of the roles and accountability mechanisms between the state and the citizens, as well as the public, private, and civil society sectors. The definition and widespread communication of rights, entitlements, and standards enable citizens to hold makers and providers of public policy to account for the delivery of social policy. The presence of a legal or normative framework of entitlements, roles, and responsibilities also involves making available means of redress for citizens who are unable to enjoy specified entitlements or social minimums.

To become operational, a guarantee requires specific institutional arrangements involving the state, the private sector, and civil society to define the precise mechanisms, to secure the budget, to implement and monitor programs that will make those rights realizable, and to enable those individuals and social groups without access to claim their rights. In this context, the state fulfills a key role as a normative and regulatory institution overseeing the realization of the social minimums associated with a guarantee and its progressive revision.

Any guarantee also has an instrumental domain—that is, the translation of the legal and institutional frameworks into functioning policies and programs designed and implemented to ensure the realization of a specific entitlement.

Although laws, institutions, and programs are essential in building the framework for introducing and regulating social guarantees, such guarantees alone do not ensure that all citizens are able to access and claim timely provision of good-quality services. Making services "work" requires budget allocations and economic resources invested in realizing the guarantee and its subdimensions to ensure sustained access to the guaranteed entitlement.

In summary, any social guarantee can be described with reference to four domains—legal, institutional, instrumental, and financial—and to the five operational mechanisms or subguarantees described earlier. Any guarantee could be described through this prism, and any social program could be assessed against these dimensions to measure the potential gaps that exist between declared and existing rights or the opportunity gaps across social groups who might have differential access to entitlements and services.

To facilitate the design of social policies using a guarantees approach, it is helpful to build a matrix such as the one shown in table 2.1. When completed, it defines the specific content of each of the five subguarantees and identifies the necessary actions to be taken in each policy domain (legal, institutional, instrumental, and financial). Such a matrix may assist in identifying the most suitable techniques for putting in place a given social guarantee. It also helps coordinate the various mechanisms associated with a social service or guarantee. In particular, it is important to establish a link between the judicial and administrative mechanisms pertaining to social programming. Using the matrix helps policy makers build a conceptual bridge that reconciles judicial categories with the administrative ones used in social planning.

The evidence discussed in the following chapters suggests that moving toward a social guarantees approach can provide multiple benefits. First, from institutional and political points of view, the definition of social guarantees strengthens governance. Arriving at a social guarantee is a technical and political process that requires establishing social and political pacts that bring different stakeholders together to agree on specific levels of and mechanisms for service delivery, monitoring, and redress. At the same time, implementing a program inspired by a guarantees framework implies developing the institutional and inter-institutional capacity required for programs to function effectively.

A system of social guarantees implies the existence of a well-crafted legal framework and a sustainable budget—both of which necessitate creation of a fiscal pact or wide political agreements that permit financing the guarantees. Fiscal expenses should be structured to allow for timely

Table 2.1. Domains and Subdimensions of a Social Guarantee

Subguarantee / Policy domain	Access	Quality	Financial protection	Continuous revision and participation	Redress
Legal					
Institutional					
Instrumental					
Financial					

Source: Authors' compilation.

and sustainable provision of a set of prioritized services. To form such a structure, policy makers explicitly should establish the funding sources and tools for these services. The tools may include budget reallocations indexed to economic growth, tax increases, new incentives for donations, changes in the structure of the tax system, loans, and so forth.

The need to achieve a wide consensus on which services should be guaranteed enables society to exercise stronger control over policies, often raising the productivity and efficiency of public spending. Thus, creating a social and fiscal pact, as required by the guarantees approach, is instrumental in strengthening democratic institutions. Fiscal pacts are rooted in political agreements and should represent diverse societal interests. In a rule-of-law system, the legislative branch represents popular sovereignty and, therefore, is best equipped to undertake this task. At the same time, the corresponding authorities from local and regional governments and from civil society should engage in this process through the participation channels available to them.

Conclusion

In summary, applying a social guarantees framework may enable governments to confront certain challenges to social policy precisely because of the approach's technical characteristics. The social guarantees approach

- Defines the precise and technical content of rights, sets a minimum level of realization, describes the corresponding legal and policy mechanisms, establishes monitoring indicators, and enables progressive revision. In this sense, the approach serves as an organizing principle for monitoring and reforming social programs.
- Bridges existing social gaps. Whereas rights are universal, effectively making them operational through social guarantees ensures that those individuals and groups without access will receive the agreed minimum entitlements. In the context of the *World Development Report 2006: Equity and Development* (World Bank 2005), a social guarantee contributes to a more equitable delivery of basic services and, hence, to an enhanced equality of opportunities among all citizens.
- Increases transparency and accountability. Given its precise nature, the approach helps reduce administrative discretion and patrimony. The guarantees contain clear definitions of rights and descriptions of

rightsholders, institutional arrangements, operational mechanisms, and budget allocations.

- Empowers vulnerable groups by ensuring that redress and enforcement mechanisms are available to them. It increases their voices and participation and offers opportunity for a more open dialogue on social entitlements. A common definition and the widespread communication of rights enable citizens to hold institutions accountable.
- Facilitates the adaptability of benefits to a country's social, economic, and political conditions. Social guarantees can be modified or updated without harming the values they protect because they take into consideration aspects such as culture, resource availability, public consensus, and the like. Therefore, social guarantees are flexible and adaptable, and they make it possible to avoid falling back on standardized solutions that may not suit the specific circumstances in which they are formulated.

References

Abramovich, Victor. 2004. "An Approximation to a Rights Approach to Development Strategies and Policies in Latin America." Paper presented at "Rights and Development in Latin America: A Working Seminar," Santiago, Chile, December 9–10.

———. 2006. "The Rights-Based Approach in Development. Policies and Strategies." *CEPAL Review* 88 (April): 33–48.

Alston, Philip. 2003. "A Human Rights Perspective on the Millennium Development Goals." Paper prepared for the Millennium Project Task Force on Poverty and Economic Development. http://www.hurilink.org/tools/HRsPerspectives _on_the_MDGs—Alston.pdf (accessed February 19, 2009).

Doyal, Len, and Ian Gough. 1991. *A Theory of Human Need*. New York: Guilford Press.

Ferrajoli, Luigi. 2000. *El garantismo y la filosofía del derecho (The Guarantees Theory and the Philosophy of Law)*. Translated by G. Pisarello, A. Estrada, and J. M. Díaz Martín. Bogotá: Universidad Externado de Colombia.

———. 2001. *Los fundamentos de los derechos fundamentales (The Basis of Fundamental Rights)*. Madrid: Editorial Trotta.

———. 2004. *Derechos y garantías: la ley del más débil (Rights and Guarantees: The Law of the Weakest)*. Madrid: Editorial Trotta.

FUNASUPO (Fundación para la Superación de la Pobreza; Foundation for Overcoming Poverty). 2007. "Garantías sociales para la superación de la pobreza en Chile." Unpublished manuscript prepared for the World Bank, Washington, DC.

Habermas, Jürgen. 1996. *Between Facts and Norms: Contributions to a Discourse Theory of Law and Democracy.* Cambridge, MA: MIT Press.

————. 1998. *The Inclusion of the Other: Studies in Political Theory.* Cambridge, MA: MIT Press.

Moser, Caroline, and Andy Norton, with Tim Conway, Clare Ferguson, and Polly Vizard. 2001. *To Claim Our Rights: Livelihood Security, Human Rights and Sustainable Development.* London: Overseas Development Institute.

Rawls, John. 1971. *A Theory of Justice.* Cambridge, MA: Harvard University Press.

Rey Pérez, José Luis. 2002. "Can We Argue for a Human Right to Basic Income?" Universidad Pontificia Comillas, Madrid. http://www.citizensincome.org/resources/Jose%20Luis%20Rey%20Perez.shtml (accessed February 19, 2009).

Theis, Joachim. 2003. "Brief Introduction to Rights-Based Programming." Save the Children, Stockholm, Sweden.

United Nations. 2006. *Frequently Asked Questions on a Human Rights–Based Approach to Development Cooperation.* New York: United Nations.

World Bank. 2005. *World Development Report 2006: Equity and Development.* Washington, DC: World Bank.

CHAPTER 3

Democratic Governance and Institution Building for Inclusive Social Policy: The Latin American Experience

Estanislao Gacitúa-Marió, Sophia V. Georgieva, and Leonardo Moreno

Over the past 30 years, Latin America has experienced wide political, social, and economic reforms responding to an evolving domestic and international environment and to emerging social risks. Aspirations toward more democratic governance and toward social equity have evolved simultaneously; nevertheless, the struggle of Latin America's young democracies for stability, equity, and inclusion continues. In July 2008, José Miguel Insulza, secretary general of the Organization of American States (OAS), highlighted social justice as the most pressing issue on the social policy agenda of the Americas, adding that it needs to be pursued in the context of consolidating democracies and responding to the challenges of globalization (Insulza 2008).

Since the mid-1970s, social policy approaches in the region have progressed from state universalism, through social investment funds, targeted programs, and, most recently, a push toward an integrated social policy model that promotes equity and inclusion (Tulchin and Garland 2000; Deacon 2005, 2007). The latest trend toward a more comprehensive social policy has come with the recognition that vulnerable groups in each state are disadvantaged not only by their low financial means and lack of access to basic services, but also by a set of social, economic, and political barriers that prevent them from taking the lead in their own development and from effectively overcoming poverty and social marginalization. The fact that the region continues to have the greatest income inequality in the world and low rates of social mobility, even after radical political changes and overall political stabilization, demonstrates that there are structural inequities in Latin American societies that neither economic growth nor political stability alone can reverse.

This chapter argues that democratic governance is an essential factor for building social equity. A focus on democracy has to be coupled, however, with an effective social policy design to help diminish inequality of opportunities over the long run. Various experiences in the Latin American context already show an emerging consensus on this topic, as well as a trend toward institutionalizing a comprehensive social policy to achieve that goal. The next section begins by discussing the links and mutually reinforcing dynamic between democratic governance and inclusive social policy. The chapter proceeds to identify some of the major challenges to inclusion and democracy in Latin America. It then elaborates on the institutional arrangements needed to support a system that is both democratic and equitable, and finishes with a section of lessons and a conclusion.

Democratic Governance and Social Policy

The assertion that social cohesion strengthens democratic governance is now well supported. In addition, there is an inverse relationship—democratic governance itself generates social cohesion. Both assertions reveal that democracy and social development (understood as social inclusion, cohesion, and accountability) should not be analyzed in isolation from each other (see World Bank 2005).

Kaufmann, Kraay, and Mastruzzi (2008:7) define *governance* as the "traditions and institutions by which authority in a country is exercised. This includes the process by which governments are selected, monitored and replaced; the capacity of the government to effectively formulate and implement sound policies; and the respect of citizens and the state for the institutions that govern economic and social interactions among them.[1]" In that context, *democratic governance* refers to the capacity of a society to manage itself and to make decisions while balancing various social demands in a free and just environment.

Based on that definition, democratic governance goes beyond free elections and a transparent and accountable government. It also entails the capacity of all actors (be they political, economic, or civil society) to operate in a defined system of rules and norms, and their active participation in defining these rules. Enabling all relevant actors to participate and influence decision making in the context of unequal societies thus would require equality in terms of basic opportunities—that is, identifying and trying to overcome all structural barriers that may prevent the meaningful participation of any group. One way to approach this task is through a more inclusive and universal model of social policy—one that enhances every person's ability to engage as an active citizen in his or her society.

Social policy may have multiple definitions. Some understand it as concerning only the social sectors (such as health, education, and social protection), whereas others view it as embodying cross-cutting concerns about equity, distribution, social justice, and livelihood security—that is, as closely associated with economic policy. It is the latter view that is discussed in this chapter. In a democratic context, this view implies that social policy in any given country would represent a *social contract* based on negotiations among different social groups and on a compromise among what is desirable, feasible, and acceptable. It also implies that this social contract will be in the spirit of promoting equal opportunities for all citizens—with regard to such basic needs as food, clothing, housing, education, and health care; and to opportunities in the labor market, chances for social mobility, and political voice, among others. Although democratic governance certainly facilitates the adoption of comprehensive social policy, the reverse is also true: an inclusive social policy itself serves to strengthen the basis for democratic governance. This two-way dynamic reveals a fundamental synergy between democracy and an inclusive social policy.

There is both ethical and instrumental value to aspiring simultaneously to democratic governance and social inclusion. Experiences in Latin America and the world at large have shown that a democratic system can function without a systematic policy to meet universal basic needs and that basic needs can be met effectively in a nondemocratic model. Viewed from the perspective of human rights, the balancing of democratic governance and inclusive social policy is especially important if governments aspire to the respect, protection, and fulfillment both of civil/political and of economic/social/cultural rights. Across Latin America, democracy is seen as guaranteeing civil and political freedoms. In consequence, the laws and policies of the various states have advanced notably toward guaranteeing civil and political rights. Efforts to safeguard the economic and social rights of citizens have been more recent; however, they are essential to the future support for democracy. The Latinobarómetro report (2008:7) argues that the meaning of democracy in Latin America always has had a strong economic dimension.

Having emerged from subsequent and tumultuous periods of frequent political change and authoritarianism, Latin American states now have the opportunity to shape a future social contract that promotes both social equity and democracy. Although democratic governance has yet to be consolidated and recognized as fully functioning in the region, there is no doubt that most Latin American states aspire to the democratic model. The notions of rights and citizenship can be instrumental to this end. As noted by OAS Secretary General Insulza, in relation to new social programs in Latin America, the transition toward more democratic conceptions of social policy in Latin America is developing hand in hand with an emphasis on the rights and obligations of citizens and the state (Insulza 2008).

Challenges to Inclusive Social Policy in the Latin American Context

Various factors have contributed to unsatisfactory social policy outcomes in Latin America—for example, periods of low economic growth, uneven tax policies, geographic barriers, and lack of an effective model to address the region's extensive ethnic diversity with limited state resources. Two particular factors that are characteristic of the region's historical experience can be singled out: (1) lack of consensus on a valid social policy model among states and, even more important, among various political actors within each state; and (2) political instability and frequent changes in leadership and policy concepts that have obstructed the sustainability of any social reform and have prevented the formation of independent and effective institutions for social policy.

The first fundamental challenge to inclusive social policy has been the shaping of Latin America's social policies by a series of drastically different approaches (see box 3.1) and the resulting mosaic of models: subsidiary, targeting, universalist, and hybrid. Consequently, the current social policy architecture in the region reflects diverse conceptual frameworks and institutional arrangements. Moreover, political actors within each state advocate for more or less fiscally conservative social policy models and, depending on their power within the state in each given period, those actors sway policies in their preferred direction. In other words, policy arrangements in Latin American states generally do not represent stable social contracts.

On the positive side, the experience with a variety of policy approaches and programs has yielded a wealth of lessons for future social policy design. For example, the recent popularity of conditional cash transfer programs

---

BOX 3.1

Social Policy in Latin America: A Historical Perspective

There have been several stages in the evolution of social policy in Latin America, and these stages have reflected the prevailing political, ideologic, and economic conditions of each period: (1) the late 19th century until 1930, during which time social services mainly were the domain of the private sector and of civil associations through charitable work; (2) 1930–80, a period associated with rising popularity of the import-substitution model, an increasing state role in social service delivery, a radical increase in school enrollments, declines in child mortality, and improvements in health facilities, water, and sanitation; (3) the 1980s to early 1990s, a decade of structural adjustment during which the state was progressively withdrawing from social service provision; and (4) mid-1990s to the present, a time when social service delivery is characterized by decentralization, stronger civil society participation in the delivery of social services, and more partnerships between the state and private providers, and when targeting and conditional cash transfers remain popular social protection approaches in the region.

None of these approaches, however, has been successful in eliminating the persistent social inequalities in the region. Public welfare programs developed in the first half of the 20th century were characterized by generous support to the formal sector, in contrast with almost nonexistent social assistance for the informal sector. This trend continues today, even though some recent social protection programs have tried to incorporate informal workers into states' social assistance schemes.

The changes in social policy approaches that the Latin American region has adopted over the past century account for some of the difficulties faced by the region in maintaining strong social policy institutions. A more consistent approach to social policy is likely to have a stronger impact in reducing socioeconomic inequities in the long term.

Source: World Bank 2008:6.

---

and, even more so, the emergence of multisectoral action plans in social policy (such as the Plan for Social Equity in Uruguay) reflect an understanding of the needs to expand state assistance to vulnerable citizens beyond the formal sector and to open opportunities in more than one area.

The second fundamental challenge to inclusive social policy in the region has been frequent political change that has held back sustainable social reforms. To be effective over the long term, social policies require a commitment reflected in the legal framework, budgetary allocations, and institutions with a clear mandate to support that commitment. Given the lack of agreement and continuity in many areas of social policy experienced in Latin American states, it has been difficult for legal, institutional, and fiscal commitments promoting social equity to be sustained over long periods. Thus, societies in the region are challenged to reach a consensus on basic universal entitlements across the political spectrum to ensure sustainable implementation (along the lines of Chile's health reforms, described in chapter 5).

Building a social contract and a related fiscal pact that can persist through political change while remaining flexible for continual improvement is a recognized but challenging goal for Latin American governments. The political discourse aspiring toward sustainable social policies and institutions has become more pronounced, as revealed by elaboration of the Social Charter of the Americas and recent high-level summits of the Americas convened to discuss trends in social policy.

The following section, based largely on Sulbrandt (2008), traces the institutional developments in Latin America that gradually are shaping a more active multisectoral approach to equity and social inclusion.[2]

Institutionalizing Inclusive Social Policy in the Region

The discussions of recent years on how to reconcile economic with social policy, universal policies with targeting, equity with efficiency, the role of the state with that of the market are intimately linked with the design of our institutions.

–José Miguel Insulza (2008:5)

Latin America's social policy institutions in education, health, social protection, and the like have developed progressively over the past century. However, their evolution in the context of democratizing and incorporating concerns for universal equity has occurred mostly since the mid-1990s. After 15 years of an exclusive policy focus on economic growth and no satisfactory evidence of declining inequality, Latin American governments and societies began to rethink the design of social policies in the mid-1990s, giving more attention to issues of inequity and exclusion. Prior to that time, the efforts to alleviate extreme poverty had centered on creating social investment funds. That approach viewed poverty and vulnerability mostly as functions of income and as transitory.

The social investment funds were targeted to extremely poor people in the belief that if their incomes increased, households would be able to overcome their marginalization. In the beginning of the 1990s, the social policy agenda was broadened to include the needs of specific vulnerable groups—women, children, and ethnic minorities. By the end of the 1990s and the beginning of the present millennium, more innovative approaches to social policy addressing the roots of inequality and exclusion began to emerge.

Some of the earliest critiques related to the structural adjustment policies of the 1980s and early 1990s were directed specifically at the weak institutional design of the social sectors that could not manage to stand up to the demands of the market economy and protect the equality of opportunity between the poor and marginalized groups and the rest of the population (Sulbrandt 2008). Each state needed a strong high-level institutional body that could negotiate with the ministries of economy and finance to reach agreement on a balance between growth and fiscal sustainability on the one hand and fulfillment of the state's responsibilities to secure basic rights and opportunities for all citizens on the other.

Acknowledging these institutional needs, in the past 5 years many Latin American states created ministries of social development or equivalent agencies with a cross-sectoral mandate. Establishing such bodies greatly enhanced the state's technical capacity to design and follow through on social policies because systems for information and control and for monitoring and evaluation as well as relevant targets and indicators began to be generated. The research, knowledge, and proposals for the design of more inclusive policies also could be channeled at the highest level to produce a grater impact on decision making.

Drawing on Sulbrandt (2008), we can identify two broad classes of current institutional arrangements across the region: (1) those whose social development policies are led by a central coordinating agency—a ministry of social development (Argentina, Paraguay, and Uruguay), a ministry of planning (Chile, Colombia, and Costa Rica), or a similar body; and (2) those that lack a high-level coordinating institution, whether because such institution was established but later reformed (Bolivia and República Bolivariana de Venezuela) or because social development responsibilities are split between various agencies and secretariats (Guatemala and Mexico) or assigned to a multisectoral social cabinet (Panama).

The establishment of ministries of social development has provided a legal and institutional basis for coordinating social development policies and has enabled the growth of technical and professional capacities in social policy at the country level. If successfully managed, ministries of social development can lead a multisectoral network of activities aimed at social inclusion, and they can find ways to engage organized civil society in meaningful dialogue with the government. Ministries of planning, such as those in Chile, Colombia, and Costa Rica, also have developed a strong technical-professional capacity to formulate and implement social policies and programs, coordinating their activities with those of other sectors. Both types of ministries already have a substantial experience with cash transfers and other social protection programs (Sulbrandt 2008).

In other states, such as Bolivia and the República Bolivariana de Venezuela, social policy agencies were created at the national level but have been subject to various reforms since their establishment. In Bolivia, social policy is ascribed to the Ministry of Planning and Development (created in 2006), which also is responsible for accepting and administering foreign aid. In the República Bolivariana de Venezuela, social policy formally is delegated to the Ministry of Popular Power, Participation, and Social Protection (established in 2005), but its functions have been reformed continuously (Sulbrandt 2008).

Also within this second general group of states are those that rely on social secretariats or agencies responsible for different social programs, affiliated either with sectoral ministries in education, health, and nutrition or with ministries of the family or of women. In this subgroup, the capacity for overall leadership and coordination of social policy generally is weak. Programs often are affiliated directly with the President's Office or, as in Guatemala, with the Secretariat for Social Works of the President's Wife. In this case, the institutional basis for social policy planning is less consolidated. One can also argue that it is less sustainable, given that its normative basis (in law or the constitution) is weaker than that of a ministry, and its activities can be discontinued more easily after a change in administration.

In Ecuador, since 2007, the institutional structure for social policy has become even more complex, with two responsible ministries—the Ministry of Social Development Coordination and the Ministry of Economic and Social Inclusion—and a cross-sectoral Social Cabinet. The function of the Social Cabinet is essential because it has the power to approve and make decisions regarding social policies. In other states, the social cabinet is important as a space for negotiation among sectors, but it does not always have decision-making powers.

Overall, social policy institutions in Latin America have undergone an intensive process of consolidation and reform, owing to the distinct political and economic views over the past 20 years. Instead of leading the process of social policy making, these institutions themselves have been shaped and reshaped by various public policy trends. In the past 5 years, the emergence of high-level social policy institutions has contributed to more active cross-sectoral planning in the areas of social inclusion and to enhancing of opportunities for vulnerable groups.

The evolution of social policy institutions in the past decade shows a growing commitment to increasing equity and social justice. Nevertheless, the impact and sustainability of recently developed institutions and programs have not been proved. To be effective in the long run, social cabinets, ministries, or equivalent institutions must have the budgetary and decision-making powers to fulfill their policies. They also need to be flexible and open to working with various nongovernmental actors in the public, private, and civil sectors to channel creative proposals into the policy-making arena and to stir and maintain an open dialogue about social policies. Achieving a social contract that is supported by all or most actors in society and by policy makers is the first and most essential goal of a coordinating social policy institution.

The value of extra-governmental agencies (such as Chile's Foundation for Overcoming Poverty, the Institute for Research and Development in Uruguay, and similar organizations) in developing proposals and steering public dialogue on innovative social policies is worth highlighting. Such agencies that combine professional expertise with nonpartisan views are well positioned to design credible proposals for social policy improvement and to promote an understanding of those proposals across political divides and diverse policy communities. Facilitating the inclusion of such extra-governmental agencies in the policy dialogue can be of great benefit to social development authorities.

Lessons and Conclusion

As democratic governance and social policy approaches continue to evolve in Latin America, it is important to remember the lessons that the rich and varied political and economic history of the region has to offer. This chapter has revealed an emerging agreement in Latin America that social policies need to address issues of equity and inclusion rather than issues of poverty reduction alone. It also has pointed out that a new and better social policy is a responsibility of both the state and its citizens within a mutually agreed-upon framework of rights and obligations. Latin American states have put significant effort into consolidating democratic governance and civil and political rights. A similar emphasis now should be placed on strengthening social inclusion and both protecting and fulfilling economic, social, and cultural rights.

In general, each Latin American state has yet to define a sustainable process by which policy reforms in the social arena would be best designed and implemented in line with the needs and priorities of its society and with its fiscal limits. Because countries need to ensure stronger continuity of policy approaches and their sustainability through periods of political change, the goals for the future of social policy in the region can be distilled as follows: (1) to reach concrete and long-term commitments to policies and programs that diminish barriers to opportunity for the most vulnerable groups, and (2) to establish strong social institutions to lead a multisectoral agenda for social equity and inclusion policies.

Latin American states are at various stages of movement toward those goals. An overarching theme in all states of the region is an effort to extend the frontiers of social citizenship by enabling all people to be active participants in society. Also needed are efforts to identify and eliminate obstacles that keep citizens from active participation. To achieve the latter, societies (policy makers and nongovernmental actors included) must establish minimums or "citizenship thresholds" above which every citizen effectively can exercise his or her fundamental rights.

The social guarantees approach discussed in this book suggests one possible framework for establishing citizenship thresholds for realizing fundamental rights and for designing policies and programs to uphold them. Applied to each specific country context, social guarantees imply the definition of universal entitlements that the society as a whole agrees to protect and fulfill. They also call for concrete definitions of the roles and obligations of citizens, the state, and all involved institutions in fulfilling those entitlements for every person who needs them. In this volume, the social guarantees approach is used as a framework of analysis that enables policy makers, development workers, and researchers to evaluate recent policies' progress and shortcomings in fulfilling fundamental rights in the region. Nevertheless, as the case of health policy in Chile demonstrates, the social guarantees framework also can be used as a basis for designing specific programs that effectively increase equity in service delivery.

Notes

1. The authors define six dimensions of governance: (1) voice and accountability; (2) political stability and absence of violence; (3) government effectiveness; (4) regulatory quality; (5) rule of law; and (6) control of corruption, including capture of the state by elites for private interests.
2. Representative gatherings include the Second Meeting of the Inter-American Committee on Social Development of the OAS, held in Washington, DC, October 22–23, 2007; the OAS First Meeting of Ministers and High Authorities of Social Development, held in Reñaca, Chile, July 8–10, 2008 (http://www.sedi .oas.org/ddse/english/cpo_desoc_minist.asp#_Hlk4); and the Technical Consultation Workshop on the Challenges for Social Development Policy in Latin America and the Caribbean, sponsored by the OAS and the World Bank, in Asunción, Paraguay, June 4–6, 2008.

References

Deacon, Bob. 2005. "From 'Safety Nets' Back to 'Universal Social Provision': Is the Global Tide Turning?" *Global Social Policy* 5 (1): 19–28.

———. 2007. *Global Social Policy & Governance*. Beverly Hills, CA: Sage Publications.

Insulza, José Miguel. 2008. Welcoming remarks at the inauguration ceremony of the Organization of American States (OAS) First Meeting of Ministers and High Authorities of Social Development, Reñaca, Chile, July 8–10. http:// www.sedi.oas.org/ddse/english/cpo_desoc_minist.asp#_Hlk4 (accessed March 23, 2009).

Kaufmann, Daniel, Aart Kraay, and Massimo Mastruzzi. 2008. "Governance Matters VII: Aggregate and Individual Governance Indicators, 1996–2007." Policy Research Working Paper 4654, World Bank, Washington, DC.

Latinobarómetro. 2008. *Informe 2008*. Santiago, Chile: Corporación Latinobarómetro. http://www.latinobarometro.org/docs/INFORME_LATINOBAROMETRO_2008 .pdf (accessed March 23, 2009).

Sulbrandt, José. 2008. "La institucionalización de la política social" (Institutionalizing Social Policy). Presentation at the Technical Consultation Workshop on the Challenges for Social Development Policy in Latin America and the

Caribbean, sponsored by the Organization of American States and the World Bank, Asunción, Paraguay, June 4–6.

Tulchin, Joseph S., and Allison M. Garland, eds. 2000. *Social Development in Latin America: The Politics of Reform.* Boulder, CO: Lynne Rienner.

World Bank. 2005. *Empowering People by Transforming Institutions: Social Development in World Bank Operations.* Washington, DC: World Bank.

———. 2008. *Realizing Rights through Social Guarantees: An Analysis of New Approaches to Social Policy in Latin America and South Africa.* Washington, DC: World Bank.

CHAPTER 4

Comprehensive Social Policy for Inclusive and Sustainable Globalization

Steen Lau Jorgensen and Rodrigo Serrano-Berthet

Worldwide, social policy increasingly is recognized as central to promoting inclusive and sustainable globalization because a comprehensive, or holistic, view of social policy, working in tandem with economic policy, helps ensure inclusive and sustainable economic growth and well-being. This shift in understanding is being led by a group of emerging and transition economies introducing comprehensive reforms focused on social cohesion and sustainable development. The emphasis at the cutting edge of this change is no longer on a social policy dealing with residual effects of economic policy, but on a renewed social compact between citizens and the state that sets the stage for congruous development paths.

The mark of our time is globalization with increased opportunities from enhanced flows of ideas, capital, and trade. However, these benefits and the downside risks of globalization are not equally distributed. Better-off, better-connected people are likely to benefit, and people who are less well-off or in sectors less well adapted to globalization will suffer. However, it also is clear that the old welfare state model—where the state acts as sole provider of social services—is no longer tenable. With increasingly open economies, the ability of governments to tax and redistribute is becoming increasingly limited. Conversely, a complete reliance on market-based systems is likely to increase inequality and severely test the social fabric, thereby undermining opportunities for sustained growth.[1] Most important, globalizing factors transform not only economies but also social and political structures, creating further opportunities and increased risks that again are unevenly distributed.

These trends call for an expansion of the concept of social policy toward a comprehensive "social contract," moving away from a model of state or market provision of welfare services to needy beneficiaries (elderly, disabled, and so forth) to a contract between the state and citizens with rights and responsibilities on both sides. It means a blurring of the boundary between economic and social policies by rethinking traditional roles and institutional setup. Although this debate is very much alive in Organisation for Economic Co-operation and Development (OECD) settings, the countries with emerging and transitional economies have moved most strongly toward these new concepts. By moving toward a system appropriate for a globalized world, these countries see an opportunity to "leapfrog" the traditional OECD countries.

Figure 4.1 illustrates a simple analytical framework for social policy in a globalizing world. As goods, services, finance, and people and ideas begin to move more freely, it is essential for sustainable and inclusive growth that a society creates a social compact framed by the three themes of inclusion, cohesion, and accountability. Inclusion enables people to see the benefits of globalization and economic growth. Cohesion is essential to restructuring the economy with little disruption and within a commonly agreed framework. Finally, accountability ensures there is trust between the citizens and the state where services are paid for and delivered. Economies can be restructured only through a strong social contract.

Figure 4.1. Analytical Framework for Globalized Social Policy

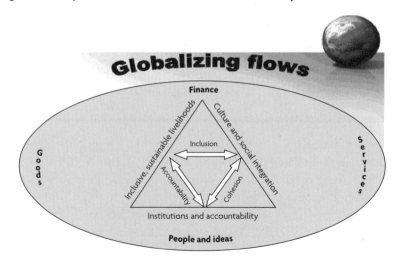

Source: World Bank 2005c.

Traditional social policy interventions are important parts of this contract. Safety nets are needed to ensure that workers are willing to accept the more flexible working arrangements that are necessary for economies to remain competitive; old-age income security is an important component of inclusion and remuneration for those people who have helped set the stage for today's well-being. In addition to these traditional social policy measures, a more comprehensive set of rights guarantees is important to help citizens engage in investments that carry both higher risk and higher return. Such investments would enable them to benefit from globalization and, thus, drive a more sustainable economic growth. For example, a comprehensive social policy would guarantee access to a minimum set of publicly or privately provided services—such as transportation, property rights, or health care—as part of a contract between the state and its citizens. This access truly would free individuals and firms to engage in free-market activities because of their greater ability to take on risks as these minimum standards are met. With greater risk taking would come greater returns and a virtuous cycle of growth and stability. Without such a compact, the increased risks from globalization might force individuals and firms to go for a "safety-first" strategy to guard against catastrophic events, thereby limiting their willingness to engage in high-risk/high-return activities.

There is some historical evidence that even small, resource-scarce economies do well when markets open up if those economies have comprehensive social policies ensuring that citizens' basic needs are met. (Holland is an example of such an economy.) The evidence so far has come mostly from Europe, so it is important to assess non-European countries carefully, given their different socioeconomic traditions and institutions.

Comprehensive, Citizenship-Based Social Policy

A comprehensive social policy is concerned not only with the sectors covered by traditional social policy (health, education, and safety nets), but also with the social dimension of all sectors that has an impact on welfare. It approaches policy making through a social justice, citizenship, and rights-based perspective.

Elements, Origins, and Implications of a Comprehensive Social Policy

There are two main parts to the definition of a comprehensive social policy: (1) it covers a variety of sectors, in addition to the traditional social sectors, to provide a broad set of guarantees or minimum standards; and (2) it uses the lens of social justice (social fairness) and citizenship (rights and responsibilities) as a yardstick for measuring policy changes. Social policy is judged by whether the proposed policy change enhances social justice; enhances the sense of fairness in a society; and, thus, supports a social compact. In other words, is the policy inclusive? Does it support cohesion, and are the institutions accountable?

For the traditional social sectors, a comprehensive approach means addressing the key social justice aspects of the policies. In public health and education, the key to supporting a social compact is equal access and basic service guarantees for everyone, regardless of who provides the service and how the service is financed. States should guarantee as part of the social contract that all citizens have access to such services through public provision, financing, or regulation. Equal access, traditional issues of efficiency, political economy, as well as clear and equal standards become critical.

In addition to health and education, traditional social policy covers safety nets (welfare payments and social assistance)—noncontributory transfer programs targeted in some manner to poor or vulnerable people (see box 4.1). Examples include

- *cash transfers* or food stamps, whether means tested or categorical (as in child allowances or social pensions)
- *in-kind transfers*, with food through school lunch programs and mother and child supplement programs being the most common types
- *price subsidies* meant to benefit poor households, often for food or energy
- *jobs on labor-intensive public works*, sometimes called workfare
- *conditional transfers,* in cash or in kind, given to poor households, subject to their compliance with specific conditions regarding education or health
- *fee waivers* for essential services, such as health care, schooling, utilities, or transportation.

Increasingly, countries are looking comprehensively at their safety net programs to ensure that they are affordable and effective. The World Bank's social protection policy states that effective safety nets are essential to enable the poor to better manage risks (World Bank 2001b). By looking at this issue through the lens of social justice, targeting criteria for benefits can be assessed on how accurately they ensure a citizenship approach whereby every citizen has access and is guaranteed a minimum

BOX 4.1

Four Critical Functions Played by Safety Nets

Safety nets can help achieve four objectives that are part of the larger poverty reduction and risk management agenda goals:

1. *Safety nets can have an immediate impact on reducing inequality and poverty, especially extreme poverty.* As a minimal function, safety nets can make poverty survivable or more bearable by getting transfers to the poorest people. In economics, on the basis of a social welfare function that weights the welfare of the poorer more than the welfare of the less poor, society benefits more if a poor person receives an extra $1 of income than if a rich person receives that amount.
2. *Safety nets can enable households to make better investments in their futures.* Safety nets can act to remedy credit market failures, allowing households to take up investment opportunities they would otherwise miss—investments both in the human capital of their children and in the livelihoods of the earners.
3. *Safety nets help households manage risks.* When families—especially poor families— face reductions in income or assets, they may have to resort to costly coping strategies that perpetuate poverty. For example, there is clear evidence that families who suffer from short-term shocks may be forced to cut back on the feeding or schooling of their children, with deterioration in nutritional or health status often more common than withdrawals from school. When risks increase, households may minimize risk by making livelihood choices that reduce their earnings. A good safety net can reduce such strategies that can trap households in a cycle of poverty.
4. *Safety nets help governments make or sustain sound policies.* They can facilitate macroeconomic and structural changes in the economy that are meant to support growth. The logic is intuitive: there is less opposition to reform when there are mechanisms to compensate losers or to assist the poor who often become poorer during a downturn. Less opposition to reform then allows better macroeconomic policy and growth (Rodrik 1997). Safety nets also can reduce the costs to growth associated with high inequality by reducing inequality over the short term. Transfers play both direct and indirect roles in reducing inequality by helping create a virtuous circle, leading to more inclusive institutions, better policy, and higher growth.

Sources: Grosh et al. 2008, and sources cited therein.

standard. This does not mean paying out an equal amount to all citizens; rather, it means that every citizen has a right to a given service if certain events happen. For example, everyone has the right to a disability payment if they become disabled; and everyone has the right to a social pension guaranteeing a dignified old age, regardless of gender, ethnicity, or employment status.

A comprehensive social policy also means applying the same criteria to other areas of public policy. Are labor market policies geared toward nondiscriminatory practices? Do transportation policies favor equal access to public transportation? Are urban policies protecting the property rights of all people, including the poor? Do financial policies create distortions that discriminate against smallholders? Are utilities regulated in a fair and transparent manner that ensures maximum, affordable access for all? The well-being of individuals and families covers many areas not included under traditional definitions of social policy. Individuals' relationships with the state include all areas of state policy and service provision, so the social compact between the state and its citizens needs to ensure that all policies and regulations address issues of social justice and fairness. In addition to providing better social policy, it may be more economically efficient to improve regulation of, say, electricity markets toward more universally affordable access than to design and raise taxes to ensure equal access through subsidies for poor or elderly people.

The Emerging Consensus: A Comprehensive, Rights-Based Approach to Social Policy

In addition to covering more than traditional social safety nets and ensuring equality of opportunity to benefit individuals (at the microlevel), a comprehensive social policy also addresses society's meso- and macrolevels by promoting the following conditions:

- equality of agency and institutional reform to benefit groups (mesolevel)
- horizontal and vertical social integration to benefit society as a whole (macrolevel).

Equality of agency is crucial if the social compact is to function. Only when different groups are empowered to influence policies and outcomes will the resulting policies be seen as fair and just. This means that the policy process must be opened to citizens and citizen groups to ensure that the voices heard are not only those of the powerful. Similarly, good social policies must promote horizontal or vertical integration and social mobility so that everyone has a chance "to make it." If individuals or groups feel excluded and see little to gain from globalization and national growth, ownership is limited and there is a danger of losing social cohesion, which can result in social unrest. In less-developed countries, those circumstances may result in violent conflict; in higher-income countries, they may lead to social disturbances, crime, or the marginalization of key groups who then are unwilling or unable to contribute to national progress.

Several emerging economies have begun to implement comprehensive social policies or, as they also may be characterized, *rights-based approaches to social policy*. These reforms imply the introduction of a set of institutions and policies within a society that secures every member's reasonable access to a social minimum (see chapter 2 of this volume; World Bank 2007). Generally, the following elements are incorporated in such an approach:

- the definition and widespread communication of rights, entitlements, and standards, which enable citizens to hold public policy makers and providers to account for the delivery of social policy
- the availability of redress mechanisms for citizens who are unable to enjoy specified entitlements or social minimums
- a universal commitment to the equitable delivery of the specified rights, entitlements, and standards.

Successful examples include both lower- and middle-income developing countries (Chile, India, South Africa, and others).

This new consensus on comprehensive and rights-based approaches has been under way for more than a decade, and it builds on the 10 principles from the March 1995 World Summit for Social Development, held in Copenhagen, Denmark. The United Nations Commission on Human Security identifies three fundamental elements of human security— survival, livelihood, and dignity—that can be expressed in three types of freedom: freedom from fear, freedom from want, and freedom to live in dignity (Jorgensen 2006). In December 2005 in Arusha, Tanzania, the World Bank convened a conference on new frontiers of social policy to mark the 10-year anniversary of the Social Summit.[2] During the conference, participants agreed on three key areas to address as the new frontiers of social policy (see box 4.2). A similar message came out of the roundtable convened by the governments of Finland and Sweden, at which social and employment policy experts from several governments, civil society organizations, and research institutes of the global South

BOX 4.2

New Frontiers of Social Policy

Leading thinkers on social policy—including academics, policy analysts, practitioners, and policy makers from developing and developed countries—gathered in Arusha, Tanzania in December 2005 to discuss and debate how to foster and augment existing social policies by giving greater attention to employment (livelihoods), social integration, and institutions. They identified three new frontiers for social policy:

1. *Transforming subjects and beneficiaries into citizens:* This refers to policies that recognize and promote the universal rights and responsibilities of citizens and that strengthen the capacity of citizens to claim their rights. Some of the most effective examples of progress on citizens' rights have come from alliances between the poor and other segments of society, suggesting that targeting public resources to the poor alone is not always the most effective way to empower them and build their capabilities.

2. *Fostering an enabling, accessible, responsive, and accountable state:* This calls for universal application of the rule of law and for equal rights under the law for all citizens. Universal rights, however, need to be accompanied by legitimate, effective, and accountable institutions for policy formulation and implementation, with rigorous monitoring of outcomes. This implies recognizing and celebrating multiculturalism as a source of strength for societies, and supporting policies that accommodate diversity in the achievement of universal rights. It also requires recognizing the role of power relationships and creating institutional mechanisms that offer redress against power inequities.

3. *Strengthening the capacity of states to mobilize revenue from their citizens, and diminishing reliance on external aid:* Domestic resource mobilization is the most effective means of enhancing citizen ownership and state accountability and of ensuring sustainability. It presupposes a stronger enabling environment and resources for accelerated development. The international community—donors, governments, international organizations, and the private sector—will have to play their parts to enable these processes.

Source: World Bank (http://go.worldbank.org/GVLVLLV790 [accessed March 27, 2009]).

and global North, as well as from international organizations, gathered in Kellokoski and Stockholm in November 2006 (Wiman, Voipio, and Ylönen 2007).

Different Starting Points: Welfare Regimes around the Globe

Adopting a comprehensive, rights-based approach to social policy does not mean that all countries around the globe should adopt the same set of policies and service provision arrangements. Each country will follow its own path. Starting points will be different, although countries share the same end point: formal security of welfare for all people. In other words, this may be described as being universalist about ends while being relativist about means. Recognizing formal security of welfare (in the sense of individual, guaranteed, nonpersonal, judicial rights independent of wealth, gender, status, or other ascribed characteristics) is understood as the most satisfactory way to meet universal human needs.

Welfare regimes is the term used to characterize the different starting points for individual countries or regions of the world. It refers to "repeated systemic arrangements through which people seek livelihood security both for their own lives and for those of their children, descendants, and elders.... it embodies the relationship between sets of rights on the one hand and the performance of correlative duties on the other. The manner in which that relationship is specified is a product of history, especially a history reflecting the interrelation in different epochs between domestic institutions and the global economy. Those interrelations circumscribe the relative autonomy and legitimacy of the state, and bring a range of non-state actors at global as well as local level into our generalized account of social policy" (Wood and Gough 2006: 1700).

At the global level, following Esping-Andersen (1990) and Wood and Gough (2006), it is possible to identify three distinct metawelfare regimes[3]:

1. *Welfare state regimes* are capitalist societies that have been transformed into welfare states. This does not include countries that happen to engage in a bit of social policy on the side, but specifically refers to societies so deeply affected by their nonresidual, pervasive social policies that they are best defined as welfare states (Esping-Andersen 1990). This definition most closely describes OECD countries that can be differentiated, in turn, according to their social democratic, conservative, or liberal matrix.

2. *Informal security regimes* are situations in which people rely heavily on community and family relationships to meet their security needs. These relationships usually are hierarchical and asymmetrical, resulting in problematic inclusion or adverse incorporation where people trade some short-term security for longer-term vulnerability and dependence. The underlying patron-client relationships then are reinforced, proving extremely resistant to civil society pressures and measures to reform them along welfare-state lines. Nevertheless, these relationships do comprise a series of informal rights and afford some measures of informal security.

3. *Insecurity regimes* are institutional arrangements that generate gross insecurity and block the emergence of stable informal mechanisms. These regimes arise in areas of the world where powerful external players interact with weak internal actors to generate conflict and political instability. Such unpredictable environments undermine stable patterns of clientelism and informal rights within communities, and can destroy household coping mechanisms. In the face of local warlords and other disruptive actors, governments often are incapable of offering governance- and security-enhancing roles. Such situations result in a vicious circle of insecurity, vulnerability, and suffering for all but a small elite, their enforcers, and clients (Esping-Andersen 1990: 1699–700).

These regimes express substantial variations in welfare outcomes (need satisfaction, subjective well-being, and so forth). In figure 4.2, selected economies and regions are clustered across different regime types. The outcomes are explained most immediately by differences in the institutional responsibility matrix, or welfare mix, of each regime—that is, "the institutional landscape within which people have to pursue their livelihoods and well-being objectives, referring to the role of government, community (informal as well as organized, such as NGOs [nongovernmental organizations] and community-based organizations), private sector market activity, and the household in mitigating insecurity and well-being, alongside the role of matching international actors and processes" (Esping-Andersen 1990: 1701).

Middle-income countries in East Asia provide a model of combined informal and formal welfare, described as *productivist welfare regimes*. Social policy is subordinated to the dominant economic policy goal of maintaining high rates of growth, concentrated in education and health

Figure 4.2. Selected Economies and Regions Classified by Type of Welfare Regime

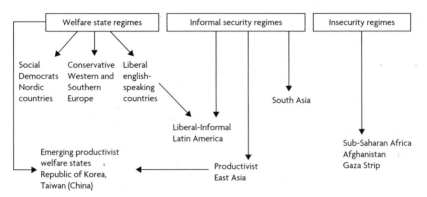

Source: Wood and Gough 2006. Reprinted with permission from Elsevier Ltd.

rather than in social protection. When the 1997 financial crisis hit East Asia, the absence of social protection measures and lack of social investment in higher education exposed vulnerabilities in the old system. Spurred by the financial crisis, some countries (such as the Republic of Korea and Taiwan [China]) are developing incipient productivist welfare states (Kwon 2005).

This comparative perspective on global welfare regimes points to the need to focus social policy on "declientelization," confirming the consensus on a new citizenship- and rights-based approach to social policy. If informal arrangements within the community are characterized by clientelism, declientelization should be the basis for improving the quality of rights and duties. Declientelizing requires establishing more formal rights to welfare and security. Institutionalized microcredit is an example of an attempt to de-link poor people from usurious moneylenders. Approaches that strengthen the voice and power of poor people in making decisions—such as community-driven development and participatory local governance—are other examples of instruments that can help countries move toward a comprehensive social policy. Civic mobilization often has been crucial to helping countries from the South move along the path of greater security and inclusion. For instance, in the Republic of Korea and Taiwan (China), advocacy coalitions comprising policy experts, grassroots civic organizations, bureaucrats, and politicians have been at the center of progress in the welfare state (Kwon 2005).

Main Debates and Challenges

The case for a comprehensive social policy approach inevitably leads to counterarguments, namely, the following:

1. Wouldn't an increase in social spending have a negative effect on growth (the traditional argument of efficiency vs. equity)?
2. Wouldn't scarce public resources be used more efficiently by targeting the "truly deserving" poor rather than by creating a universal provision?
3. Is this affordable? Can public budgets sustainably finance the expanded mandates implied in this comprehensive approach?

A brief response to each of these concerns is offered here.

Debate 1. Equity and Efficiency Trade-offs—A False Dichotomy

An entrenched view in public finance and social policy debates has been that high levels of social spending inevitably will harm growth—that is, taxing some people to pay others who earn little will reduce national output and cause deadweight losses of net national well-being. The principal argument is there will be costs on both sides of the tax-transfer system. On the taxation side, "higher tax rates infamously cut incentives to work, invest, and take risks, causing a loss of GDP and well-being" (Lindert 2003: 3). On the recipients' side, there is also a presumed disincentive to produce because "for each extra dollar a low-skilled person earns with extra work, part or all of that dollar will be taken away from them because they have less 'need' for income support—a clear disincentive to work" (Lindert 2003: 4).

Contrary to those assumptions, recent reviews of OECD experience critique older literature in ways that largely discount the concern that high expenditures on well-designed social protection systems slow growth (see Grosh et al. [2008] for a review of the literature). Econometric analysis has shown that "a bigger tax bite to finance social spending *does not* correlate negatively with either the level or the growth of GDP per capita" (Lindert 2003: 2). Therefore, "within the range of true historical experience, there is no clear net GDP cost of higher social transfers" (Lindert 2003: 10).

A review of the experience of European Union accession countries also finds that the European Union's greater social spending requirements had not harmed growth in accession countries: "Social spending varies widely around the OECD average, with no evidence that growth has been slower in high-spending countries or higher in low-spending countries. Poland, with one of the highest levels of public pension spending of the accession countries, has the strongest growth performance over the period since 1989; Slovenia, with the highest pension spending, is the next best growth performer" (Barr 2005: 19).

Here are several explanations for what Lindert (2003) calls the "free lunch puzzle":

- Higher-spending states have more pro-growth tax packages than do lower-spending states.
- Welfare states have minimized young adults' work disincentives.
- Early retirement subsidies are not very costly to gross domestice product (GDP), in part because they are skewed toward lower-productivity workers.
- Unemployment programs raise the number of people who are unemployed, but also raise the productivity of those who are employed and therefore have little effect on GDP.
- Even after accounting for the effects of taxes to support spending, many social transfer programs raise per capita GDP.

These findings are based on two methodological critiques of the traditional models underpinning conventional arguments. First, the models used to describe the labor-reducing effects of tax and transfer policies are too simplistic and extreme and, thus, are misleading. Second, the assessments of the cost of the welfare state have focused on costs in terms of growth but have not calculated the benefits that may be derived from the programs and, as such, are misspecified.

Some economists have identified the design features of real-life social protection policies that limit their potential distortions. Blank (2002), for instance, categorizes the ways in which program design can minimize inefficiencies: by supporting those unlikely to work (the elderly, children, and the disabled); by imposing job search, work, or study requirements on those who can work (as in the "activation" reforms in industrial countries, conditional cash transfer programs in middle-income countries, or public works jobs in low-income countries); or by investing in human capital development (as in many programs for young children, including those linked to their health or education and possibly even general child allowances).

Finally, it is important to understand the implications of OECD literature for developing countries (Grosh et al. 2008):

- The literature is concerned with the complete package of social protection or of social protection and health insurance, so that the transfers considered average 21 percent of GDP for the OECD countries and range up to 30 percent for the highest spenders—an order of magnitude more than the range of spending on safety nets in developing countries (Grosh et al. 2008: 58–59). This implies that developing countries spending little on safety nets may be able to spend a bit more without undue harm to their economies.

- OECD countries essentially have added their social protection systems to the list of government's other social service and infrastructure duties. Social protection has not come directly as a trade-off between, say, establishing universal education or good road systems but in addition to them. In a low-income setting, debates on safety nets often are couched as transfers versus development. Perhaps the question should be whether safety nets are an important (additional) component of development policy.

- As Lindert (2003) argues, the highest-spending countries have chosen a relatively efficient pattern of taxation, more so than some of the lower-spending ones. Thus, the impact of social protection on growth depends not only on the size of the sector, but also on how the social protection is financed.

- The OECD literature covers long-standing systems so that the benefits of them may be realized and captured in effects on growth as a counterbalance to their costs. This suggests that the findings easily could apply to developing countries that have well-designed safety nets, but less so to those whose programs are poorly designed or are ineffective as a result of other challenges.

Debate 2: Not Targeting versus Universalism, But Targeting That Meets the Citizenship Test

A call for a comprehensive, rights-based approach to social policy raises a second highly contested issue: targeting versus universalism. For much of the history of social policy, there has been tension over whether the core principle behind social provisioning should be "universalism" or selectivity through "targeting." Under universalism, the entire population receives social benefits as a basic right; under targeting, eligibility for social benefits involves some type of means testing to identify the people who are "truly deserving." However, policy regimes very seldom are purely universal or purely based on targeting. Instead, they tend to lie somewhere between the two extremes and are often hybrid.[4] Where they lie on that continuum can be decisive in spelling out an individual's life chances and in characterizing the social order (Mkandawire 2005).

Both universalists and targeters understand that current budgets do not allow a meaningful provision of transfers in most developing countries and that targeting experience is far from uniformly excellent. It is a case of two glasses half empty (or half full), where universalists and targeters disagree on which glass can be filled:

- *Universalists* are optimistic that the social unity resulting from standardized provisions will garner sufficient budget to provide meaningful protection (nationally financed in middle-income countries and donor-assisted in low-income countries). They view targeting as a narrow approach to enhancing the efficiency of redistributive spending— an approach that is unsatisfactory to date; uninspiring of hope for the future, given the potential for increasing social tension; and detrimental to efforts to increase the budget.
- *Targeters* are more optimistic than universalists in seeing hope that the bad past world experiences can be replaced, improved on, and maybe even made better. Targeters, seeing both political and technical obstacles that would prevent sufficient meaningful universal benefits, believe universalism is not practical (Grosh et al. 2008).

On the continuum between pure targeters and pure universalists, the current global consensus seems to be on targeting that meets the citizenship test, or in the words of Skocpol (1991), "targeting within universalism."

Targeting That Meets the Citizenship Test. Whether it is based on work requirements or on sending children to school, eligibility for conditional transfers implies that beneficiaries should be "deserving." Although such a description is likely to be more palatable politically to the middle class, it breaks the fundamental principle of equal rights for all citizens. When proponents of conditional cash transfers argue the necessity of such restrictions, they often compare them to unconditional, untargeted transfers. In fact, many of the arguments for conditional cash transfers are couched in terms of increased targeting efficiency; however, those are two very different issues that should be handled as such. For example, if a universal right to transfer is offered to those whose income is below a certain level, then the transfer would meet the citizenship test by treating all citizens the same while lowering the fiscal costs, compared with an untargeted transfer. However, when the state decrees that transfers can be accessed only if one's income is low, *and* if certain obligations are fulfilled, then the beneficiaries are just that—beneficiaries—and therefore no longer can be considered citizens with equal rights and obligations. Economically, there are externalities associated with forcing parents to send their children to school, an argument for additional fiscal incentives for parents to do so. However, it would be more equitable and efficient to lower the barrier for school entry (for example, by eliminating school fees and uniform requirements) before making it mandatory that poor people send their children to school (Jorgensen 2006).

Targeting within Universalism. After a careful examination of the history of U.S. public policy, Skocpol (1991) reached three main conclusions supporting universal programs: (1) when antipoverty efforts have targeted the poor alone, they have not been politically sustainable and have stigmatized and demeaned the poor; (2) some kinds of universal policies have been successful politically; and (3) room exists within certain universal policies for extra benefits and services that may help less-privileged people without stigmatizing them. Skocpol indicates that throughout the history of modern American social provision, targeting within universalism has delivered extra benefits and special services to poor groups. In other words, targeting should be used to direct and fine-tune extra benefits to low-income groups within the context of what are fundamentally universalist policies.

A recent literature review of the targeting debate supports this view, based on analysis of the political economy and the budgetary implications of targeting (Mkandawire 2005). Some of the main conclusions are the following:

- Targeting tends to lead to reduced budgets devoted to poverty and welfare, so that "more for the poor mean(s) less for the poor" (Gelbach and Pritchett 1997, cited in Mkandawire 2005: 13). This conclusion is based on models in which voters determine the program budget and voters' interest in funding a program relates to their likely direct benefits from a program (for example, see Gelbach and Pritchett 2002; Pritchett 2005). In such models, universal programs generally have larger sustaining budgets and more instances where narrowly targeted programs would end up with no allocation at all. Some of the more Interpretive literature follows a similar line of reasoning (Esping-Andersen 1990).[5]

- In developing and middle-income countries, universal access is the best way to ensure political support for the middle-class tax-based financing of welfare programs.

Debate 3: Affordability and Budgetary Implications

The comprehensive approach also faces concerns about budgetary implications and affordability. Terms such as *comprehensive* and *rights* too often are associated with other terms such as *fiscally unsustainable* or *unaffordable*. However, this approach is not about expanding the budget in a fiscally irresponsible and unsustainable way; rather, it is about allocating the budget to advance equity and fulfillment of basic rights for all citizens. It is a departure from the traditional approach to social policy budgeting in at least three important ways: (1) it reclaims the budgeting process as an eminently political, rather than technocratic, process and argues for politics based on principles of equity and rights; (2) it defines accountability and transparency of the budget process as a core element of social policy; and (3) it claims that all sectors in the budget (not merely the traditional social policy sectors) should be scrutinized from equity and citizenship perspectives.

A budget is an expression of the social contract between citizens and the state. It is an integral part of a comprehensive, rights-based approach to social policy. Such an approach shifts the focus away from "what can we afford to finance with the available social policy budget?" to "how should the whole budget be allocated to ensure all individuals have access to the benefits the state has agreed to provide for its citizens?" The central idea of this shift is to set the level of benefits where provision for all is possible. Budgetary agreements are the result of struggle within the political process and consensus building. The role of social policy is to facilitate that process in a way that advances the fulfillment of the rights of all citizens.[6] As stated previously, a universal approach is more likely to elicit larger and more sustainable budgets for social spending than is a targeted approach.

Many governments have the resources to solve their poverty problems; however, they are limited by the political nature of the budgetary process. For example, Brazil has the resources necessary for solving its poverty problems through redistributive transfers alone and without raising taxes (World Bank 2001a). The income gap constitutes 1.6 percent of GDP, less than 5 percent of the income of the wealthiest 10 percent of Brazilians, and is small in comparison with total social spending in Brazil (World Bank 2001a: 7).

Public spending often is highly inequitable or inefficient, with the redistribution of resources frequently benefiting people who are better-off (see box 4.3). Safety nets may serve as more efficient ways of redistributing income than does creating alternate policies. No new expenditures are created; instead, the safety nets act as alternatives to other redistributive instruments. Indonesia's large new cash transfer program is not an additional burden on the budget; rather, it is a low-cost substitute for energy subsidies. Safety net programs often are areas of ineffective spending by governments.

BOX 4.3

"Successfully" Reaching Nonpoor People

There are many cases of public resources redistribution to nonpoor people. Here are a few:

- Energy subsidies are highly regressive and often more costly than safety nets. The Arab Republic of Egypt spent 8 percent of its GDP in 2004 (World Bank 2005a) and Indonesia spent up to 4 percent of its GDP between 2001 and 2005 on fuel subsidies (World Bank 2007).
- Insolvent contributory pension funds are bailed out by transferring general revenues to support them. The expansion of Brazil's well-targeted conditional cash transfer program, Bolsa Família, effectively to cover the bottom quintile of the population is raising some eyebrows about whether the country can afford to redistribute so much funding. It cost 0.4 percent of GDP in 2006. But the deficit in the main federal pension programs covered from general revenues is nearly 10 times that amount, at 3.7 percent of GDP. The federal pension programs deliver more than 50 percent of their benefits to the richest quintile of the population (Lindert, Skoufias, and Shapiro 2006). This pattern is not unusual, at least in Latin America. Safety nets are progressive but tiny, compared with the amount that goes to finance pension deficits.
- Financial sectors receive bailouts. In the East Asian financial crisis, for example, Indonesia's bank bailout cost 50 percent of its GDP (Honohan and Klingebiel 2000). However, spending on the accompanying safety net for the poor was about 2.4 percent of GDP in fiscal 1998/99, including food subsidies, public works, targeted scholarships, and fee waivers for health care (APEC 2001). In the Republic of Korea, the bank bailout cost 27.0 percent of GDP (Honohan and Klingebiel 2000), whereas spending on the safety net tripled from about 0.6 percent in 1997 to nearly 2.0 percent in 1999 (APEC 2001).

Sources: Grosh et al. 2008, and sources cited therein.

As previously mentioned, a comprehensive approach also regards budget transparency and accountability as elements of social policy. These two elements conveniently offer common ground between budget specialists and social rights advocates, two very different knowledge communities who often share a "dialogue of the deaf." Budget specialists typically value restraint, place emphasis on trade-offs, and are very concerned with moderating claims. They are largely allergic to entitlements, one of the main methods of identifying rights. These specialists view entitlements as a threat to budget management because they can lead to uncontrolled demands on public resources. By contrast, rights advocates place emphasis on building poor people's capacities to make claims, and, for obvious reasons, they lean toward absolute moral arguments (Norton 2007).

However, there is common ground between the two groups, based on the values of transparency, accountability, and efficiency. A rights-based approach promotes participation in the budget process, which is a means of increasing efficiency, reducing corruption, and reducing waste—thereby reinforcing values shared by budget specialists. A rights-based approach also means a focus on equity because the claims that derail budget processes tend to come from nonpoor people (Norton and Elson 2002).

The past decade has seen an explosion of innovations through which citizen participation can bring transparency and accountability to the budgeting process, as marked by the worldwide trend toward decentralized government. Participatory budgeting across Latin America often has led to a reversal of priorities in public spending, making the spending much more progressive and pro-poor (Baiocchi 2003; Faguet 2004). Citizen report cards, citizen charters, and public expenditure tracking are examples of the convergence between the concerns of budget specialists and those of rights-based advocates.

Finally, all sectors and cross-cutting themes should be examined within the framework of the rights-based approach. For example, gender budgeting, which entails looking at gender issues comprehensively within the budget, is an illustration of a cross-cutting theme that should be part of a more comprehensive approach to social policy.[7]

Moving Forward: Social Guarantees and Social Authorities

There are many policy instruments and interventions that can advance a comprehensive, rights-based approach to social policy in practice. Through recent work, there has been an attempt to conceptualize the operational side of a rights-based social policy by the idea of social guarantees. Social guarantees differ from social rights. These guarantees are sets of legal and administrative mechanisms specifying entitlements and obligations that states put in place to realize a certain right. Although economic, social, and cultural rights often are realized progressively, guarantees imply immediate obligations. Social guarantees are defined in a precise manner, with reference to specific beneficiaries. They are defined legally, thus resulting in explicit state responsibility. These guarantees are flexible revisable and may differ across countries or historical periods. They reflect the underlying political and social consensus achieved in a society, as well as the level of economic development, the budgetary commitments, and the state institutional landscape (see chapter 2).

Other chapters of this book explain in greater detail both the concept of social guarantees and how they can be made operational. Here, as a conclusion to this chapter, we want only to highlight what we consider one of the key challenges of this new approach—namely, developing effective institutional arrangements to coordinate and provide a sense of direction to efforts that, by definition, are scattered across an array of actors: ministries and agencies in the public sector; state and local governments; all types of civil society organizations; private sector organizations at local, national, and international levels; and multilateral agencies.

Creating a "social authority" to coordinate the social agenda has been a long-standing aspiration of many governments in Latin America. Although many of their experiences have been unsuccessful, others seem to be moving forward. The government of Uruguay, for instance, is implementing a comprehensive approach to social policy through its Plan for Social Equity. Creating and strengthening the Ministry of Social Development and a multisectoral Social Cabinet provided the institutional foundation for this approach. The ministry has played a critical role in moving toward an integral social policy model. Created in 2005, its assigned mission was to lead a comprehensive effort in the promotion of equity and social rights. The ministry coordinates the government's policy in a variety of sectors (nutrition, education, health, housing, work, social security, and all activities concerning the enjoyment of a healthy environment). The Social Cabinet, chaired by the minister of social development, comprises the ministers of economy and finance; education and culture; labor and social security; public health; and housing, territorial planning, and environment. The Ministry of Social Development has taken the lead in ensuring cooperation among sectors that impact general welfare, while making policies more cost effective, given past overlap in functions and beneficiaries associated with previous programs. For this reason, in the new Plan for Social Equity, the Ministry of Social Development is the only ministry in charge of a number of cross-sectoral programs.

Careful study of global experience with "social authorities" in Latin America and other regions, and understanding what made some of these experiences more effective than others, are critical pieces of the puzzle of operationalizing a more comprehensive approach to social policy based on a social guarantees framework.

Notes

1. There is emergent evidence that high levels of inequality can be costly to growth and poverty reduction (for extensive literature reviews, see de Ferranti et al. [2004]; World Bank [2005c]), and they can slow economic growth and development itself. As Rao (2006) indicates, in the context of great political and wealth inequalities, policy choices that lead to the generation of rents for particular groups may be preferred above policy choices that encourage broader-based growth. The various dimensions of inequality (in wealth, power, and social status) interact to protect the rich from downward mobility and to prevent the poor overcoming their marginalized status, thus creating and sustaining inequality traps.

2. The Arusha Statement and a commentary by nine top social policy specialists can be found in the December 2006 issue of the journal *Global Social Policy*.

3. Countries and regions can combine elements of all three types within a single social formation.

4. Even in the European welfare states that have gone the furthest in universal provision of child allowances, education, and health insurance, and have quite extensive minimum wage laws, labor market activation, and the like, there still are last-resort, needs-based programs that are very tightly targeted (Grosh et al. 2008).

5. For sources of political support that would favor a targeted approach, see Grosh et al. (2008).

6. An analytical tool to facilitate the political process for comprehensive social policy reform is a Poverty and Social Impact Analysis (PSIA). A PSIA provides a structured instrument to ask the question about winners and losers in policy reform. Eventually, many different stakeholders will contribute their own analytical input to a public debate over policy change, enhancing the plurality of opinions and choices and debating their trade-offs. To achieve such an organic

forum, a PSIA must be anchored in a country's policy-making process, and both process and results must be owned by national decision makers.

7. To date, the experience with "gender budgeting" has been mixed. A recent review concluded that to become more useful, gender budgeting should be integrated into budget processes in a way that generates tangible improvements in policy outcomes. Fiscal authorities should take into account the external benefits of reducing gender inequalities and remove from fiscal legislation any arbitrary discrimination against women (Stotsky 2007).

References

APEC (Asia and Pacific Economic Consortium). 2001. "Safety Nets and Response to Crisis: Lessons and Guidelines from Asia and Latin America." Unpublished manuscript, World Bank, Washington, DC.

Baiocchi, Gianpaolo. 2003. "Participation, Activism, and Politics: The Porto Alegre Experiment." In *Deepening Democracy: Institutional Innovations in Empowered Participatory Governance*, ed. Archon Fung and Erik Olin Wright, 45–76. London: Verso.

Barr, Nicholas A. 2005. "From Transition to Accession." In *Labor Markets and Social Policy in Central and Eastern Europe: The Accession and Beyond,* ed. Nicholas A. Barr, 1–30. Washington, DC: World Bank.

Blank, Rebecca M. 2002. "Can Equity and Efficiency Complement Each Other?" Working Paper 8820, National Bureau of Economic Research, Cambridge, MA.

de Ferranti, David M., Guillermo Perry, Francisco H. G. Ferreira, and Michael Walton. 2004. *Inequality in Latin America: Breaking with History?* Washington, DC: World Bank.

Esping-Andersen, Gøsta. 1990. *The Three Worlds of Welfare Capitalism.* Cambridge, U.K.: Polity Press.

Faguet, Jean-Paul. 2004. "Does Decentralization Increase Responsiveness to Local Needs? Evidence from Bolivia." *Journal of Public Economics* 88 (3/4): 867–93.

Gelbach, Jonah B., and Lant H. Pritchett. 1997. "More for the Poor Is Less for the Poor: The Politics of Targeting." Policy Research Working Paper 1799, World Bank, Washington, DC.

———. 2002. "More for the Poor Is Less for the Poor? The Politics of Means-Tested Targeting." *Topics in Economic Analysis & Policy* 2 (1): article 6. http://www.bepress.com/bejeap/topics/vol2/iss1/art6/ (accessed April 1, 2009).

Grosh, Margaret E., Carlo del Ninno, Emil Tesliuc, Azedine Oeughi, with Annamaria Milazzo and Christine Weigand. 2008. *For Protection and Promotion: The Design and Implementation of Effective Safety Nets.* Washington, DC: World Bank.

Honohan, Patrick, and Daniela Klingebiel. 2000. "Controlling the Fiscal Costs of Banking Crises." Policy Research Working Paper 2441, World Bank, Washington, DC.

Jorgensen, Steen Lau. 2006. "Freedom from Want and Freedom from Fear: New Frontiers in Social Policy." Paper presented at the conference, "Social Protection Initiatives for Children, Women, and Families: An Analysis of Recent Experiences," New York City, October 30–31.

Kwon, Huck-Ju. 2005. *Transforming the Developmental Welfare State in East Asia.* Social Policy and Development Programme Paper Number 22. Geneva, Switzerland: United Nations Research Institute for Social Development.

Lindert, Kathy, Emmanuel Skoufias, and Joseph Shapiro. 2006. "Redistributing Income to the Poor and the Rich: Public Transfers in Latin America and the Caribbean." Social Protection Discussion Paper 605, World Bank, Washington, DC.

Lindert, Peter H. 2003. "Why the Welfare State Looks Like a Free Lunch." Working Paper 9869, National Bureau of Economic Research, Cambridge, MA.

Mkandawire, Thandika. 2005. *Targeting and Universalism in Poverty Reduction.* Social Policy and Development Programme Paper Number 23. Geneva, Switzerland: United Nations Research Institute for Social Development.

Norton, Andrew. 2007. "Human Rights, the Budget Process, and Social Policy." Paper presented at United Nations Children's Fund Open Dialogue, "Eyes on the Budget as a Human Rights Instrument," January 30.

Norton, Andrew, and Diane Elson. 2002. *What's Behind the Budget? Politics, Rights and Accountability in the Budget Process.* London: Overseas Development Institute.

Pritchett, Lant. 2005. "A Lecture on the Political Economy of Targeting." Social Protection Discussion Paper 0501, World Bank, Washington, DC.

Rao, Vijayendra. 2006. "On 'Inequality Traps' and Development Policy." *Development Outreach* (February): 10–13.

Rodrik, Dani. 1997. *Has Globalization Gone Too Far?* Washington, DC: Institute for International Economics.

Skocpol, Theda. 1991. "Targeting within Universalism: Politically Viable Policies to Combat Poverty in the United States." In *The Urban Underclass,* ed. Christopher Jencks and Paul E. Peterson, 411–36. Washington, DC: Brookings Institution Press.

Stotsky, Janet G. 2007. "Budgeting with Women in Mind." *Finance and Development* 44 (2). http://www.imf.org/external/pubs/ft/fandd/2007/06/stotsky.htm (accessed March 5, 2009).

Wiman, Ronald, Timo Voipio, and Matti Ylönen, eds. 2007. *Comprehensive Social and Employment Policies for Development in a Globalizing World: Report Based on an Expert Meeting at Kellokoski, Finland, November 1–3, 2006.* Helsinki, Finland: Ministry for Foreign Affairs. http://www.globalaging.org/agingwatch/events/CSD/2007/socialpoliciesfordevelopment.pdf (accessed March 5, 2009).

Wood, Geof, and Ian Gough. 2006. "A Comparative Welfare Regime Approach to Global Social Policy." *World Development* 34 (10): 1696–712.

World Bank. 2001a. *Brazil: Attacking Brazil's Poverty.* Sector Report 20475-BR. Washington, DC: World Bank.

———. 2001b. *Social Protection Sector Strategy: From Safety Nets to Springboards.* Washington, DC: World Bank.

———. 2005a. "Egypt—Toward a More Effective Social Policy: Subsidies and Social Safety Nets." Draft Report 33550-EG, World Bank, Washington, DC.

———. 2005b. "New Frontiers of Social Policy: Concept Note of Arusha Conference." Unpublished manuscript, World Bank, Washington, DC.

———. 2005c. *World Development Report 2006: Equity and Development.* Washington, DC: World Bank.

———. 2007. *2007 World Development Indicators.* Washington, DC: World Bank.

———. 2008. "Realizing Rights through Social Guarantees: An Analysis of New Approaches to Social Policy in Latin America and South Africa." Report 40047-GLB, World Bank, Washington, DC.

PART II

IMPLEMENTING SOCIAL POLICIES
WITH A RIGHTS-BASED FOCUS:
EXAMPLES FROM THE CARIBBEAN,
LATIN AMERICA, AND SOUTH AFRICA

CHAPTER 5

Implementing Social Guarantees: The Regime of Explicit Guarantees in Health in Chile

Leonardo Moreno and Mauricio Rosenblüth

Chile has considerable experience implementing various social policy approaches ranging from welfare and universalist reforms, to a market-oriented system and social protection strategy (Raczynski 1994, 2000a, 2000b; Castiglioni 2005). In Chile, as in most countries in the region, social policy responses to the economic crises have been different, but a broad rights perspective has informed the conceptualizing of many social programs (Filgueira and Lombardi 1995; Abel and Lewis 2002). It is important to highlight, however, that few (if any) of the social policies conceived with a rights perspective have developed the institutional, programmatic, and financial mechanisms to ensure the full protection of the entitlements that these rights imply. Only recently has the notion of a social guarantee been introduced as a way to operationalize a rights-based perspective and translate its basic principles into the design, implementation, and evaluation of social programs.

Chile stands out in the region for having one of the few practical experiences in this line: the Regime of Explicit Guarantees in Health (REGH),[1] a curative health program (to a lesser extent including prevention, rehabilitation, and palliative care) that has been conceived and implemented within a social guarantees framework. This program incorporates a set of explicit guarantees (access, quality, opportunity, and financial protection) as well as redress and enforcement mechanisms. Although the REGH still faces some challenges, it clearly is a social guarantee program that can be used to illustrate some key implementation issues.

In the case of Chile, the REGH has achieved the highest level of technical development in terms of applying the concept of social guarantees, even though recent social policies in other areas of concern have incorporated a similar structure.[2] The incipient development in the majority of other programs indicates that better definitions of procedures and mechanisms will be required to make the notion of guarantees operational in other sectors. Among other things, that effort will involve defining not only clear criteria for access and quality of services, but also mechanisms for redress and for revision or continual improvement of services.

The Health System in Chile: Background

Prior to 1980, the Chilean health system was fundamentally public, financed through social security and public funds. After the health reform in 1981, the modality of risk insurance was introduced whereby a market mechanism regulated the level of protection. Thus, a dual public-private system emerged. Workers could be affiliated either with the public health system through the National Health Fund (Fondo Nacional de Salud; FONASA), whose distribution rationale favors solidarity, or with private health insurance institutions (instituciones de salud previsional; ISAPREs). Despite the obligatory nature of the insurance, the latter operate under the logic of private insurance, which is associated with individual risk (Sojo 2006; see also Hernandez, Sandoval, and Delgado 2005; Drago 2006).

Thus, until 2001 the Chilean health system operated under a dual modality in which the public system and the private system were completely separate from each other. They did not coordinate or complement each other to achieve a set of health objectives defined by society (Drago 2006). This duality led to a strong segmentation of the health care system in Chile, with clear differences in quality and access to services across social groups. At the same time, it led to an overburdening of the public system, which often attended to private affiliates who were unable to afford all private services but who contributed nothing to the public system.

Under this dual system, FONASA offered a universal health plan to its beneficiaries. Given its resource constraints, the public system was unable to ensure timely and high-quality services. The private system, however, discriminated by financial means, forcing many members to seek attention in the public system when their health plans (based on income) did not cover a particular service or health condition. The level of protection in the private sector was derived, on the one hand, from the amount of required monthly contributions and, on the other hand, by the medical risks associated with each individual (as estimated by age, gender, family medical history, and so forth). Monthly contributions to ISAPREs could exceed the obligatory amount of 7 percent of the salary, and the coverage of services varied according to each plan. There was no minimum standard and the law allowed for variation in the plans, based on preexisting health conditions. Therefore, two people paying the same contribution, but with different risk levels, received different coverage and benefits.

Over time, this situation generated increasing criticism from civil society organizations, political parties, and professional associations linked to the health sector, all of whom called for structural reforms in health care that would address the needs of the population more adequately (FUNASUPO 1999). These reform proposals echoed the principles stated by the democratic government coalition in the early 1990s. Although some of these ideas were in the agenda from the beginning of the Concertación[3] administrations in 1990, the initial reforms focused on other (more politically volatile) sectors, such as education and housing. In the health sector, early health policy initiatives by the Concertación were limited to infrastructure and hospital inputs, improved access to primary health care, and wages for health workers (Chile, Ministry of Planning 2006).

The main criticisms of the dual system raised by the various stakeholders included the following (FUNASUPO 1999):

- A coherent and consensual state policy dealing with health issues in an integral manner was lacking.
- The structural segmentation of the health system resulted in the low-income and/or high-risk population being treated mainly by the public sector and the high-income and/or low-risk population being treated by the private sector.
- The health system did not account for changes in the population's demographic and epidemiologic profiles, leaving out health conditions linked to sedentary or changing lifestyles and aging (Morales 2005).
- The prevalence of certain pathologies or health conditions increasingly was polarized. Existing data showed that the health indicators' rates of improvement were faster among the top income quintiles and much slower in poorer sections of the population. An indicator of this phenomenon is that the prevalence of contagious diseases is higher among low-income households.[4]

- An important segment of ISAPRE beneficiaries faced a lack of security resulting from their plans having no coverage for certain health conditions. Such was the case for women of childbearing age who either had to pay higher premium rates or had to opt for health plans without pregnancy-related coverage, and for elderly people who had less coverage and fewer benefits unless they opted for higher premiums. Expenses related to HIV/AIDS also were not covered by the private sector plans.
- Resources were overallocated to healthy and young individuals in the private system, as a result of insurance market distortions, and that overallocation prompted superfluous uses of existing resources.
- There was an underinvestment in preventive medicine and health promotion.
- Beneficiary copayment for services in addition to the general contributions to the system presented a high burden for some households.
- Referral problems existed in the public sector (primary network versus hospitals) as well as between the public and private sectors (no entry mechanisms to allow someone from the public sector to receive services in the private network).
- Despite significant increases in the sector's budget, hospitals, health clinics, and posts in the public health sector were not modernized, and improvements in the volume and quality of available services were too slow.
- Persistent labor issues resulted in frequent strikes by the various unions and other health workers' organizations.

Opening the Door for Reform

To address these institutional, regulatory, and epidemiologic problems, the administration of President Ricardo Lagos (2000–06) recognized that a drastic reform of the health system was required—namely, a movement away from the dual system and toward a coordinated mixed system with modern and effective state regulation. The new system would have to protect the health policy goals and objectives of the country in light of the current social context and health profile of the population.

Early in his term of office, President Lagos established an interministerial committee to study and propose reforms in the health system. The committee included representatives from the Ministry of Finance, the Ministry of

Labor and Social Protection, the General Presidential Secretariat (a policy coordination body), and the Ministry of Health. It was chaired by the Minister of Health (then Michelle Bachelet, Chile's president at the time of this writing). The committee's executive secretariat, headed by surgeon Hernán Sandoval, was responsible for elaborating proposals and congressional bills for the potential health reform. This multisectoral committee began its work by identifying the main challenges facing the health system—among them, the aging of the population, which increases the cost of health services, and the growing inequalities in health care among different socioeconomic groups. Committee members recognized that addressing these challenges would involve changes in the composition and quality of services, as well as in the mechanisms for their delivery. It also would require bringing services up-to-date with modern technical requirements and meeting the rising demands of the users as they became more conscious of their right to health care.

On May 9, 2001, the committee delivered a report proposing the objectives, principles, and funding sources for a potential health reform, and President Lagos presented to the public some of the essential elements of the plan. Four key objectives to be sought over the following decade were highlighted: (1) improving the existing health indicators; (2) addressing the new demands derived from aging and from the changing health profile of the population; (3) closing health gaps and inequalities across socioeconomic groups; and (4) improving the scope and quality of services and access to them, according to the expectations of the population (Aguilera et al. 2002).

All sectors represented in the committee agreed that there was a need to identify concrete objectives for a health reform, to specify guaranteed and redressable health entitlements, and to improve equity in the system. The funding mechanisms for the reform, however, were less clear. Because the explicit guarantee of services was expected to burden the available fiscal resources, the core of the committee's discussions—namely, between the health sector and financial authorities—focused on financial arrangements. The committee's executive secretariat referred to a mid-1990s proposal from the Ministry of Health, the University of Chile's economics department, and the Foundation for Overcoming Poverty—the Guaranteed Plan for Health Services. This plan defined in great detail the services that the state would commit to provide on a universal basis. Thus, the secretariat was able to give the Ministry of Finance the much more concrete estimate of required costs that it needed to support the reform. On the basis of the data included in the earlier proposal, the committee dedicated itself to estimating more precisely the costs that would be associated with the proposed reform to be discussed in the National Congress (Lenz 2007).

Having defined the challenges and targets for health reform, the interministerial committee proposed the following four legislative bills:

1. a law that would create the Plan for Universal Access to Explicit Guarantees (Plan AUGE [Plan de Acceso Universal y Garantías Explícitas], later renamed Regime of Explicit Health Guarantees) establishing the scope of the regime (for both FONASA and ISAPRE affiliates) and the dimensions around which services would be guaranteed—access, quality, opportunity, and financial protection
2. a law on health authorities and public management that would strengthen the regulatory role of the Ministry of Health and improve the management of public health establishments
3. a law that would establish new regulations for the ISAPREs
4. a law regarding the financing of health reform and the Chile Solidario Program (which proposed increases in taxes on tobacco, alcohol, diesel fuel, and gambling) and an increase in value added tax (VAT) from 18.00 percent to 18.25 percent.[5]

These four bills were presented to congress in May 2002. On a FONASA initiative, another bill regarding the rights and obligations of patients was completed in 2001 to mitigate potential controversies with medical professionals over the reform. The committee did not recognize this last bill as a priority, but it was publicized by the president and his administration as part of the reform package. Even though it was not approved with the other four bills, the bill on patient rights and obligations was revised and submitted again in August 2006. At the time of this writing, it had been approved by the Chamber of Deputies (the lower house) and was awaiting approval by the Senate (the upper house) of the National Congress.

From the beginning of the technical-political debate, two strong and conflicting positions emerged regarding the content of the reforms and the way they should move forward. The debate was between supporters of a state-based model and supporters of a privatized model. The conflict became increasingly politicized and held back the discussion and processing of reforms (Boeninger, cited in Drago 2006:51). The statists tolerated, but reduced to a minimum, the role of the ISAPREs (and the private sector in general) under a strict regulation. Their vision was represented by the center-left sectors of the ruling coalition, which rejected the concept of private profit in social provision and who were more willing to trust the mechanisms that the regulatory agency could implement to correct market imperfections. The privatizers considered market forces to be the best regulator for delivering health services. To them, the principal problem was the public management of health services, which needed to increase its efficiency and flexibility in interacting with the private sector. Thus, representatives of the ISAPREs pushed for development of portable subsidies. Such subsidies could be used by public sector subscribers, if necessary, to seek attention in private health centers—for example, when they could not receive the service in the public sector within the time needed. This measure would make the two sectors compete for subsidies under the REGH.

To break the statist-privatizer stalemate, the Lagos administration opened up dialogue with a wide spectrum of stakeholders beyond the political parties. Representatives of the Colegio Médico (an association of medical doctors), the National Confederation of Health Workers (an association of paramedics, nurses, and other health workers), and the ISAPREs were invited to the dialogue. Given the political context at that time (in the run-up to parliamentary elections), the reforms had to wait for a postelection window of opportunity (2002–03), when there was more political openness and discussions could be less partisan and politicized.

When presented in congress, the four bills immediately were rejected by the medical professionals' organizations. Health workers mobilized and caused significant disruption in the health system for approximately 6 months, asking for the bills to be withdrawn. The president stepped in to support the reform, and his involvement resulted in a series of sociopolitical accords with health workers, including projects on a "new institutional structure" and on the "status of public employees."

As the bills entered the senate, a third position emerged, distinct from that of the statists or privatizers—one that supported an integrated health system. This new vision was based on the belief that the two subsectors (public and private) could be coordinated and could operate under a common system of rules, seeking an optimal allocation of existing resources. This third way implied the need for profound reform, both in public health care and in the private providers. At the same time, however, it helped modify and moderate some of the proposed bills to make them acceptable to all affected groups.

The bills regarding reforms in the public system easily found support in the Senate. The ones regarding the ISAPREs were modified further, mostly because of the rejection of the proposal to create a solidarity fund that would transfer funds from private affiliates. The law on the financing of reform also was modified, particularly to exclude the increase of taxes (except the VAT) and instead to include improved measures for tax collection. Thus, the reforms were moderated so there would be no absolute winners or losers and so a solution could be found that supported the interests of multiple stakeholders. Ultimately, all reform projects were approved by a large majority in the Senate. This broad passage allowed their subsequent approval (with only a few dissenting votes) in the Chamber of Deputies.

The health reform would not have progressed had it not been for (1) the consistent and energetic support of the executive branch; (2) the counteraction of political opposition that ultimately resulted in a change of ministers and public communication campaigns to disseminate the content of the reforms; (3) the use of a rights perspective in the discussion of reform; (4) the role of the Senate in mediating between conflicting interests of stakeholders and in making acceptable modifications; (5) a public campaign on the part of the government to win public support and mitigate the opposition and long strikes of health professionals by claiming that the new REGH would put more order in the delivery of health services and eliminate long waits and other existing disruptions; and (6) the emergence of mediating actors, such as civil society organizations, that managed to involve all political actors in a broader and less politicized discussion (Drago 2006).

Lenz (2007) analyzes some of the key political aspects of negotiating the Chilean health reform that were as important to its success as were the surrounding technical negotiations. First, the decisions to create a new multisectoral body such as the reform committee and to include both important political actors and technical experts allowed for innovative discussions that would not have been possible if restricted only within the Ministry of Health. Second, the Lagos administration noted and relied on the political potential of the social guarantees concept. The use of the concept of guarantees helped gain wide public approval for the reforms, even though the design of the new regime was quite complicated and, at first, not easily understood by the average citizen. Moreover, the fact that guarantees were explicit and legally subject to redress brought the hope of a more just system for patients. Public spending that guaranteed a certain level and quality of products and services proved to have strong political advantages.

Third, the president adopted a risky, but eventually rewarding, strategy by transferring discussions from inside the executive branch to the legislative branch before all details of the reform were set in concrete terms. Thus, some final decisions on its content—for example, the bills regarding the ISAPREs or the sources of funding for the reform—were flexible and still open for discussion. The Christian Democratic Party (a moderate party, part of the Concertación government following the military regime) played a key role in this strategy. It became an intermediary that managed to negotiate the details of the reform with its opponents within congress and eventually to mitigate the resistance on the part of both the extreme right and the extreme left.

Opposition from medical professionals was one of the strongest impediments to the reform. The initial REGH proposals were met with a long strike by health care workers. The decision to send the new health bills to congress at an early stage of the discussion was partly a response to that resistance: it made it more difficult for the associations of health professionals to press their demands because the interests represented in the congress were much more diverse and complex to influence than were those interests represented in the initial working committee.

Another important aspect of the political negotiations surrounding the explicit guarantees regime was the opportunity that rightist parties and private health providers saw in increasing their legitimacy and social acceptance. Being part of a common framework of guaranteed services, regulated in a manner equal to the public system, generated a favorable social climate for the much-criticized ISAPREs. Because of these benefits to the legitimacy of the private system, parties on the extreme right hesitated to reject the reform completely and focused only on a few concrete aspects: (1) preventing any redistribution policies between FONASA and ISAPRE affiliates, and (2) preventing an increase in taxes. Their demands were reflected in the REGH bills, gaining the ultimate approval from the right-leaning political parties.

Implementing the Reform with Explicit Guarantees

The new legal framework on health, passed between 2003 and 2004, was of great significance from both social policy and legal perspectives.[6] It was the first legal installment of a rights-based social guarantees program incorporating and defining the principles of access, quality, opportunity, and financial protection and specifying mechanisms for redress. It also pioneered new funding mechanisms for the health system that were agreed by a parliamentary majority. In addition, the REGH framework introduced institutional changes in the health system, creating the Office of the Superintendent of Health, a new ministerial subsecretariat, and the REGH Advisory Council (Consejo Consultativo).

The REGH is an instrument for organizing health services provision in a way that guarantees a certain set of services for all users. It prioritizes health problems, based on the epidemiologic danger they present and the feasibility of solutions. The regime defines the medical response or treatment for each disease and condition, and recognizes the importance of primary care and early detection of symptoms. In addition, it defines the set of activities, procedures, and technologies necessary for treating the medical condition (subguarantee of quality); a maximum waiting period for receiving services at each stage (the subguarantee of opportunity); and both the copayment and the maximum amount a family can spend per year on health (subguarantee of financial protection).

Thus, the REGH is a significant change from the prior health system in which the user was subject to the existing offer of services, and the offer of services in the public system was limited by resource allocations. Affiliates of the private system could accede to services only if they could afford all necessary copayments. In the case of specialized diseases or medical plans with less coverage, private system copayments often were unaffordable. In those cases, ISAPRE users frequently turned to the public system, which could not deny them the service. From that situation came one of the biggest distortions in the health system—that is, an affiliation with the private system by users who had no major health problems and an overload of the public system (which had to provide services to all people who could not finance their treatment individually or through their private insurance plans).

The system of explicit guarantees regulates such discrepancies under a mixed and complementary public-private regime that ensures timely access and quality of services for a prioritized list of health conditions. Access to these services can be described as universal, given that it is guaranteed equally by the public and private sectors. The guarantees are not targeted only to the poorest people but to the entire population. The regime establishes each citizen's maximum threshold of financial contribution for access to health services. These thresholds differ across the population, according to income level, to avoid the abuse of the system under a universalist argument. In that way, the regime protects the principles of equity, inclusion, and redistribution.[7]

The legal basis of the guarantees regime lies in Law 19.966, which establishes the REGH and ascribes the elaboration of a list of health conditions and guaranteed services to an administrative decree to be issued jointly by the Ministry of Health and the Ministry of Finance. Supreme Decree (SD) 170, enforced in 2005, established the first 25 health conditions with guaranteed services to be provided to all citizens. A year later, SD 228 added 15 conditions, expanding the total list to 40. Subsequently, SD 44 in 2007 extended the regime to 56 medical conditions (see annex A for a complete list). Currently, a pilot plan to include more health conditions on the REGH list is under way as part of former President Lagos's commitment to expanding the list to 80 conditions. In January 2009, a list of 24 additional medical conditions was presented to the REGH Advisory Council with the expectation that they would be included in the regime by 2011. This strategy of gradually expanding the scope of guaranteed services has been at the core of the new health regime. It is worth mentioning that even though the REGH officially entered into force on July 1, 2005, it had been pilot-tested since 2002—beginning with three medical conditions and gradually expanding to five in 2003 and to 17 in 2004.

To decide on the medical conditions included in the explicit guarantees regime, health professionals reviewed and ranked all major health problems in the country, according to their frequency, seriousness, and treatment cost. The principal ranking criterion was the number of years of healthy life lost, which quantifies how serious the disease or condition is, as determined by an indicator that combines early mortality with the disability that the disease can cause to those who survive it. Because of the issue of disability, both mental health conditions and conditions that generate partial disability and, therefore, prompt a significant decline in the quality of life were considered priorities.

Once the priorities for the health regime were defined (according to the indicator of years of healthy life lost), the possibility of affecting the outcomes of the condition through medical treatment was assessed, together with the feasibility of guaranteeing such treatment to all citizens, regardless of geographic location and socioeconomic status. The latter necessitated a comprehensive analysis of the existing public and private health infrastructure. In addition, the process considered citizens' demands. Although consideration of them was excluded from the described methodology, those demands constituted serious social problems and had to be addressed (for example, cystic fibrosis). As a result of this process of prioritization, 56 health conditions were identified by 2007, accounting for approximately 70 percent of the years of healthy life lost out of all considered medical conditions.

Various funding mechanisms were discussed to support the new regime. Ultimately, Law 19.888 stipulated that resources would be derived from (1) an increase in consumer tax from 18 percent to 19 percent between October 1, 2003, and October 1, 2007 (President Bachelet subsequently decided to retain the tax increase for a longer period); (2) a budget increase from tobacco tax; (3) a budget increase from customs; and (4) the sale of state minority shares in public enterprises (for example, water and sewerage management or residential maintenance companies). As additional funding sources, the reform also considered preexisting FONASA funds, an increase in copayments, budget increases from economic growth, and reallocation of resources from other sectors.

It should be noted that the 1 percent increase of consumer tax constitutes regressive financing and prompts serious doubts from the point of view of equity, given that this tax increases the cost of goods that are important in maintaining health, such as food and basic sanitary supplies.

To mitigate fiscal pressure, the reform was implemented in stages and progressively added medical conditions to the list of priority diseases. The new Office of the Superintendent of Health absorbed the functions of the previous superintendent of the ISAPREs and was placed in charge of the FONASA budget covering REGH services. Thus, the Office of the Superintendent of Health became the first body to supervise public and private funds together.

The four explicit guarantees built into the new health regime under Law 19.966 are as follows:

1. *Access,* defined as the obligation of FONASA and the ISAPREs to ensure the provision of guaranteed services to all of their users for the medical conditions established by law in SD 170 of 2005, which refers to 25 medical conditions; SD 228 of 2006, which adds 15 health problems; and SD 44 of 2007, which puts 16 more health conditions on the priority coverage list. The decrees elaborate in detail all services to which patients are entitled.

2. *Quality,* defined as the provision of health services by a registered or accredited provider, according to Law 19.937 (which concerned sanitary authorities, and was published on February 24, 2004, in Chile's official journal, *Diario Oficial de la República de Chile,* where all new

laws, decrees, treaties, and other legal documents adopted in Chile are published). The guarantee of quality is still in the initial stages of implementation: clinical guides (protocols) have been created and approved as best-practice guidelines by medical professionals. The guidelines are not obligatory, however, and patients may not use them as a sole basis for redress. The system of accreditation and certification related to the REGH has been designed but is not yet operational.

3. *Opportunity*, defined as the maximum waiting period for receiving a service, as established by the respective decree that regulates provision of that service. Proper functioning of this guarantee implies that a reasonable period of time is set for the diagnosis, treatment, and follow-up care for each medical condition covered by the REGH. During that period, the health provider should supply the specified services. If the provider does not comply with the time periods specified in the respective decrees, the patient's insurance agency— FONASA or an ISAPRE—must assign a different provider within 2 business days.

4. *Financial protection*, defined as a limit on a user's out-of-pocket costs for a health service. The costs cannot exceed 20 percent of the "market price" for the service, as determined by the Ministry of Finance. Low-income groups are exempt from all out-of-pocket costs.

To uphold the state's commitment to fulfill these guarantees, the regime incorporates an administrative system of redress and envisions a continuous revision of the guarantees and services to ensure that they are up-to-date and efficient. Annex B presents a detailed matrix of the legal, institutional, instrumental, and financial frameworks used to make each of the four explicit guarantees operational. It also describes the provisions established to realize effective channels of redress and a system of continuous revision.

Results of the REGH

By July 2008, the REGH had attended to 5,419,604 cases. Of those cases, 85.6 percent were in the primary health care sector (for example, consultations and visits to the physician's office), and 14.4 percent involved more specialized hospital services. Those facts are important because they show an efficient use of the infrastructure resources in the health system. Moreover, they reveal the significance and frequent use of primary health centers that focus largely on public health issues, prevention, and early detection of medical problems. Fifteen of the 56 medical conditions currently included in the health guarantees account for 91.4 percent of cases. At the top of the list of most-used services, with 1.5 million cases, have been those services associated with essential arterial hypertension. Services related to acute respiratory infections, dental problems, diabetes, and depression also have been among the most frequently used (Vega 2008).

Given that the REGH is relatively recent, the National Budget Office has not completed a comprehensive evaluation of the degree to which it has fulfilled its objectives.[8] Nevertheless, the positive effects of the regime already can be demonstrated, particularly with regard to access to services (Barría 2008):

- *Diabetes:* In 2003, approximately 250,000 individuals were treated for diabetes mellitus, type 2. After this condition was included in the REGH list, the number of patients rose to about 450,000 in 2007.
- *Depression:* The population under treatment rose from 50,000 (2003) to 250,000 (2007).
- *Cataract:* Between 1996 and 2004, the annual average number of cataract surgeries did not exceed 7,000. Between 2004 and 2008, the average rose to almost 30,000 operations each year.
- *Palliative care:* Noncurative care to reduce symptom severity rose from an annual average of 30,000 cases (1998–2003) to 70,000 cases (2004–08) after the REGH was introduced.
- *Breast cancer:* In the framework of the explicit guarantees regime, late detection of breast cancer was reduced from 20 percent to 5 percent of the cases, and early detection increased from approximately 40 percent to 65 percent.

Those are only a few examples of the regime's impact on access to essential health services. It was made possible by prioritizing spending in a way that guaranteed coverage for listed services and expanded the number of working hours available to attend to the covered services. Between 2004 and 2007, 70 percent of medical working hours were allocated to REGH patients. More resources also were allocated to new technology, such as mammography, echotomography, and arteriography equipment. Overall, after the introduction of the REGH, the health sector budget rose from \$288 million to \$466 million between 2003 and 2008 (Barría 2008).[9]

An important guarantee offered by the new regime is that of the opportunity to receive services and attention in a timely manner. Under the REGH framework, medical attention was delayed in 299,587 cases, or 5.18 percent of all cases between 2005 and 2008. Compared with the prior situation, this result is considered a tangible improvement in the timeliness of services (Barría 2008).

The Office of the Superintendent of Health has initiated a series of public opinion surveys to measure citizens' perceptions of the new system. In January 2008, the office presented the following results of its surveys (Chile, Office of the Superintendent of Health 2008)[10]:

- A large proportion of citizens still is not completely aware of the services guaranteed under the regime. Only 45 percent of the people interviewed knew what the regime consisted of, and 28 percent knew partial details about it.
- When asked about the specific guarantees included in the REGH, 54 percent of respondents alluded to the guarantee of access, 48 percent knew of the financial protection mechanisms for a set of medical services, 36 percent mentioned the opportunity guarantee for timely service, and 25 percent referred to the guarantee of quality.
- The above responses are probably a result of the fact that most of the citizens interviewed had never needed to use any of the guaranteed services. Only 12 percent of the sample had a personal experience using the system, and approximately 30 percent knew about it through friends and relatives who had used it. Still, 58 percent had no point of reference—direct or indirect—with the new health regime. Hence, it can be expected that citizens' knowledge of, use of, and feedback on the system will improve with time, based on their experience with it.
- A subsample of people—those who had used the services in the REGH—was asked to rate the quality of the personnel, equipment, and infrastructure of the health center where they received the services. The rating used a 1–7 scale, with 1 being lowest and 7 being highest. Most of the FONASA and ISAPRE patients rated services at 6 or 7 (maximum quality)—a much higher grade than in previous evaluations (Chile, Office of the Superintendent of Health 2007b).

- In a different evaluation, 69 percent of respondents declared that health care has improved since the introduction of the REGH: improved a lot (21 percent of respondents) or somewhat (48 percent). In the same evaluation, 39 percent of those interviewed felt that their health was better protected under the new system, and 51 percent felt it was as protected as before. Only 5 percent felt they were less protected than before (Chile, Office of the Superintendent of Health 2007a).[11]
- According to the March 2007 study, the guarantee most appreciated by citizens was that of access (mentioned by 34 percent of respondents), followed by those of opportunity and quality (mentioned by 23 percent and 21 percent, respectively), and finally that of financial protection (mentioned by 18 percent). Access was the most valued guarantee across all socioeconomic groups (Chile, Office of the Superintendent of Health 2007a).
- Both FONASA and ISAPRE beneficiaries noted improvements in the speed and quality of services (60 percent and 59 percent, respectively). FONASA users mentioned the better attitude toward patients (30 percent), while users of ISAPREs highlighted the reduction in costs (20 percent).

These public opinion data show that over the short period of its existence, the REGH has had a tangible effect on the population. This finding speaks to the potential of the reform, especially given that the full list of 56 medical conditions has been in force since only July 2007.

Nevertheless, an overall judgment of the extent to which the REGH fulfills the objectives and targets of the national health system requires a longer time frame to assess its results fully. Studies in 2006 conducted by the Equity in Health Initiative of the Ministry of Health reveal that important health targets for 2010 still are not being addressed properly. Progress has been achieved in maternal and infant health care, for example, but such other issues as smoking, obesity, and suicide have grown at a rate that raises concern. The new health plan is expected to show results in those areas only in the medium term (Barría 2006).

These results indicate that the regime has had some important preliminary effects on access, efficiency, and people's perceptions of the health system—a satisfactory result, given that it has been in force since only 2005. What makes the REGH a rights-based regime—apart from the four universal guarantees—is the presence of an administrative mechanism that allows for the redress and enforcement of health entitlements if and when those guarantees are not being fulfilled (see box 5.1).

BOX 5.1

Mechanisms for Redress—The Role of the Superintendent of Health

A survey initiated by the Office of the Superintendent of Health analyzed REGH users' opinions about the regime's mechanisms for redress. The mechanisms are regarded as *secondary guarantees*—that is, those that seek to correct violations of the established entitlements and to enforce the *primary guarantees* of access, quality, opportunity, and financial protection. The survey, conducted by Datavoz, was based on 680 cases, randomly sampled from a total of 1,899 claims resolved during the first half of 2006. Here are some of the prominent results of this survey:

- For the most part, citizens who have used the new regime have been informed of its mechanisms for redress through the mass media. About 50.3 percent of the participants responded that they learned of the redress mechanisms through "general knowledge"; 23.5 percent learned from an ISAPRE or a FONASA health worker; 12.9 percent knew about them from a friend, parent, or acquaintance; 5.5 percent learned of them in the workplace; and 7.6 percent learned from other sources. Only 48 percent of interviewees who have used redress think that sufficient information is available concerning the system of redress.
- With regard to the waiting period for resolving claims, half of the respondents stated they were informed of how long the period of redress would last. Thirty-one percent noted that their claims were solved in more than 1.5 months. These results are consistent with the 51-day average set by the Office of the Superintendent of Health. The average waiting period for resolution in arbitration cases was 74 days, and it was 48 days for administrative cases.
- Fifty-seven percent noted that their cases were delayed beyond the 51-day limit, to an average of 99 days. Arbitration cases were delayed most—on average, to 117 days. Middle- or low-income respondents pointed out that their cases were delayed, on average, to 121 days, and higher-income interviewees reported an average delay of up to 88 days. This gap in delays between different income groups sheds light on possible inequities in the attention and resolution of claims on the part of the Office of the Superintendent's staff.
- Forty-eight percent of the respondents who had experienced delays thought that their case delays were reasonable, 44 percent thought that the delays were too long, and 6 percent considered the waiting period short. This marks an improvement in perceptions from a survey conducted in August/September 2006 (Chile, Office of the Superintendent of Health 2006).

(continued)

Mechanisms for Redress—The Role of the Superintendent of Health
(*continued*)

- Less than half of the respondents (38 percent) declared that they were informed how to check the status of their claims. The lack of guidance in this respect diminishes the empowerment of citizens that derives from the existence of a system of redress. The system originally was designed so that citizens could follow up or check their claims by telephone and Internet.
- There are observable differences in the evaluations of different segments of the redress system: citizens with arbitration cases have given better evaluations than those who have used administrative channels for redress. The same can be observed when comparing cases that have been resolved in favor of the claimant with those resolved in favor of the provider.
- A positive aspect of the system is the capacity of the superintendent's office to communicate claims resolutions to the citizens involved. Nine of 10 respondents indicated that the resolution letter from the superintendent's office was easy to understand; eight of 10 indicated that it was clear on the steps to be followed to make the resolution effective; and seven of 10 thought it contained solid arguments to support the decision.
- Finally, about 60 percent of all respondents were satisfied with the resolutions of their claims, and 40 percent reported that they were not satisfied. Claimants in arbitration cases, men, seniors, high-income claimants, and ISAPRE affiliates were likely to be satisfied with the results. This issue deserves further study because it could indicate certain discriminatory practices toward young people, women, and middle- and low-income groups. It is worth noting that regardless of the final resolution, seven of 10 respondents thought that making the claim was worth the effort, and only three of 10 reported it was not.

Source: Chile, Office of the Superintendent of Health 2007a.

Lessons and Conclusions

The government of Chile has developed a comprehensive rights-based system with explicit guarantees of access, quality, opportunity, and financial protection; has established well-defined mechanisms for redress; and has made a commitment to continuous improvement. Rather than introducing more services for the poor, this system integrates the poor into a universal system—that is, those who require the most support are enabled to access goods and services on equal terms with the rest of the population. In the first public opinion survey conducted after the health reform was implemented, 42 percent of respondents believed that the REGH benefited mainly public system subscribers, and only 32 percent considered it to be of benefit to the entire population. Two years later, 53 percent of interviewees were convinced that the explicit guarantees regime works in favor of both public and private users, with 31 percent believing that it is a program primarily for the benefit of FONASA users (Chile, Office of the Superintendent of Health 2007a). Further analysis of REGH functioning will provide more specific information about which groups are benefiting most from the program, and about possible areas of discrimination. Current results, however, demonstrate the already substantial impact the REGH has had on coverage of services related to some of the top-priority health conditions.

In addition to the innovative technical approach (determining priority services and coordinating distinct health insurance systems), various political lessons can be drawn form the successful implementation of the REGH. The political timing is one of those lessons. Legislative negotiations were postponed until after congressional elections to avoid additional politicizing of the discussions. The role of the Christian Democratic Party in negotiating the terms of reform with the more extreme left and right parties in the national congress allowed all interests to be taken into account and moderated the reforms accordingly. The fact that the government presented a flexible reform proposal rather than pushing for a reform on very strict terms facilitated an agreement and revealed its commitment to sustainable reform. The open discussion of budget alternatives and willingness to pursue nontraditional sources of health funding reiterated that commitment.

The policy structure of the REGH—particularly codifying institutional responsibilities and procedures (including funding) in legal documents—was of utmost importance for the proper functioning and transparency of the system. It gave clarity to the process rather than only to the overall targets of the reform, making sure that all affected actors follow established norms and standards. It also made possible the complex coordination between the public and private insurance sectors. In addition, the mechanism of researching, negotiating, and adding new health conditions to the regime was tested and established, reinforcing the progressive nature of this policy.

Finally, the element of redress was given ample attention in this initiative, unlike in most social programs in Chile and the rest of the region. Together with the definition of explicit entitlements and guarantees, the redress and enforcement mechanism is what distinguishes the REGH as a rights-based policy. It avoids the solely judicial protection of health rights. Instead, the administrative redress system—through the insurance providers and the Office of the Superintendent of Health—presents a faster and more affordable route for all citizens to claim their health entitlements. The issues of public information and citizens' awareness of their entitlements are still challenges to be overcome as the regime gains popularity.

In the words of former Minister of Health Osvaldo Artaza, a key actor in the approval of the guarantees regime, "A health system based merely on purchasing power or targeted and paternalist assistance programs generates inequity, inefficiency and quality discrepancies. On the contrary, a system that is able to offer universal (basic and modern) services in priority areas, defined through cost-benefit analysis, can promote greatly the sustainable exercise of the right to health.... The guarantee of the right to health, similar to other social guarantees, has meaning only in a democratic society. Democracy is increasingly conceived not only as a political but also a social and economic system that allows simultaneously for growth and equity, for economic development and quality of life..." (Artaza 2002:6).[12]

Annex A.

Table 5.A.1. Medical Conditions Included in the REGH, by Stage of List Expansion

First stage (July 2005–July 2006)

1. Chronic terminal renal insufficiency
2. Operable congenital cardiopathy for people younger than age 15
3. Cervical cancer
4. Palliative care for advanced forms of cancer
5. Acute myocardial infarction
6. Diabetes mellitus, type 1
7. Diabetes mellitus, type 2
8. Breast cancer for people age 15 or older
9. Spinal dysraphism (development abnormalities of the spine)
10. Surgical treatment of scoliosis for people younger than age 25
11. Surgical treatment of cataracts
12. Hip endoprosthesis for people age 65 or older suffering from hip arthrosis and severe functional limitations
13. Cleft lip and palate
14. Cancer for children younger than age 15 (leukemia for children under age 5, lymphomas and solid tumors for children under age 15)
15. Schizophrenia
16. Testicular cancer for people age 15 or older
17. Lymphomas in people age 15 or older
18. HIV/AIDS
19. Respiratory infections of a low degree and ambulatory treatment for infants younger than age 5
20. Community-acquired pneumonia, for ambulatory treatment for people aged 65 or older
21. Primary arterial or essential hypertension for people age 15 or older
22. Nonrefractory epilepsy for people between ages 1 and 15
23. Integral oral health for children younger than age 6
24. Prematurity: general, retinopathy, hypoacusia (deafness), and dysplasia
25. Cardiac disorders that require a pacemaker in people age 15 or older

Second stage (July 2006–July 2007)

1. Preventive cholecystectomy of gallbladder cancer for people between ages 35 and 49
2. Stomach (gastric) cancer

3. Prostate cancer for people age 15 or older
4. Vision disorders caused by hypermetropy, myopia, or astigmatism
5. Strabismus for children younger than age 9
6. Diabetic retinopathy
7. Nontraumatic rhegmatogenous retinal detachment
8. Hemophilia
9. Depression in people age 15 or older
10. Benign prostatic hyperplasia
11. Orthesis (joint support) for people age 65 or older
12. Ischemic cerebrovascular accidents (brain stroke) for people age 15 or older
13. Ambulatory treatment of chronic obstructive pulmonary disease
14. Moderate and severe bronchial asthma for children younger than age 15
15. Respiratory distress syndrome in newborns

Third stage (July 2007–July 2008)

1. Medical treatment of light or moderate hip and knee arthrosis for people age 55 or older
2. Subarachnoid hemorrhage in the skull area surrounding the brain
3. Surgical treatment of primary central nervous system tumors for people age 15 or older
4. Surgical treatment of herniated lumbar disc
5. Leukemia for people age 15 or older
6. Ambulatory dental emergencies
7. Integral oral health for adults older than age 60
8. Severe trauma affecting more than one organ/system of the body
9. Emergency treatment of moderate or severe cranio-encephalic trauma
10. Severe eye (ocular) trauma
11. Cystic fibrosis
12. Rheumatoid arthritis
13. Dependency or detrimental consumption of alcohol or drugs in people younger than age 20
14. Analgesia (pain relief) during labor and birth
15. Severe burn
16. Bilateral hypoacusia (deafness) that requires an audiophone for people age 65 or older

Source: Chile, Ministry of Health (http://www.redsalud.gov.cl/gesauge/ges.html).
Note: REGH = Regime of Explicit Guarantees in Health.

Annex B.

Table 5.B.1. Legal, Institutional, Instrumental, and Financial Aspects of the REGH in Chile

Guarantee	Legal framework	Institutional framework	Instrumental framework
Overall health reform	– Art. 19, No. 9, of the Constitution: guarantees citizens' right to health protection – LD 1/2005: establishes public and private health system – LD 725/67, Sanitary Code: regulates health promotion, protection, and recovery – Law 19.966: establishes the REGH – SD 228/05: determines services and guarantees in the framework of the REGH law (published in the **Official Journal of Chile** in January 2006) – Decree 68/06: establishes minimum financial coverage offered by REGH – SD 136/05: sets norms on the effectiveness of REGH and additional financial coverage – SD 369/85: regulates the public health care system – Resolución Exenta 1052[a]: regulates preventive medical exams – Decree 594/99: establishes basic sanitary and environmental standards for the workplace	*Institutions at the national/country level:* – Ministry of Health – Office of the Superintendent of Health (managed independently from the Ministry of Health) – Subsecretariat of Public Health – Ministry of Finance – REGH Advisory Council *Regional institutions:* – 13 regional ministerial secretariats of health – Regional branches of the Office of the Superintendent of Health *Insurance agencies:* – ISAPREs – FONASA *Institutions at the local level:* – Closed network of primary health care centers affiliated with the ISAPREs – Public network of primary health care centers	– 56[b] health conditions, with related clinical guidelines and explicit guarantees of access, quality:[c] opportunity, and financial protection – A functioning system of mediation and redress – Procedures for the realization of explicit guarantees under the REGH

(continued)

Table 5.B.1. Legal, Institutional, Instrumental, and Financial Aspects of the REGH in Chile (continued)

Guarantee	Legal framework	Institutional framework	Instrumental framework
Access	Law 19.966 defines the guarantee of access as the obligation of FONASA and the ISAPREs to ensure provision of the guaranteed services to all of their users for the medical conditions established by law (SD 170 of 2005 that refers to 25 medical conditions, SD 228 of 2006 that adds 15 health problems, and SD 44 of 2007 that adds 16 health conditions) and declares that the same guarantees apply to all services. A patient with any of the health conditions specified in SD 44 can access the REGH and the services specified in the decree. This supreme decree elaborates in detail the services to which patients are entitled, related to the diagnosis, treatment, and follow-up for the listed health conditions. No other health services are guaranteed in this manner, unless needed in the context of one of the heath conditions listed in the decree. FONASA users can access services only through their corresponding network of providers through the primary health centers. Users of the ISAPREs can access the guaranteed services through a provider determined by their insurance institution.	*National regulating institutions:* – Ministry of Finance – Ministry of Health *Central planning institution for the design of the REGH:* – REGH Council *Insurance institutions at regional/local levels:* Services in the REGH are provided through the main public and private insurance channels already existing in the country— FONASA and the ISAPREs: – FONASA includes all public health centers and some private ones that are part of a REGH agreement. It includes primary health centers; family health centers; and primary emergency services, hospitals, and public hospital emergency rooms. The FONASA network covers all cities and villages and a large part of all other rural settlements. – ISAPRE affiliates receive REGH services through a REGH Providers Network that includes professional health centers with which ISAPREs have signed agreements specific to REGH services. These centers are present in all large and medium-sized cities in the country.	Fifty-six health programs have been created corresponding with the 56 health conditions of the REGH. Services within them are supplied by the corresponding public or private health providers. *Private sector:* Affiliates of ISAPREs, concurring with the diagnosis of the physicians in their institution, would be assigned to an appropriate provider within the REGH Providers Network. The explicit guarantees associated with the regime (for example, financial protection) will not be effective unless the services are received from a provider in this network. *Public sector:* REGH services are received through the existing network of providers, first going through primary health centers and then through the appropriate secondary and/or tertiary public institutions, depending on the complexity of the pathology. FONASA affiliates have to be referred by the primary health center where they are registered. In case of emergency, FONASA users can turn to primary emergency services or a public hospital emergency room. The primary health care network has to ensure that it has the capacity necessary to respond to the

Access to the REGH is not automatic for FONASA or ISAPRE users. It must be requested specifically and be supplied by a provider to which the FONASA or ISAPRE assigns the patient. If this process is not being followed, services are provided according to the general health regimen (that is, not according to the regime's explicitly guaranteed norms).

Continuous provision is contingent on the user's continuing to be a patient for the listed medical condition and following the required procedures to access the guaranteed services.

Nevertheless, for some services in the regime—promotional, preventive, palliative, or rehabilitation-related—there is a need to define more explicitly the time period for which the services are guaranteed. Some of the medical guides and descriptions of pathologies in the REGH framework address this issue.

Local providers:
– *Individuals:* Health professionals who are individually authorized to offer health care services in their respective areas (present in all communities in the country)
– *Institutions:* Health centers, such as hospitals, clinics, consultancies, laboratories, or other medical centers; the primary health care system has an Assistance Network in all communities of the country; the hospital network for more specialized services has more limited coverage; private health centers are present only in larger urban areas.

requirements of the explicit guarantees regime to be able to provide timely supply and quality of services specified in the REGH normative framework.

Both private and public sectors are bound by the same protocols or medical guidelines for the provision of REGH services. The objective is to provide adequate attention, including, among others, algorithms for diagnosis, confirmation of diagnosis, therapy, and follow-up activities, depending on the medical condition. These guidelines or protocols are not obligatory and are not financed by the Superintendent of Health. Nevertheless, they contain generic guidelines for how services should be structured and, thus, attempt to protect quality of services within the regime. They are part of the guarantee of quality.

As indicated by the Ministry of Health, the clinical protocols are general guidelines that contain the best available evidence on how to approach each of the medical conditions in the REGH. However, given the complexity of treatment associated with each health problem and considering the ongoing evolution in research and clinical knowledge, these guidelines are subject to modification at any time. That is why the guidelines, as published, are considered recommendations for best

(continued)

Table 5.B.1. Legal, Institutional, Instrumental, and Financial Aspects of the REGH in Chile (*continued*)

Guarantee	Legal framework	Institutional framework	Instrumental framework
			practice but in no way take precedence over the physician's judgment in individual cases. In 2004, the Ministry of Health published 17 working documents as Protocols of Attention. By the end of 2005, a total of 25 clinical guides (including the 17 from the previous year) were published, corresponding with the first 25 pathologies included in the first regime of explicit guarantees, in force since July 1, 2005. In 2006, 15 more clinical guides were added, corresponding to the new pathologies included in the regime through SD 228. The latter increased to 40 the total number of health conditions under the REGH. In 2007, 16 more guides were published, corresponding with the pathologies added through SD 44 in 2007; and some of the previous guides were revised.
Quality	Law 19.966 on the REGH defines quality as provision of health services by a registered or accredited provider, according to Law 19.937 (on sanitary authorities), published in Chile's official journal. *Diario Oficial de la República de Chile*, on February 24, 2004.	*Regulating institutions at the national level:* – The Ministry of Health is responsible for formulating and controlling health policy, which includes, among other responsibilities, "establishing the minimum standards to which all health institutions (hospitals, clinics, and all types of health centers) should adhere so that all services comply	Law 19.966 indicates that to fulfill the set quality standards, two complementary instruments need to be established: one for institutional providers (health establishments) and another for individual providers. Although these instruments are not yet in force, the following are in the process of being established:

Law 19.966 also declares that the guarantee of quality will be subject to redress when the systems for certification, accreditation, and registration of the Office of the Superintendent of Health enter into force. Currently, the guarantee of quality is not fully implemented.

The Code of Accreditation for Health Provider Institutions was published on July 3, 2007 (SD 15). However, it is not yet in force, so the guarantee of quality within the REGH cannot be subject to redress.

with the required quality standards and ensure the security of patients."

National and regional fiscal institutions:
– The Office of the Superintendent of Health is responsible for financing the processes of accreditation and certification.

National certification and accreditation bodies:

Certification and accreditation of providers in the REGH will be realized by neutral and independent national agencies, such as
– Certification agencies for individual providers—public or private agencies, such as universities, authorized by the Ministry of Health
– Accreditation agencies of institutional providers—public or private bodies authorized by the Office of the Superintendent of Health to grant accreditation to providers, according to established regulations.

The institutions in charge of certification and accreditation should maintain a list of providers who have been certified/accredited by them and who successfully have passed the most current required evaluations.

– Systems for accreditation of institutional providers:the accreditation is defined by law as the periodic evaluation of compliance with the minimum health standards, according to the type of health establishment and the complexity of services.
– A system for certification of professionals in health specializations and subspecializations:certification is defined as the process of recognizing that an individual health provider has mastered a body of knowledge and experience relevant to a given area of medical practice that qualifies him or her to practice in that area.

Currently, the two instruments listed above are applied voluntarily by health providers. However, the law indicates that they should become obligatory for the services in the REGH framework when they are functioning fully.

In addition, the following quality mechanisms are envisioned in the REGH framework:

1. instruments and procedures for evaluation, related to the certification and accreditation processes and undertaken by independent evaluating bodies
2. a public health provider registry to contain the following up-to-date information:
   – all certified individual health providers

(continued)

Table 5.B.1. Legal, Institutional, Instrumental, and Financial Aspects of the REGH in Chile (*continued*)

Guarantee	Legal framework	Institutional framework	Instrumental framework
		– all accredited institutional health providers – certifying institutions for medical specializations and subspecializations – accrediting institutions for institutional providers.	
Opportunity	Law 19.966 defines the guarantee of opportunity as the maximum waiting period for receiving a service, established by the decree that regulates the provision of that service. The functioning of this guarantee implies the following: 1. A reasonable period for the diagnosis, treatment, and follow-up health care for each medical condition in the REGH is determined, during which time the health provider should supply the specified services. 2. If the provider does not comply with the periods specified in the respective decrees, the patient may turn to his or her insurance agency (FONASA or an ISAPRE), which has 2 business days to assign a different provider. Recently, more channels for this type of claim have emerged: offices for information, claims, and advice; a Web page; and a telephone hotline.	*Regulating institutions at the national level:* – Office of the Superintendent of Health regulates the procedures with which FONASA and the ISAPREs must comply, according to the law on the REGH. *Coordinating institutions at regional/local levels:* – FONASA and ISAPREs implement the procedures necessary to comply with the legal guarantee of opportunity. *Local implementing institutions:* – Public or private health establishments, assigned by formal agreement to perform services in the REGH framework	The instrumental framework consists of a set of supervision and control mechanisms through which the Office of the Superintendent of Health ensures that FONASA and the ISAPREs comply with their legal obligations under the REGH. The most important mechanism or instrument with regard to the guarantee of opportunity is the Integrated Information System for the Management of Explicit Guarantees in Health, which contains online information for each REGH patient. Through this system, the services provided to the patient, including waiting times and other medical data, may be monitored. Doctors, nurses, and other health professionals are responsible for keeping this database up-to-date. The system thus allows for timely monitoring and follow-up on the waiting lists. It also contains alerts when waiting deadlines are about to be reached so that timely actions may be taken. In addition, it supports the financial management of the REGH.

3. If the FONASA or ISAPRE does not make the necessary referral to a new provider or if the new provider is not able to supply the service, the user may turn to the Office of the Superintendent of Health, which is responsible for assigning a third provider in no more than 2 business days. The regime's normative framework states that the guarantee of opportunity may be suspended for 1 month or more in the case of a serious epidemic or other health threat that demands urgent attention.

Financial protection	Law 19.966 defines financial protection as the declaration that a user's out-of-pocket costs cannot exceed 20 percent of the "market price" for a service, as determined by the Ministry of Finance. (Some users are completely exempt from out-of-pocket costs, as explained below.) SD 44 includes a detailed list of the covered services with their costs and expected user contributions (20 percent) for each of the health problems associated with the REGH. The regime covers the entire cost of services for lower-income beneficiaries of FONASA (groups A and B), all people included in the Health and Rights Reparation and Integration Program,[d] health workers, and senior citizens older than age 65 (that is, these users contribute nothing for services).	*Insurance institutions at the national level:* – FONASA covers the entire cost of REGH services for groups A and B (the lowest-income affiliates in the system), as referred to in Art. 29 of Law 18.469. It also can offer additional financing to groups C and D (generally middle- and lower-middle-income groups), referred to in the same article, according to the norms established in Title IV of Law 18.469. – ISAPREs are obliged to ensure the provision of services and the financial coverage considered a minimum by FONASA in its "free choice option,"[e] as determined by the law.	A system of defined contributions, exemptions, and additional benefits determined by the income level of users and the cost of services

(continued)

99

Table 5.B.1. Legal, Institutional, Instrumental, and Financial Aspects of the REGH in Chile (continued)

Guarantee	Legal framework	Institutional framework	Instrumental framework
	The REGH also includes an "additional financial coverage" benefit to cover the additional costs in cases where the out-of-pocket expense exceeds a deductible equivalent to 29 monthly contributions for affiliates of ISAPREs and members of FONASA group D (middle class), or where it exceeds 21 monthly contributions for FONASA group C users.		
Mechanisms for redress	Law 19.966 envisions that all beneficiaries of the REGH would demand services first from their respective insurance agency. If that agency does not comply with its obligations, users may present claims against FONASA or the ISAPRE at the Office of the Superintendent of Health, according to LD 1 of 2005. At the same time, the law permits REGH affiliates to submit claims to the Office of Health Insurance Funds (part of the Office of the Superintendent of Health), which may act as an arbiter in the resolution of conflicts if the case has not been resolved through mediation.	*First step—institutions receiving claims and administering solutions at the local level:* FONASA or ISAPREs are obligated to take actions to resolve claims. *Second step—institutions receiving claims at regional and national levels:* Office of the Superintendent of Health receives claims and, in the case of non-compliance, may suspend the authorization of a health provider to supply services under the REGH or under the FONASA free choice option. *Third step—institutions that regulate mediation:* (Used in case the aforementioned mechanisms of redress fail or the client is not satisfied with the solution. This mechanism is available for all patients in the health system, within or outside the REGH. Lawsuits cannot be filed without first passing through a stage of mediation.)	*Administrative mechanisms for redress:* Protocols that establish all procedures and time frames for filing, processing, and resolving claims *Extrajudicial mechanisms for redress—mediation:* Mediation Regulations for Claims against Public Health Institutions or Their Employees and Private Health Providers In the case of private providers, mediation has to be facilitated by mediators accredited by the Office of the Superintendent of Health. The mediation is free of cost. The Office of the Superintendent of Health is responsible for maintaining an integrated list of accredited mediators. Mediation is initiated by filing a claim with the State Defense Council (against a public health provider) or with the Office of the Superintendent of Health (against a private health provider).

	A specific normative framework also exists (for example, for nonprovision of services in the case of FONASA or negligent services in the case of ISAPREs) when noncompliance is the direct result of the agency's actions: — Mediation Procedures established in Art. 43 of Law 19.966 — Mediation Regulations for Claims against Public Health Institutions or Their Employees and Private Health Providers (published in the official journal on June 23, 2005).	State Defense Council (for the public system) or the Office of the Superintendent of Health (for the private system) designates one or more mediators for the case. *Fourth step: judicial arbitration or trial:* (Used if the measures described above fail) Courts of justice	The time frame for the entire mediation process is a maximum of 60 days, counted 3 days after the first summons notice is sent to the health provider. This period can be extended for a maximum of another 20 days at mutual agreement of the parties. *Judicial redress:* Follows the criteria and procedures established by the judicial branch
Continual revision	The process of elaborating explicit guarantees indicated in Law 19.966 presupposes a periodic evaluation (every 3 years) and, if necessary, revision of the guaranteed services. The explicit guarantees and their modifications enter into force on the first day of the sixth month following their publication in the official journal. In some circumstances, clarified in the respective decree that regulates the guarantee, modifications can enter into force in less than 6 months.	The following agencies participate in defining and revising guarantees within the regime: — Ministry of Health proposes explicit guarantees based on available research and evaluations. — Ministry of Finance determines the resources that will be available for the National Health Fund and the amount that citizens will contribute when explicit guarantees first are being defined. — REGH Council monitors activities of the Ministry of Health in all aspects related to the analysis, evaluation, and revision of the explicit guarantees. To complete its functions, the council can use other research and technical expertise or studies, complementary to the ones already considered by the Ministry of Health.	Proposals for new social guarantees or modifications of the existing guarantees need to be based on research that determines a list of health priorities for the country and suggested interventions; the effectiveness of the proposed interventions; their contribution to extending life expectancy or the quality of life; and, if possible, a cost-benefit analysis of the suggested intervention. Subsequently, the per-user cost of the proposal is verified through another set of studies. The completed proposal is discussed by the nine-member REGH Council, which consists of recognized authorities in the areas of medicine, public health, economics, bioethics, sanitary rights, and related disciplines.

(continued)

Table 5.B.1. Legal, Institutional, Instrumental, and Financial Aspects of the REGH in Chile (*continued*)

Guarantee	Legal framework	Institutional framework	Instrumental framework
		– FONASA and ISAPREs provide information solicited by the Ministry of Health or other authorized entities, according to the Law on REGH and relevant decrees, to facilitate the process of evaluating and revising the regime.	After the proposal is evaluated by the council, it is considered by the Ministry of Health and the Ministry of Finance, which elaborate the final proposal to be sent to the president of the republic. The president issues the respective decree. The independent research and studies that serve as a basis of these health proposals are of great importance because they ensure that the selection of guaranteed services and health conditions will not be subject to political discretion, although the specific services to be provided in the regime are determined in light of the budget that the Ministry of Finance makes available.

Source: Authors' compilation.

Note: FONASA = National Health Fund; ISAPRE = private health insurance institution; LD = Legislative Decree; REGH = Regime of Explicit Guarantees in Health; SD = Supreme Decree.

a. Resolución Exenta is a resolution exempt form the control of the government agency responsible for monitoring the public administration spending.

b. President Michelle Bachelet has committed to including a total of 80 medical conditions in the REGH. In addition to the 56 conditions already included, 7 more are in the stage of research and piloting.

c. The guarantee of quality is still in the process of implementation. Its functioning would require the creation and installment of an entirely new system to regulate the certification, accreditation, and monitoring of certification and accreditation procedures for health professionals and health establishments associated with the REGH services. Designing this new framework and setting up the necessary institutions to implement and maintain it are slow and costly processes. In addition, the Ministry of Health has to be cautious in introducing new quality and authorization standards so that health professionals do not perceive them as threats. The functioning of the quality subguarantee also has been delayed by the discussions surrounding the health protocols or clinical guides that refer to quality standards and good practices associated with the 56 medical conditions included in the REGH. Originally, these protocols were intended for use as a basis for redress of the quality subguarantee. However, organizations of medical professionals strongly opposed the use of these guidelines as a basis for redress and suggested that they be used instead as "good-practice guidelines" that should not overrule the physician's judgment for each particular case. Currently, the clinical guides have been created and have been endorsed widely as good practices by the community of health professionals. The certification and accreditation system is also close to becoming operational. Thus, even though the quality guarantee has not yet been fully implemented as intended, the described advances have been very relevant and, overall, have had a positive impact on health care.

d. This includes people recognized as victims of the military regime by the National Truth and Reconciliation Commission or by the National Reparation and Reconciliation Corporation (according to Law 19123) or the spouses, parents, mothers of biological children, siblings, or children of victims under the age of 25 (or at any age in the case of disability).

e. FONASA offers its affiliates an "institutional service option," a "free choice option," or both. Under the former option, users should be registered with a primary public health center through which they can be referred to other specialized health establishments within the public system as needed. This option is accessible to all FONASA users. Under the second option, users can access any public health center—including private ones affiliated with FONASA—and may choose their physicians. This option is accessible to FONASA groups B, C, and D (that is, all but the lowest-income group of affiliates).

REGH Financial Framework

The following is a presentation of consolidated budget data for the REGH between 2002 and 2006 (tables 5. B. 2 and 5. B. 3).[a] Unfortunately, it does not show the budget changes effected with the introduction of 16 new conditions in July 2007, which extended the list of medical problems from 40 to 56. In the period 2002–06, a total of $1.35 billion was spent on the new health regime. Fifty-one percent of that sum was spent in 2006 alone because 15 new health conditions were financed, and there was an overall increase in investment. Thus, there is a large difference between the level of spending on the regime in its initial years and that in the period 2004–06. Because this policy was designed to grow progressively, so too did the resources allocated to it. Between 2002–03 and 2004–06, spending in the REGH had grown by more than 100 percent.

Data on REGH spending are drawn from the budgets of its related institutions because there are no cost centers that allow a more detailed look into the spending for each operational area of the regime. This is one limitation in presenting the exact operational costs of the program.

The fiscal data presented here are based on an official analysis performed by the Foundation for Overcoming Poverty using data from the Budget Office of the Ministry of Finance.

Table 5.B.2. Spending in the REGH Based on Budget Allocations Only
2006 US$ millions

2002[a]	
Item	Spending
Equipment (purchase plus 7-year maintenance)	n.a.
Personnel	35.2
Additional personnel required by the REGH	n.a.
Total	35.2
2003	
Item	Spending
Equipment (purchase plus 7-year maintenance)	n.a.
Personnel	53.3
Additional personnel required by the REGH	n.a.
Total	53.3
2004	
Item	Spending
Equipment (purchase plus 7-year maintenance)	14.7
Personnel	138.9
Additional personnel required by the REGH	18.0
Total	171.6

2005

Item	Spending
Equipment (purchase plus 7-year maintenance)	30.3
Personnel	387.5
Additional personnel required by the REGH	2.6
Total	420.4

2006

Item	Spending
Equipment (purchase plus 7-year maintenance)	37.6
Personnel	673.9
Additional personnel required by the REGH	8.3
Total	719.8

Source: Foundation for Overcoming Poverty, based on data supplied by the Budget Office of the Ministry of Finance.

Note: n.a. = not applicable.

a. This budget analysis begins in 2002 because a pilot plan of the explicit guarantees regime with three medical conditions was introduced in 2002 and gradually was expanded to five conditions in 2003 and to 17 in 2004. Only on July 1, 2005, did the first REGH decree with 25 medical conditions enter into force.

Table 5.B.3. Aspects of Spending in the REGH Based on Budget Allocations Only

2006 US$ millions

Year	Spending (US$ millions)	Annual variation in spending (%)	Proportion of total social spending (%)	Proportion of total institutional spending (%)
2002	35.2	n.a.	0.2	0.8
2003	53.3	51.4	0.4	1.1
2004	171.6	222.2	1.1	3.2
2005	420.4	144.9	2.5	7.5
2006	719.8	71.3	4.1	11.1

Source: Foundation for Overcoming Poverty.

Sources of funding:
- Budget support
- Obligatory worker contributions (more workers will be contributing and a higher proportion of contributions will be allocated to the REGH as more medical conditions are included and as the amount of the obligatory contributions rises).
- Improvements in the health care and financial systems that promote higher efficiency in the collection of citizen contributions and the reallocation of public resources. Typically, contributions to the health system have been collected through an obligatory deduction from workers' salaries, which the employer deposits into either FONASA or the ISAPREs. However, the large number of informal or self-employed workers and microenterprises (many of whom pay no contributions but can access public health care for free) has challenged this system. To address the challenge, the government has introduced incentives for voluntary contributions and other legal mechanisms to help formalize the collection of contributions from the informal sector.
- Economic growth that would help increase salaries and employment and, hence, the amount collected in citizen contributions.

Conditions:
- Increase of the state's budget support to FONASA is equivalent to the cost of new health activities that it needs to finance or is proportional to the increase of the contributions required for low-income groups (Art. 14 of the Law on REGH).

Notes

1. The REGH (Régimen de Garantías Explícitas en Salud; GES) is also known as the Plan AUGE (Plan de Acceso Universal y Garantías Explícitas).

2. An example is the pension reform considered by President Michelle Bachelet's administration.

3. The Coalition of Parties for Democracy (Concertación de Partidos por la Democracia), more often known as the Concertación, is an alliance of center-left political parties founded in 1988. It has won every presidential election since Chille's return to democracy in 1990. The coalition member-parties include the Christian Democrats, the Party for Democracy, the Social Democrat Radical Party, and the Socialist Party.

4. Figueroa (1998) notes that the morbidity and mortality for tuberculosis are linked directly to socioeconomic determinants. He shows that in health services areas where the rate of indigence is 8.5 percent of the population and that of poverty is 20.1 percent, the rate of mortality from tuberculosis rises to 5.5 per 100,000 inhabitants, the rate of morbidity for all forms of tuberculosis is 56.6 per 100,000, and the rate of pulmonary bacillus tuberculosis is 31.0 per 100,000. However, in health services areas where the rate of indigence is 3.4 percent and that of poverty is 10.0 percent, the rate of mortality from tuberculosis reaches only 2.9 per 100,000 inhabitants, the rate of morbidity from all forms of tuberculosis is 26.2 per 100,000, and the rate of morbidity from pulmonary bacillus tuberculosis is only 10.8 per 100,000. In other words, in areas where poverty is high, rates of mortality and morbidity from tuberculosis are double and triple, respectively, the rates where there is less poverty. Allende (2005) also notes that mortality rates for tuberculosis among manual workers in Chile are much higher than those among other employees.

5. Except for the value added tax, these proposed tax increases were not approved. However, measures were taken to improve the efficiency of tax collection.

6. The framework includes Law 19.882 and Law 19.888 (both approved in 2003) that regulate, respectively, the new personnel policy for public employees and the financing of health reform; and Law 19.966 (approved in 2004), which establishes the REGH.

7. For example, FONASA has four groups of affiliates (A, B, C, and D). Group A is the lowest-income group and group D is the highest-income group among all the users of public health care. Traditionally and prior to the REGH, these groups have had different contribution obligations: group A is exempt from contributions and from out-of-pocket costs; group B pays contributions but is exempt from copayments; group C pays both contributions and defined copayments; and group D pays contributions and higher out-of-pocket costs than does group C. The higher-income groups of FONASA affiliates generally

correspond to poverty quintiles III and IV of the population. Quintile V typically is affiliated with the private health system. Under the REGH, groups A and B are exempt from all costs in any stage of treatment and for any required inputs.

8. The National Budget Office (Dirección de Presupuestos de la Nación), part of the Ministry of Finance, is responsible for allocating resources to ministries and programs. Its duties include conducting evaluations of spending and controlling the fulfillment of commitments and targets by the programs financed.

9. These numbers were calculated on the basis of the budget allocated at the beginning of each year plus adjustments and special laws. Drawn from a homogenous series, based on budget changes by the National Central Procurement Office of the National Health System (http://www.cenabast. cl/ingles/links2.html) and the Fondo Único de Prestaciones Familiares (Family Benefits Fund). Also see the presentation by the Pan American Health Organization (http://www.paho.org/English/AD/DPC/NC/global-health-08-chile.pdf). The number presented here includes only budget line spending and does not consider debt service, financial investments, or final cash balance.

10. The study was conducted by the Criteria Consulting firm. It employed both interviews with users and a household survey. The study included 1,227 adult men and women (age 18 or older) representing different socioeconomic groups and users of FONASA and ISAPREs and residing in the greater Santiago area and in other regions of the country.

11. This study was conducted by the Datavoz consulting agency, using a sample of 1,034 people interviewed in their homes. It used a method of probability sampling with a ± 3 percent margin of error and a 95 percent level of confidence. The sample consisted of FONASA and ISAPRE users.

12. The administration of President Bachelet has committed to expanding the list of health conditions under the REGH from 56 to 80. As mentioned previously, research and a pilot plan for including 7 more medical conditions are under way. The REGH Advisory Council has signaled the importance of including guarantees for public health promotion (for example, for psychological and physiological/nutritional services).

References

Abel, Christopher, and Colin M. Lewis. 2002. "Exclusion and Engagement: A Diagnosis of Social Policy in Latin America in the Long Run." In *Exclusion and Engagement: Social Policy in Latin America,* ed. Christopher Abel and Colin M. Lewis, 3–53. London: Institute for the Study of the Americas, University of London.

Aguilera, Ximena, Claudia González, Andrea Guerrero, Paula Bedregal García, Vivian Milosavijevic, Marisol Rivera, Jeannette Vega, Judith Salinas, Fernando Otaíza, Francisco Espejo, and Consuelo Espinosa. 2002. "Objetivos sanitarios para la década 2000–2010." *El Vigía 5* (15). http://epi.minsal.cl/epi/html/elvigia/vigia15.pdf (accessed March 8, 2009).

Allende, Salvador. 2005. "Medical and Social Reality in Chile." *International Journal of Epidemiology* 34: 732–36. http://ije.oxfordjournals.org/cgi/reprint/34/4/732 (accessed March 27, 2009).

Artaza, Osvaldo. 2002. "Derechos humanos y reformas a la salud." Report 254. *Asuntos Públicos.* http://www.asuntospublicos.org/web/pdf/254.pdf (accessed March 27, 2009).

Barría, María Soledad. 2006. "Objetivos sanitarios para el 2010: índices están estancados." Interview for "La Nación." December 8. Santiago, Chile. http://www.lanaciondomingo.cl/prontus_noticias/site/artic/20061207/pags/20061207221836.html (accessed March 8, 2009).

———. 2008. "AUGE 2005–2008: Implementación de garantías explícitas en salud." Ministry of Health, Santiago, Chile.

Castiglioni, Rossana. 2005. *The Politics of Social Policy Change in Chile and Uruguay: Retrenchment versus Maintenance, 1973–1998.* Latin American Studies: Social Sciences and Law Series. New York: Routledge.

Chile, Ministry of Planning. 2006. "Balance de seis años de las políticas sociales." Ministerio Secretaría General de Gobierno, Santiago, Chile.

Chile, Office of the Superintendent of Health. 2006. "Informe nacional: 'Conocimiento de la superintendencia.'" Plataforma de Atención Presencial (Platform to the President's Attention). Consultation, Santiago, Chile, August 21–September 1, 2006. http://www.supersalud.cl/568/articles-3257_recurso_8.pdf (accessed March 31, 2009).

———. 2007a. "Public Opinion Survey and Market Investigation, Final Report, Evaluation of the Degree of Satisfaction with Using the Services of the Superintendent of Health and the System for Resolving Claims." Santiago, Chile.

———. 2007b. "Resultados entregados en el marco del seminario: Avances y perspectivas de la reforma del sector salud." Santiago, Chile.

———. 2008. "Estudio de opinión a usuarios del sistema de salud: Conocimiento y posicionamiento de la superintendencia de salud, GES-AUGE y otros aspectos de la reforma." Santiago, Chile.

Drago, Marcelo. 2006. "La reforma al sistema de salud chileno desde la perspectiva de los derechos humanos." Social Policies Series 121, Economic Commission for Latin America and the Caribbean, Santiago, Chile.

Figueroa, Alex. 1998. "Política de salud del gobierno del Presidente Frei, para 1998 y 1999. Énfasis y prioridades." *Boletín de la Academia Chilena de Medicina.* Santiago, Chile.

Filgueira, Carlos, and Mario Lombardi. 1995. "Social Policy in Latin America." In *Social Policy in a Global Society*, ed. Daniel A. Morales-Gómez and Mario A. Torres, 123–69. Ottawa, Canada: International Development Research Centre.

FUNASUPO (Fundación para la Superación de la Pobreza). 1999. "Propuestas para la futura política social 1999." Santiago, Chile.

Hernandez, Sandra, Hermán Sandoval, and Iris Delgado. 2005. "Sistema de salud: Las diferencias entre lo público y lo privado." In *Determinantes Sociales de la Salud en Chile: En la Perspectiva de la Equidad*. Santiago, Chile: Chilean Initiative for Equity in Health.

Lenz, Rony. 2007. "Proceso político de la reforma AUGE de salud en Chile: Algunas lecciones para América latina. Una mirada desde la economía política." Serie Estudios Socio/Económicos 38. Santiago, Chile.

Morales, María Eugenia. 2005. "Chile Envejece: Prospectiva de los impactos políticos y sociales de este fenómeno hacia el bicentenario." Programa Interdisciplinario de Estudios Gerontológicos de la Universidad de Chile, Santiago. http://www.gerontologia.uchile.cl/docs/chien.htm (accessed March 8, 2009).

Raczynski, Dagmar. 1994. "Políticas sociales y programas de combate a la pobreza en Chile: Balance y desafíos." *Colección Estudios CIEPLAN* 39: 9–73.

———. 2000a. "Chile: Progress, Problems, and Prospects." In *Reforming Social Policy: Changing Perspectives on Sustainable Human Development,* ed. Daniel A. Morales-Gómez, Necla Tschirgi, and Jennifer L. Moher, 45–82. Ottawa, Canada: International Development Research Centre.

———. 2000b. "Overcoming Poverty in Chile." In *Social Development in Latin America: The Politics of Reform*, ed. Joseph S. Tulchin and Allison M. Garland. Latin American Program of the Woodrow Wilson International Center for Scholars. Boulder, CO: Lynne Rienner.

Sojo, Ana. 2006. *Health Benefits Guarantees in Latin America: Equity and Quasi-Market Restructuring at the Beginning of the Millennium*. Serie Estudios y Perspectivas. Economic Commission for Latin America and the Caribbean, Mexico City, Mexico.

Vega, Jeannette. 2008. "La garantía del derecho a la salud en Chile: Un balance del Plan AUGE." November 4. Ministry of Health, Santiago, Chile.

CHAPTER 6

The Role of the Courts in Realizing Rights to Housing and Health: The Case of South Africa

Sibonile Khoza

The advent of constitutional democracy in South Africa brought hope to the great majority of the people who were deprived of access to a whole range of resources and opportunities during the dark years of Apartheid. The inclusion in the Bill of Rights of a comprehensive list of social, economic, civil, and political rights as justiciable rights signified South Africa's unequivocal commitment to achieving social transformation and signaled that such transformation would take a rights-based approach. The 1996 Constitution has encouraged a culture of entitlement to recourse and opportunities and a "culture of justification" for failure on the part of government to ensure such access.

The greatest hope for social change has been in the areas of housing and health care services. Apartheid arguably did some of the greatest injustices in these sectors. It adopted and implemented a series of discriminatory and segregative laws and policies that resulted in black populations being forcibly removed from and dispossessed of their land; viciously evicted from their homes; and inhumanely relocated to remote, racially defined areas outside of the cities and far away from economic activities. The legacy of these acts is glaringly visible in the residential setup in the country. The majority of black and poor people live in poorly resourced rural areas, dense townships, and uninhabitable informal settlements; whereas their white counterparts (with a group of black middle-class people) live in the well-resourced residential areas (the so-called suburbs).

The South African health system also was divided according to race and geographic location during Apartheid. There were 14 departments in all: 10 Bantustan health departments for blacks; 1 each for coloreds, Indians, and whites; and the National Department of Health. The Bantustan, or homeland, system was intended to ensure that blacks received health care services that were inferior to those received by whites (Schneider, Barron, and Fonn 2007). Spending on the public and private health sectors was disproportionately skewed in favor of whites. Black people in homelands and townships were denied access to basic sanitation, clean water supply, and other components of public health. They also were refused access to health care services in private hospitals because of their race, geographic location, or indigence (Baldwin-Ragave, de Gruchy, and London 1999), and were discouraged from pursuing careers in medicine. The result was world-class, well-resourced medical care for whites and overcrowded, filthy, and underserviced health facilities for blacks.

As Arthur Chaskalson[1] once remarked, these conditions preexisted the Constitution "and a commitment to address them and to transform our society into one in which there will be human dignity, freedom and equality, lies at the heart of our constitutional order."[2] Therefore, the post-Apartheid government had to undertake the enormous challenges of transforming, reconstructing, and developing a country that had been systematically destroyed by its earlier system of social organization and by colonialism. The rights of access to housing and health care services therefore were guaranteed constitutionally to ensure redress of the historical imbalances. Everyone has access to housing and health care as a matter of entitlement rather than charity, so social transformation in these two sectors is driven by people's entitlement to these social services and goods.

It is not simply the protection of housing and health rights that demonstrates South Africa's commitment to social transformation in these sectors. It is the recognition of the principle of interdependence of human rights that is demonstrated by the comprehensive nature of the list of justiciable rights that are guaranteed. The comprehensive protection of these rights is particularly important, given South Africa's historical background. The protection is based on the notion that human rights should be treated holistically to safeguard human welfare (Liebenberg 2006). However, the Constitution's key feature was the justiciability of the socioeconomic rights provisions, which directed the courts to play a significant role in realizing these rights, thereby helping achieve social transformation.

This chapter focuses on this role of the courts. It seeks to answer the following questions: (1) What has been the role of the courts in realizing health and housing rights in South Africa? (2) To what extent have the courts' decisions influenced social change and social policy? Put differently, have those decisions made any difference in the lives of poor, homeless, and diseased people? and (3) What factors contributed to the courts' relative success? Before examining the role of the courts in realizing these rights, however, it will be worth discussing the housing and health policy contexts that prevailed prior to adoption of the Constitution to address the legacy left by Apartheid and to set the tone for a rights-based approach to social transformation.

Laying the Foundations for a Rights-Based Social Policy

At the beginning of Apartheid's end in the early 1990s, there were major shifts toward a human rights culture and democratic principles in all aspects of life. South Africa's rights-based approach to social policy was expressed for the first time in 1994, with the adoption of the Reconstruction and Development Programme. This policy expressly acknowledged housing and health care as human rights. It thereby committed the government to delivering those services in a manner consistent with human rights standards and the democratic principles of inclusiveness, participation, and transparency. The program paid special attention to the basic needs of poor people, women, children, and other vulnerable groups. It was the most comprehensive policy framework to be adopted by the democratically elected government, and it informed the adoption of the subsequent social policies.

Housing Policy

A major policy to be developed in the housing sector was the White Paper on a New Housing Policy and Strategy in South Africa. It had four main objectives: (1) to provide housing to the homeless and alleviate overcrowding, (2) to improve the quality of housing through the provision of formal top structures (that is, buildings), (3) to increase tenure security and promote ownership, and (4) to develop "sustainable human settlements." This White Paper set out the framework to be followed in developing the national housing laws, policies, and programs.[3]

It aimed, first, to address the housing crisis directly through the scale of delivery of subsidized housing for low-income households, both for ownership and for rental. Second, it sought to create an environment in which the subsidized housing market can operate normally as part of the broader, nonsubsidized housing market. The key policy aimed at implementing the right to adequate housing was the Housing Subsidy Scheme, adopted in 1995, which provided a one-off housing grant to people who had dependents, earned less than R(rand) 3,500 per month, and had never owned a home.[4] In the years following the adoption of the Constitution in 1996, the courts played a key role in the evolution of housing policy—a role that is outlined in detail in subsequent sections of this chapter.

Health Policy

Prior to the Reconstruction and Development Programme, the African National Congress developed the National Health Plan (ANC 1994), which set out policies and principles for radical reform of the health care system. That plan was followed by the White Paper on the Transformation of the Health System of South Africa, which articulated the direction, strategies, and pace of reform (South Africa, Department of Health 1997). This White Paper aimed at (1) unifying the fragmented health system; (2) giving priority to primary health care and making it available and accessible to all people; (3) ensuring the availability of safe and good-quality essential drugs; (4) giving special attention to the health needs of vulnerable groups, such as the poor, elderly people, women, and children; and (5) promoting the participation of community structures in health care delivery.

The reforms began with the dismantling of the racially fragmented health care system. The 14 Apartheid-era departments of health were unified into one national department and decentralized into nine provincial departments. The National Health Act 61 of 2003, which went into force in 2005, was enacted to bring about the reforms in the health service. The act gave women and children access to free health care services in the public sector. It also gave special protection to people needing emergency treatment by outlawing the refusal to provide such treatment.

A central tenet of public health care is universal access to a package of essential health services. The government has developed a framework for implementing public health care over a 10-year time frame. This framework involves, among other things, creating a decentralized district health system consisting of 50 health regions and 170 districts (van Rensburg 2004) and bringing communities into the planning and organization of health care services. Both public health care and the district health system call for a fundamental shift in the allocation of health care resources through the dismantling of racial and urban biases. The health budget is being diverted from academic and tertiary hospitals to fund public health care and the district health system. From 1996 to 1998, there was a funding shift of 8.0 percent away from hospital services and 10.7 percent toward district health services (van den Heever and Brijlal 1997). In addition, a massive program of clinic building and upgrading constructed about 500 new clinics in rural areas between 1994 and 1999 (Abbott 1997).

The government's first step toward improving access to health care services was a 1994 presidential decree granting free care at public health facilities to pregnant women and children under age 6 (South Africa 1994). Since that time, access to free health care in primary health care facilities has been extended to the entire population (van Rensburg 2004). Another legislative measure, the Choice on Termination of Pregnancy Act 92 of 1996, radically has transformed access to abortion services. Section 2(1)(a) of the act allows free termination of pregnancy on request of the woman during the first 12 weeks. Although rural women still experience problems in accessing abortion services, access generally has increased vastly.[5]

The foregoing policy contexts laid the foundation for a rights-based approach to social policy and transformation. They also aimed at addressing the huge challenges left by Apartheid. Although the courts have been instrumental in engaging with issues of rights and in shaping social policies, and have been active in the allocation of budgets and the development of laws since the Constitution was adopted in 1996, the policy foundations or shifts prior to that supreme law coming into force made the courts' role a little easier. Essentially, the tasks that the judicial system then had were to carve out its role in social transformation discourse and set the human rights standards (based on the Constitution) on which such social transformation must take place.

The Courts: Carving Out a Role in Realizing Socioeconomic Rights

From the beginning of constitutional democracy, the courts saw themselves as key agents for social change in South Africa. However, this role was contested. Even before the 1996 Constitution was certified, the question of whether to include socioeconomic rights along with civil and political rights in the Bill of Rights ignited a wave of academic and public debate.[6] During the certification case[7] before the Constitutional Court (hereafter, the Court), some groups objected to the inclusion of socioeconomic rights on conventional grounds that these rights were "not universally accepted fundamental rights," were "inconsistent with the principle of separation of powers," and were "unenforceable in the court of law."

The Court rejected these claims, first arguing that although socioeconomic rights were not universally accepted fundamental rights, the constitutional principles emanating from the 1993 Interim Constitution permitted inclusion of these rights as supplements to the universally accepted fundamental rights.[8] Second, it argued that the enforcement of socioeconomic rights does not always have budgetary implications and, thus, does not always result in the breach of separation of powers. It further pointed out that the enforcement of civil and political rights—such as the rights to a fair trial, to vote, and to equality—also has budgetary implications, but that aspect does not preclude their being enforced by the courts.[9] It added that the fact that socioeconomic rights would almost invariably give rise to budgetary implications is not, in and of itself, a bar to their justiciability. At a minimum, socioeconomic rights can be protected negatively from improper invasion.[10]

Following that decision, socioeconomic rights were included in the Bill of Rights, equally enforceable in the courts as are civil and political rights. The certification decision paved a way for a more challenging role of the courts to give meaning to socioeconomic rights. It also signaled the Court's willingness to enforce those rights. However, the question of the justiciability of socioeconomic rights was not over. It was brought up again in the famous case of the *Government of the Republic of South Africa and Others v. Grootboom and Others* (hereafter, *Grootboom*). The Court laid the issue to rest by stating categorically that these rights—according to the certification decision and their inclusion in the Bill of Rights—are justiciable. The Court therefore pointed out that it is the method of enforcement that should be determined on a case-by-case basis.[11]

In subsequent cases, the Court demonstrated its institutional capability and skills to enforce positive obligations and grant remedies without usurping the powers of the executive branch. It asserted its role not as one of second-guessing the decisions of the government, but as one of scrutinizing against the Constitution both the measures adopted by government to realize rights and the government's conduct. All courts have scrutinized laws and policies of government that were challenged by some groups in society. Most of the socioeconomic rights cases have dealt with housing rights and health care provisions.

The Courts' Record on Housing and Health Rights

As noted above, no other socioeconomic rights have received as much attention from the courts as have health and housing rights provisions. In other words, the courts have breathed life into these rights. Although 1997's *Soobramoney v. Minister of Health (KwaZulu-Natal) and Others* was the first case to consider the enforceability of health care and socioeconomic rights in South Africa, it was only in *Grootboom* that the Court made a major breakthrough. *Grootboom*, and significant subsequent cases that were influenced by the precedents set in that case, are described below.

Government of the Republic of South Africa and Others v. Grootboom and Others

This case, brought before the Court in 2000, involved a group of adults and children who had moved onto private land to escape bad conditions in an informal settlement. The group was evicted and its building materials were destroyed, rendering group members unable to construct shelters. They applied to the High Court of South Africa: Cape of Good Hope Provincial Division (commonly referred to as the Cape High Court) to be provided with temporary housing until they got permanent accommodation, relying on the right of access to adequate housing provided in section 26(1) and the right of children to shelter addressed in section 28(1)(c) of the Constitution.

The Cape High Court said that there was only a violation of the right of children to shelter and not a violation of the right to adequate housing. In reviewing the case, the Constitutional Court set out the standard of "reasonableness" as a guide to deciding whether the government's housing program met constitutional requirements. According to this standard, the government's measures to provide adequate housing must be comprehensive, coherent, and coordinated;[12] be capable of "facilitating the realization of the right";[13] be balanced and flexible; provide appropriately for short-, medium-, and long-term needs;[14] clearly allocate responsibilities and tasks to the different spheres of government and ensure that financial and human resources are available;[15] be reasonably formulated and implemented;[16] and provide for the urgent needs of those in desperate situations.[17]

This reasonableness standard was used accordingly and developed further in a number of subsequent cases on socioeconomic rights.

Minister of Health and Others v. Treatment Action Campaign and Others

In 2002, the Treatment Action Campaign (TAC) challenged the limited nature of government measures to prevent mother-to-child transmission of HIV/AIDS. It set its challenge on two grounds: (1) unreasonable prohibition against administering an essential drug, nevirapine, at public hospitals and clinics, except at a limited number of pilot sites; and (2) failure to produce and implement a comprehensive national program for the prevention of mother-to-child transmission of HIV/AIDS.

The Cape High Court and the Constitutional Court, applying the reasonableness test developed in the *Grootboom* case, decided that the government program was unreasonable in restricting access to a potentially life-saving drug to only a few sites. Both courts also found that the state's program to prevent mother-to-child transmission of HIV/AIDS did not comply with its obligations in terms of sections 27(1) and 27(2) of the Constitution, in that restricting the program to a few sites excluded a significant number of people desperately in need of the drug. The Constitutional Court ordered the government to remove those restrictions and roll the program out nationwide

EN and Others v. Government of the Republic of South Africa and Others

In the *EN*[18] case, the TAC and 15 HIV-positive prisoners from the Westville Correctional Facility in KwaZulu-Natal sought an order from the High Court: Durban and Coastal Local Division (Durban High Court) to compel government to remove all obstacles preventing the 15 prisoners and other similarly situated prisoners from accessing antiretroviral treatment in the facility. They also sought an order that would compel the government to provide these prisoners with antiretroviral drugs in accordance with the existing Operational Plan for Comprehensive HIV and AIDS Care, Management and Treatment.

The Durban High Court found that the implementation of the Operational Plan was unreasonable, inflexible, and not responsive to the urgent needs of the affected prisoners. The court granted the orders sought by the applicants. However, the government was unwilling to implement the court order, choosing to appeal it on technicalities.[19] When the government applied to stop implementation of the court orders pending the outcomes of the appeal, the court held that such stoppage would be unfortunate because prisoners would suffer irreparable harm if the implementation were delayed and the orders set aside. This harm, the court held further, was far greater than the inconvenience likely to be incurred by the state.[20] It then went on to vent its frustration over the government's attitude toward court orders, which showed no respect for the courts, the rule of law, and the separation of powers.[21]

Occupiers of 51 Olivia Road and Others v. City of Johannesburg and Others

The *Olivia* case was brought to court by more than 400 occupiers of two dilapidated buildings in Johannesburg. They were resisting eviction, which was to take place in pursuit of the City of Johannesburg's regeneration program. The program was intended to revamp the city by, among other things, rehabilitating all buildings in disrepair. In the High Court: Witwatersrand Division, the applicants argued that they could not be evicted without being provided alternative accommodation. The Witwatersrand High Court found that the city's program fell short of the requirement to provide suitable relief for people in the city. Relying on *Grootboom*, it ordered the city to devise and implement, within available resources, a comprehensive and coordinated program for those people in desperate need of housing.

On appeal, the Supreme Court of Appeal found that the buildings were unsafe, and it authorized the evictions of the occupiers. It gave the occupiers one month to move out or be evicted forcibly. It also ordered the city to provide alternative temporary shelter to those people who were desperately in need of housing. On further appeal by the occupiers, the Constitutional Court ordered the parties to engage meaningfully with each other in an effort to resolve amicably the differences and difficulties raised in the application. Parties also were ordered to file affidavits on the progress and results of their engagement, by a stipulated date. The city, in short, was ordered to consult with the occupiers before making decisions that adversely affected them. The negotiations resulted in an agreement on interim measures the city would adopt to make the buildings safer and more habitable for the occupiers.

Effects of Court Judgments on Housing Rights

The decisions of the courts do not always translate into immediate and radical changes in the lives of the affected parties, even if those parties are victorious in the courts. For example, the *Grootboom* decision—although highly acclaimed as progressive—has not changed the deplorable conditions in which the triumphant Wallacedene community lives. Irene Grootboom died in her shack in August 2008, despite having fought successfully for a decent house (see *Citizen* 2008).[22]

However, it is important to note that the Constitutional Court's judgment in this case did not order the government to provide houses to the litigants. It ordered the government to develop a comprehensive policy to provide for people in desperate need of housing so that people such as the litigants have access to emergency housing in the future. Therefore, the key measure of court decision success is whether such a reasonable emergency housing program is instituted in response to the order. The Court also did not prioritize the victors. It did not order that, when developed, the emergency housing program had to make the Wallacedene community the first people to benefit from it. There could be communities that are even more desperate than the Wallacedenes, and they have to be prioritized according to the severity of their needs.

The *Grootboom* decision has influenced changes in state policy and conduct to ensure benefits to the broader society, not only to the litigants. This is informed by the Constitutional Court's inclination to the ethos of distributive rather than corrective justice (Mbazira 2008). Two policies that emerged as a result of the *Grootboom* decision are the Housing Assistance in Emergency Circumstances Program (2004) adopted as Chapter 12 of the National Housing Code, and the Informal Settlement Upgrading Program adopted as Chapter 13 of the code.

The emergency housing program aims to assist people in urban and rural areas who have urgent housing needs as a result of natural disaster; eviction; demolition; imminent displacement; or immediate threat to life, health, and safety. Through this program, administered by municipalities, beneficiaries receive assistance in the form of alternative land, infrastructure, and basic services. Qualified beneficiaries also may apply for permanent housing subsidies (Khoza 2007).

The informal settlements program allows municipalities to apply for a community-based or area-based subsidy that is not linked to individual households but rather is based on the actual cost of improving an informal settlement. It discourages municipalities from relocating informal settlements from expensive or geotechnically unsuitable land to new housing developments on the outskirts of cities and towns. Instead, it enables land already occupied to be made habitable (Mbazira 2008).

Though not as a direct result of the *Grootboom* decision, the government also moved away from an approach directed simply at providing housing to one aimed at developing sustainable human settlements. The Comprehensive Plan for Sustainable Human Settlements of 2004 (also known as Breaking New Ground) is the key policy in this regard. It prioritizes upgrading of informal settlements and the integrated planning for sustainable human settlements. The N2 Gateway Housing Project is the first project delivered in accordance with the Breaking New Ground program. It is hoped that the sustainable settlements program may succeed in addressing the urgent needs of the country's 2.4 million informal settlers in the medium to longer term. However, it has taken more than 2 years to complete the N2 Gateway Housing Project,[23] which has been riddled with administrative and political problems, including alleged corruption in the issuing of tenders.

The *Olivia* decision demonstrated the Constitutional Court's innovative approach of addressing social problems by compelling parties to engage with each other to find an amicable solution with minimal judicial intervention. Although the case gave some publicity to Johannesburg's grand plan to rehabilitate the city, it also revealed that the government's conduct amounted to implementing such a plan at the expense of the poor. Had the Court not intervened in the manner it did, the more than 400 occupiers would have been thrown into the street, rendered homeless, and exposed to all sorts of life-threatening elements.

The case put pressure on the city to respond more humanely to the plight of the poor. The interim order of the Court also was implemented before the relocation was effected at San Jose and 197 Main Street (Mbazira 2008). It was reported that more than 450 residents voluntarily were moved to better housing by the city (Harthon, Royston, and Wilson 2008). Before that, the city had restored the supply of water and provided portable toilets, refuse removal services, and fire extinguishers in the buildings in accordance with the terms of the interim order. The city also took charge of the relocation, providing trucks, movers, and security (Mbazira 2008).

However, huge challenges remain in the housing sector. For example, there is no policy for groups with special housing needs, such as women (especially abused women), people with HIV/AIDS, the elderly, children, and people with disabilities (Chenwi 2006). Farm evictions have been increasing since 1994. It is estimated that about 940,000 black South Africans were removed forcibly from farms during the period 1994–2004 (Wegerif 2006). Wegerif argues that this is a failure of rights and the law.

There is a need for political will and strong civil society activism to hold government accountable for its constitutional obligations and its policy and legislative commitments, and to monitor the government's compliance with court decisions and orders.[24]

Other cases on evictions include the *City of Cape Town v. Neville Rudolph and Others*,[25] *President of the Republic of South Africa and Another v. Modderklip Boerdery (Pty) Ltd and Others (hereafter, Modder klip)*[26] and *Port Elizabeth Municipality v. Various Occupiers*.[27] The recurrence of evictions despite the plethora of cases on them, including *Grootboom*, suggests that government is not taking these judgments seriously. It does not reflect much on the failure of the courts to pronounce on these rights, but it does reflect on the courts' limitations to compel government to obey the rule of law.[28]

Effects of Court Decisions on Health Rights

Although there are many problems with the health system in South Africa, cases concerning health mainly have been on HIV/AIDS—not surprising, given the endemic nature of HIV/AIDS in South Africa and the civil society activism around it. The TAC consistently and vigilantly has fought for access to treatment for people with HIV/AIDS. In doing so, it has used all avenues—political and judicial—and has done so successfully.

As noted, *Grootboom* set a precedent for subsequent cases on socio-economic rights. The Treatment Action Campaign very closely monitored the implementation of the *TAC* decision. When government dragged its feet on compliance, the TAC threatened legal action (Heywood 2003). Antiretroviral treatment was rolled out nationwide. Today, antiretroviral drugs are available and accessible (on medical grounds) in both public and private health establishments, including health clinics that geographically are closer to the people.

Following the *TAC* case, the government developed the Operational Plan for Comprehensive HIV and AIDS Care, Management and Treatment.[29] As the *EN* case illustrates, however, the government did not implement that plan in a satisfactory manner until the Durban High Court pressed it to do so. The plan now is instrumental in providing access to antiretroviral treatment in South Africa. Recent figures suggest that the plan is being implemented with some measure of success. For example, it is reported that the number of prisoners receiving treatment has risen and was projected to increase by 76 percent in 2008 (see 24News.Com 2008).

Flowing from the operational plan is the recently adopted HIV and AIDS and TB Strategic Plan for South Africa 2007–11, which represents a multi-sectoral response to the challenge of HIV/AIDS.

Both the *TAC* and the *EN* cases illustrate government's reluctance to overhaul the health system to extend HIV/AIDS treatment to everyone—and the role of the courts in dealing with this reluctance. The limited success or failure of the courts can be attributed to the failure of the state to comply with court orders (Mbazira 2008). However, there is hope that government leaders will take court orders more seriously. In the recent case of *Dingaan Hendrick Nyathi v. Member of the Executive Council for the Department of Health Gauteng, and Another*,[30] the Constitutional Court invalidated section 3 of State Liability Act 20 of 1957, which protected state officials from liability for noncompliance with court orders.[31] That decision has widened the possibilities of securing compliance with the orders.

Do Socioeconomic Rights Impose Minimum Core Obligations on Housing and Health Rights?

Some people in South Africa believe that the Constitutional Court could have done more to improve the lives of the poor and vulnerable by accepting that constitutionally mandated socioeconomic rights impose minimum core obligations on the state. By rejecting the minimum core standard in *Grootboom* and *TAC*, these people argue, the Court simply protected plaintiffs' right to "inclusion" in policy development and implementation, but failed to define the needs of poor and vulnerable people as priorities (Bilchitz 2003).

Other people contend that the minimum core obligation represents the standard of rights provision necessary to meet the basic needs of vulnerable groups. Through this standard, they argue, vulnerable groups experiencing severe socioeconomic deprivation would have a directly enforceable right to a basic level of material assistance from the state. Furthermore the state would have to realize a certain minimum level first, without delay, and improve the level of provision beyond the minimum level over time (progressive realization). This standard would place the burden on the state to demonstrate that it marshaled all resources at its disposal to satisfy, as a matter of priority, its minimum core obligation.

According to some commentators, the practical implication of the Constitutional Court's rejection of the minimum core argument is that the poor will not receive direct individual relief, although they may benefit indirectly from the positive order of the court (Liebenberg 2002). The fact that Irene Grootboom did not get immediate direct relief (a house) from the positive judgment is an example in point. The *Grootboom* relief entitles a successful litigant to a reasonable policy that would pass constitutional muster only if it included people in desperate need of a service (a house or health care service). However, individuals bear a heavy evidentiary burden to prove that the challenged government policy is unreasonable.

Because the Court is unlikely to move beyond assessing the reasonableness of government measures, human rights practitioners, including supporters of the minimum core obligation, are now focusing their energies on developing a more robust standard of reasonableness as a way to respond to the basic needs of the poor. Initial supporters of the minimum core standards argument also have found solace in the fact that the Court has acknowledged the potential role of the minimum core standard in the reasonableness review process (Liebenberg 2004).[32] The Court said that for a program to be reasonable, it must include short-term measures for vulnerable groups in desperate need and living in intolerable conditions. This element of the reasonableness review generally is regarded as an element of the minimum core standard.

The minimum core element in the reasonableness standard resonates with the social guarantees approach that the South African policy has taken already. As can be seen in the social guarantees approach presented in annex A of this chapter, measures have been taken to ensure that those who are in desperate need of minimum health care and housing services are defined clearly in health and housing policies. Thanks to victories in court, health policies provide access to medically approved essential drugs, such as nevirapine for the prevention of mother-to-child transmission of HIV/AIDS and antiretroviral drugs for people living with the virus or the syndrome. The policies also provide free primary health care to all citizens and free health care for children under age 6, pregnant and lactating women, and citizens with moderate to severe disabilities (Reconstruction and Development Programme and the White Paper on Health).

Housing policies also clearly define the minimum services to be provided to the people. As a result of court cases, it is now a well-established principle that the right to be protected from arbitrary eviction means that no one should be evicted without, at a minimum, being provided with alternative temporary shelter or accommodation to give protection from the natural elements. The housing policies also provide subsidized housing for certain eligible beneficiaries—households earning less than R 1,500 are eligible for a noncontributory housing subsidy and those earning between R 1,500 and R 3,500 must contribute some money to get the subsidy (National Housing Subsidy Scheme).

As a general minimum standard, housing and health policies also prohibit discrimination in access to housing and health care services (Reconstruction and Development Programme, White Papers on Housing and Health).

Factors Leading to the Courts' Relative Success

From the beginning of the new political order in South Africa, the courts, led by the newly established Constitutional Court, vigilantly have asserted their role in realizing the dreams and hopes of millions of people in South Africa. It is through the socioeconomic rights cases that the courts have been robust in holding government accountable on the constitutional promises of a better life for all citizens. Before delving into the record of the courts, it is important to discuss briefly the factors that led the Constitutional Court to adopt a progressive mindset toward enforcement of socioeconomic rights and its success in doing so.

Newness and Composition of the Constitutional Court

The first factor is that the Court was a new institution, free of historical association with the Apartheid regime. Even more important, the judges who first were appointed to the Court have outstanding human rights and liberation struggle credentials and vast knowledge of and expertise and skills in law.[33] Some of them were involved closely in drafting the Interim Constitution, and they have assisted in drafting the constitutions of other countries.[34] Because of these justices' human rights and liberation struggle credentials, the government respected them and had faith and confidence in their contribution to social transformation. These factors have enabled them to scrutinize policies, conduct, and laws and to assess whether those are consistent with the human rights standards they fought and worked so hard for and with the vision of the Constitution. In enforcing socioeconomic rights, the justices therefore not only were fulfilling South Africa's dreams, but were fulfilling their own as well. Because the Court is the highest court in constitutional matters, the justices' task is to guard the Constitution.

Attitude of the Court toward Social Rights Claims

The second factor leading to the measured success is the positive attitude with which the courts took on socioeconomic rights claims. Historically, those rights have not been regarded as *real* rights deserving of judicial enforcement. As noted, the courts were considered institutionally incapable and inappropriately placed to determine issues that had serious social policy and budgetary implications. However, the courts felt that they possessed the necessary capacity and skills to adjudicate on those rights without breaching the doctrine of separation of powers. They noticeably have been doing this on an incremental-approach basis.[35]

Legal Culture of Constitutionalism

The third factor is the institutionalized culture of constitutionalism (that is, the supremacy of the Constitution over parliament) that came with democracy—a culture nurtured in large part by the judges of the Court. Section 39 of the Constitution permits the Court, when interpreting human rights in the Bill of Rights, to import and apply comparative foreign law. And all courts in South Africa are free to assert their views independently.

Research Capacity and the Role of Expert Organizations

The fourth factor is the resources available to the courts in writing sound judgments. Numerous specialist organizations have intervened in cases involving the rights of access to housing and health care.[36] These interventions have given the courts expert information on a range of human rights issues and have contributed significantly to the development of laws and policies that are responsive to the needs of the poor. In addition to having a well-resourced and equipped library, judges of the Court have the services of research assistants. However, judges of the lower courts do not always have the same luxury of research assistants as do the apex court judges.

Expanded Locus Standing and Access to Justice

The fifth factor is the broad nature of the provision of locus standing in the Constitution through which people gain access to courts and justice. According to section 38, a broad range of individuals and groups may approach the court, alleging that a right in the Bill of Rights has been violated or threatened.[37] This provision empowers not only affected individuals, but also groups and organizations using the power of human rights on behalf of affected individuals and groups of people to approach the court, challenging the government's policy decision that violates or threatens their rights.

Although anyone is permitted to approach the courts to invoke his or her right, socioeconomic inequalities actually keep some people from doing so. There are three main issues that make it difficult for poor people to access the courts: (1) the costs of legal representation, (2) the lack of direct access to courts, and (3) the length of litigation. The first issue is made worse by South Africa's not having a general right to legal representation at state expense in civil and constitutional matters.[38] Unlike socioeconomically empowered groups and individuals, poor people cannot afford the often exorbitant costs of hiring lawyers and advocates. They have to rely on public interest litigation organizations (for example, the AIDS Law Project; the Legal Resources Centre; Lawyers for Human Rights; or Legal Aid clinics, including the university law clinics[39]) or on civil society groups and social movements (such as the TAC) to take up cases on their behalf. With the increasing emphasis on legal practitioners performing pro bono services, indigent people also may seek free legal services from law firms and advocates.[40]

Second, poor people without legal representation do not have direct access to higher courts. The Constitutional Court is extremely reluctant to act as a court of first and last resort in constitutional matters, unless those are matters on which it has exclusive powers (for example, determining the constitutionality of a provincial constitution or of a presidential decree). Because of that reluctance, some people have claimed that the Court has failed to be an institutional voice for the poor (Dugard 2006). In her research, Dugard found that many litigants are turned away by the Court and advised to seek legal representation, irrespective of the merits or urgency of their claims. The High Court assists poor litigants only when their cases have been brought before it through other judicial processes (Dugard 2006).

Time is the third issue that keeps poor and disadvantaged people from the full protection of the courts. Cases often take too long to complete—some as long as 1 to 5 years. For example, it took 4 years and four courts (two high courts, the Supreme Court of Appeal, and the Constitutional Court) to address the evictions matter in *Modderklip*.[41]

Litigation Combined with Social Mobilization Strategies

The sixth factor behind the success of the court is the vibrant culture of civic activism. There is a range of active civil society organizations that takes up housing and health rights issues on behalf of poor and marginalized people. These organizations include the TAC, organized in 1998 to advocate for treatment for people living with HIV/AIDS; the Anti-Eviction Campaign; the Landless Movement, which lobbies for fair land redistribution and restitution; the Homeless People's Alliance, which mobilizes the poor against homelessness; and the People's Housing Process, which encourages self-help in building houses.

It is important to note that these post-Apartheid struggles are located within the country's constitutional and human rights frameworks. Civic organizations have demonstrated the power of using the rights-based approach to fight for access to adequate housing and health care and to influence government policy on treatment and prevention of HIV/AIDS. TAC, for example, is skilled in using a combination of political negotiations, mass mobilization, and such adversarial strategies as litigation to achieve its goals. TAC's well-documented success demonstrates how the rights-based approach can be invoked to legitimize specific social claims.[42]

However, there remains an overall lack of capacity to monitor the implementation of court judgments within civil society. Although it has threatened government over noncompliance, the TAC did little implementation monitoring, focusing its energies more on the broader impact of the *TAC* case on access to treatment (Berger 2008). According to Berger, the TAC admitted it was a mistake to take its eye off the ball in this regard.

Conclusion

The courts have played a central role in achieving social transformation in South Africa. Although the decisions of the courts have not made significant changes in the lives of the poor, the homeless, and the diseased, broadly speaking, they have made significant inroads in bringing about policies that respond to the needs of the large majority of the people. Distributive justice has triumphed over corrective justice. For example, although the Wallacedene community (and Irene Grootboom) did not get houses following their celebrated victory, the *Grootboom* decision has had serious implications for the housing sector and other socioeconomic sectors, including health care.

There are many factors that made the courts' role easier. First, the foundations of a rights-based approach were laid before the Constitution was adopted. These foundations contributed to shaping subsequent programs and actions related to social transformation. Second, the courage and willingness of the court judges to enforce socioeconomic rights were informed by myriad factors, including the judges' backgrounds in human rights and liberation struggles, their involvement in drafting the Constitution, their qualifications and respected legal skills, the conducive legal environment after 1994, the vibrancy of social and human rights activism, and the contributions of specialist human rights organizations during court cases.

In some instances, the limited impact of the judgments is attributable to the failure of the government to comply with court orders. Invalidating the section of the law that gives impunity to government officials prompts hope that the government attitude toward court orders will change. Clearly, the shock of the political transformation in 1994 created unusual conditions, but there are lessons to be drawn. What is striking about South Africa in terms of economic and social rights is the extent to which rights specified in the Constitution have become major features of the social policy landscape.

Annex A. Seeing Housing and Health through the Framework of Social Guarantees

In table 6.A.1, the author poses questions to summarize various key developments and features of South Africa's housing and health regimes, in terms of the subguarantees framework discussed in chapter 2 of this book.

Table 6.A.1. Housing and Health Aspects of Social Guarantees in South Africa

Subguarantee	Housing	Health
Access		
Are the beneficiaries and services clearly defined?	The Constitution guarantees the following: • Everyone has the right to have access to adequate housing (§26[1]). • No one may be evicted from his or her home, or have his or her home demolished, without a court order made after considering all the relevant circumstances (§26[3]). • Children have a right to shelter (§28[c]). Some policies provide for the following: • Subsidized housing for certain eligible beneficiaries; for example, households earning less than R 1,500 are eligible for a noncontributory housing subsidy, and those earning between R 1,500 and R 3,500 must contribute some money to receive the subsidy (Housing Subsidy Scheme).	The Constitution guarantees the following: • Everyone has the right to have access to health care services, including reproductive health care (§27[1]). • No one may be refused emergency medical treatment (§27[3]). • Children have a right to basic health care (§28[c]). • Prisoners and detained people have a right to adequate medical care (§35[e]). Some policies provide for the following: • free primary health care for all citizens • free health care for children under age 6, pregnant and lactating women, and citizens with moderate to severe disabilities (all levels of care) (RDP and White Paper on Health)
Are there institutional procedures for monitoring access?	A Directorate of Policy and Programme Monitoring, within the Department of Housing, monitors the implementation of housing policy and programs. Provinces are required to submit conditional grant reports and provide the information in terms of the approved guidelines and to make additional information available as necessary. The Department of Housing submits expenditure reports and nonfinancial information on a quarterly basis to heads of departments, ministers, and members of the Executive Council at meetings where the content is discussed in detail. The SAHRC also monitors progress in realizing housing rights in general.	Monitoring and evaluation fall under the Health Information, Evaluation, Epidemiology and Research Program, managed by the Deputy Director General of Health Service Delivery. Additionally, there is an Office of Standards Compliance, and under that office is a Directorate of Quality Assurance. The directorate is responsible for developing systems and methods of quality assurance. The SAHRC collects information, using questionnaires (or protocols) from government departments, and compiles a report on progress made in realizing the right to health care, among others.

| Are there legal or institutional mechanisms that ensure nondiscrimination in access to services? | The Promotion of Equality and Prevention of Unfair Discrimination Act (2000) gives legislative protection against discrimination.

The Home Loan and Mortgage Disclosure Act

The Draft National Action Plan to Combat Racism in the Housing Sector notes that beyond existing patterns of inequity, racism and other forms of discrimination (such as discrimination against foreigners and people living with HIV/AIDS) sometimes occur in the allocation of housing resources.

Numerous policies also prohibit discrimination in the provision and access to housing (for example, the RDP and White Paper on Housing).

People who have been discriminated against may lodge complaints with the SAHRC or may approach the courts, including the Equality Courts. If it is a dispute between the landlord and the tenant, a complaint may be lodged with the Rental Housing Tribunal. | The Promotion of Equality and Prevention of Unfair Discrimination Act (2000) provides legislative protection against discrimination.

The National Health Act and the Medical Schemes Act of 1998 specifically outlaw discrimination against people on the basis of their disabilities and health conditions.

Numerous policies also prohibit discrimination in the provision of and access to health care services (for example, the RDP and White Paper on Health).

People who have been discriminated against may lodge complaints with the SAHRC or may approach the courts, including the Equality Courts. |

Quality

| Are there clear quality standards? | The National Home Builders Registration Council regulates the quality of housing and provides a warranty for houses built under the subsidy scheme. | Quality assurance programs in all provinces include clinical audits and monitoring of mortality and morbidity. Programs provide health teams with important information that enables them to address weaknesses in the provision of medical care. |
| Are programs being evaluated on a regular basis? | Mechanisms to evaluate programs exist both inside and outside the Department of Housing.

Through the SAHRC's monitoring mandate, housing policies regularly are evaluated for compliance with the rights-based approach to social service provision. | Mechanisms to evaluate programs exist both inside and outside the Department of Health.

The Health Systems Trust regularly evaluates specific programs; for example, it often evaluates and monitors the prevention of mother-to-child transmission of HIV/AIDS.

Through the monitoring mandate of the SAHRC, health care policies regularly are evaluated for compliance with the rights-based approach to social service provision. |

(continued)

131

Table 6.A.1. Housing and Health Aspects of Social Guarantees in South Africa (*continued*)

Subguarantee	Housing	Health
Are standards and evaluation results communicated effectively to the public?	The standards are available, but people need to be empowered to access information about them.	The standards are available, but people need to be empowered through training and education to access information about them.
Opportunity		
Are services guaranteed for the amount of time needed?	Not applicable	There is free primary health care for all citizens and free health care for children under age 6, pregnant and lactating women, and citizens with moderate to severe disabilities (all levels of health care).
Is there a maximum waiting period for receiving a service?	No	No
If the service is unavailable within the prescribed waiting period, what is a guaranteed alternative (in the same time period)?	Generally not applicable; in the case of evictions, however, people often are given alternative accommodations where they may stay temporarily until their long-term housing needs are addressed.	Not applicable
Financial protection		
Do beneficiaries need to contribute to the cost of service?	Households earning less than R 1,500 are eligible for a noncontributory housing subsidy, and those earning between R 1,500 and R 3,500 must contribute some money to receive the subsidy (Housing Subsidy Scheme).	They do not need to contribute to primary health care.
Are services accessible to beneficiaries who cannot contribute to the cost?	According to the Minister of Housing, the contribution requirement will be discontinued formally.	Yes, they are accessible.

Is this information communicated effectively to the public?	Information is available on government and civil society organizations' Web sites. It also is accessible in a user-friendly manner, in the local languages at local offices of the housing department, and through civil society organizations that run community-level information-sharing workshops. But information is not always communicated effectively by government departments.	Information is available on government and civil society organizations' Web sites. It also is accessible in a user-friendly manner and in the local languages at clinics and hospitals, as well as at community-based organizations and district offices of health. But information is not always communicated effectively by the departments.

Redress and enforcement

Are there mechanisms allowing citizens to claim adequate provision of the services guaranteed?	Adequate provision may be claimed administratively (if a person is on a housing waiting list). Complaints may be lodged with the SAHRC. A complainant also may approach the Rental Housing Tribunal and the courts if the matter involves rent.	The National Health Act requires every province to have a formal complaints system covering all levels of care. Provinces report that increasing numbers of patients have the confidence to make formal complaints. The existence of telephone hotlines has made the process easier. Provinces monitor the pattern of complaints and performance in responding to complaints. Complaints may be lodged with the SAHRC. A complainant also may approach the courts.

Continuous revision and participation

Are there mechanisms that allow for continuous improvement of services?	The Department of Housing, through engagement with other interested parties, is responsible for drawing up policy proposals that can form part of new and improved programs (for example, the Comprehensive Plan for the Development of Sustainable Settlements, which recommits the department to delivering more and sustainable housing).	The Department of Health is responsible for policy documents and strategic plans that aim for the improvement of services.

(continued)

Table 6.A.1. Housing and Health Aspects of Social Guarantees in South Africa (*continued*)

Subguarantee	Housing	Health
Do civil, parent, and community organizations have a concrete role in the design, implementation, and monitoring of the program?	Government often calls on civil society organizations when designing policy. There is also the parliamentary process in the case of legislation, where civil society organizations are asked to comment on policy at parliamentary hearings. Civil society organizations are involved in monitoring the programs through the SAHRC.	Government may call on civil society organizations when designing policy, although this is discretionary. There is also the parliamentary process in the case of legislation, where civil society organizations are asked to comment on policy at parliamentary hearings. Civil society organizations are involved in monitoring the programs through the SAHRC.
Which law or institution guarantees citizens' involvement?	The Constitution is founded on the values of openness, accountability, and transparency. Parliament is constitutionally obliged to facilitate public involvement in law-making processes (§72). The Constitutional Court has enforced this provision in *Doctors for Life International v. Speaker of the National Assembly and Others* (12 BCLR 1399 [CC 2006]).	The Constitution is founded on the values of openness, accountability, and transparency. Parliament is constitutionally obliged to facilitate public involvement in law-making processes (§72).

Source: Author's compilation.

Note: RDP = Reconstruction and Development Programme; SAHRC = South African Human Rights Commission.

Notes

1. Chaskalson was president of the Constitutional Court of South Africa from 1994 to 2001 and chief justice of South Africa from 2001 to 2005.
2. *Soobramoney v. Minister of Health, KwaZulu-Natal and Others,* 1 SA 765 (CC 1998).
3. The first piece of legislation promulgated under this framework was the Housing Act of 1997, which repealed the discriminatory Apartheid housing laws, dissolved all Apartheid housing structures, and created a new nonracial system of implementing housing policy. It also clarified the roles and responsibilities of the national, provincial, and municipal levels of government. Other housing laws enacted between 1997 and 1999 included (1) the Extension of Security of Tenure Act, which provided tenure security and protection from arbitrary eviction for people who occupy land belonging to someone else in rural and peri-urban areas; (2) the Prevention of Illegal Eviction from and Unlawful Occupation of Land Act, which provided a framework for protecting against unlawful occupation and simultaneously ensured that unlawful occupiers are treated with dignity; (3) the Housing Consumers Protection Measures Act of 1998; (4) the Rental Housing Act of 1999, which set out the relationship between and the duties of landlords and tenants and permitted the Minister of Housing to establish Rental Housing Tribunals to deal with disputes between landlords and tenants; and (5) the Home Loan and Mortgage Disclosure Act, which promoted fair lending practices and sought to ensure that financial institutions are serving the housing credit needs of the communities, without discrimination.
4. Over time, however, this ownership program was extended to households earning less than R 1,500. (Households earning between R 1,500 and R 3,500 are required to contribute R 2,479 to access their subsidy.) There also was an increased emphasis on building core structures of houses. All subsidized housing delivery had to conform to the national minimum norms and standards—a unit of 30 square meters (usually one room with a toilet) on a 250-square meter plot of land. With regard to rental housing, the delivery of well-constructed units has been limited by the fact that many people are unable to afford them (Rust 2006).
5. The act took effect on February 1, 1997. From February to July 1997, 12,887 abortions were performed. By December 1997, the number had risen to 26,406. Under the earlier law—the Abortion and Sterilization Act of 1975—an average of 800–1,200 abortions were performed annually (South African Institute of Race Relations 1997).
6. See, for example, Corder (1992), Mureinik (1992), Sachs (1992), de Villiers (1994), South African Law Commission (1994), and Liebenberg (1995).
7. *Ex parte Certification of the Constitutional Assembly: In re Certification of the Constitution of the Republic of South Africa,* 4 SA 744 (CC 1996); BCLR 1253 (hereafter, *First Certification*).

8. *First Certification,* par. 76.
9. *First Certification,* par. 77.
10. *First Certification,* par. 78.
11. *Grootboom,* 1 SA 46, par. 20 (CC 2001).
12. *Grootboom,* par. 40.
13. *Grootboom,* par. 41.
14. *Grootboom,* par. 43.
15. *Grootboom,* par. 39.
16. *Grootboom,* par. 42.
17. *Grootboom,* par. 44.
18. *EN and Others v. Government of Republic of South Africa and Others,* 6 SA 543, 568, 575 (D 2006) (hereafter, *EN*).
19. The government argued that the judge should not have heard the case because his daughters position as one of the lawyers for the prisoners created a conflict of interest.
20. *EN,* par. 42.
21. The court said, "If the government of the Republic of South Africa has given such an instruction [to disobey the court order], then we face a grave constitutional crisis involving a threat to the doctrine of separation of powers. Should that continue the members of the judiciary will have to consider whether their oath of office requires them to continue on the bench" (*EN,* par. 32).
22. Following her death, the provincial government provided a house to her family.
23. This major intergovernmental housing delivery project involved the national and provincial departments of housing as well as the city of Cape Town. It was aimed at delivering housing to more than 100,000 residents from poor backgrounds living in the city.
24. One of the problems facing South Africa today is the government's increasing disregard for court orders, particularly on social security cases, in the Eastern Cape and KwaZulu-Natal provinces.
25. *City of Cape Town v. Neville Rudolph and Others,* 11 BCLR 1236 (C 2003).
26. *President of the Republic of South Africa and Another v. Modderklip Boerdery (Pty) Ltd and Others,* 8 BCLR 786 (CC 2005) (hereafter, *Modderklip*).
27. *Port Elizabeth Municipality v. Various Occupiers,* 12 BCLR 1268 (CC 2004).
28. For more discussion on other cases, see Berger (2008).
29. Details of the plan are available at http://www.info.gov.za/otherdocs/2003/aidsoperationalplan.pdf (accessed March 9, 2009).
30. *Dingaan Hendrick Nyathi v. Member of the Executive Council for the Department of Health Gauteng, and Another,* 9 BCLR 865 (CC 2008).
31. That section of the act states, "No execution, attachment or like process shall be issued against the defendant or respondent in any such action or proceedings or against any property of the state, but the amount, if any,

which may be required to satisfy any judgment or order given or made against the nominal defendant or respondent in any action or proceedings may be paid out of the National Revenue Fund or a Provincial Revenue Fund as the case may be."

32. Liebenberg, the initial supporter of the minimum core argument, regards the reasonableness test as giving the courts a flexible, context-sensitive tool to adjudicate positive socioeconomic rights claims. She sees it as allowing the Constitutional Court to respect the role and competencies of the other branches of government, while abdicating its responsibilities to enforce the positive duties imposed by socioeconomic rights.

33. For example, Arthur Chaskalson, the former chief justice and first president of the Constitutional Court of South Africa, worked for many years as a human rights lawyer fighting in the courts for social justice. He represented the poor and the politicians during the ugly days of Apartheid. Before joining the Court, Justice Albie Sachs was a highly acclaimed academic and human rights activist.

34. Chaskalson served as a consultant on the Namibian Constituent Assembly for the period December 1989–March 1990, during the drafting of the Namibian Constitution.

35. The Court started by taking a conservative, cautious stance on socioeconomic rights cases in *Soobramoney* when it would not intervene or second-guess the rational decisions made in good faith by the government (*Soobramoney*, par. 29). In *Grootboom*, the Court made its sting felt when it found that government policy did not meet the reasonableness standard and, thus, was unconstitutional, and when it made a declaratory order for the government to fix the policy. In *TAC*, the Court found the government effort to restrict the rollout of antiretroviral drugs to a few pilot sites to be unreasonable and unconstitutional. It ordered the government to remove the barriers and implement the plan nationwide. This record shows that the Court steadily and progressively has been putting its foot down on unconstitutional actions and omissions.

36. For example, owing to its socioeconomic rights focus and expertise and its interest in the case, the Community Law Centre at the University of the Western Cape intervened in the Constitutional Court cases of *TAC, Grootboom*, and *Modderklip* and, more recently, in the Supreme Court of Appeal evictions case of *City of Johannesburg v. Rand Properties(Pty) Ltd and Others* (253 [SCA 2006]).

37. Section 38 states that "anyone listed in this section has the right to approach a competent court, alleging that a right in the Bill of Rights has been infringed or threatened, and the court may grant appropriate relief, including a declaration of rights. The persons who may approach a court are: (a) anyone acting in their own interest; (b) anyone acting on behalf of another person who cannot

act in their own name; (c) anyone acting as a member of, or in the interest of, a group or class of persons; (d) anyone acting in the public interest; and (e) an association acting in the interest of its members."

38. Only in criminal cases is there a clear right to legal representation at state expense. According to section 35(3)(g), "every accused person has a right to a fair trial, which includes the right to have a legal practitioner assigned to the accused person by the state and at state expense, if substantial injustice would otherwise result...."

39. University law clinics have been central in providing free services on eviction issues to the poor and the disadvantaged communities.

40. It is becoming increasingly necessary that legal practitioners provide eligible clients with pro bono services to ensure access to courts by those who cannot afford such support. For example, Cape Law Society Rule 17 obliges attorneys to perform pro bono work for poor people for a stipulated amount of time each year. Some large private law firms (for example, Webber Wenzel Bowens in Johannesburg) have established public interest litigation or pro bono services units.

41. *Modderklip,* 8 BCLR 786 (CC 2005).

42. For examples of TAC's successes, see Mbali (2005) and Friedman and Mottiar (2006).

References

Abbott, Geoff. 1997. "Upgrading Health Facilities." In *South African Health Review,* 119–27. Durban, South Africa: Health Systems Trust.

ANC (African National Congress). 1994. "National Health Plan for South Africa." Johannesburg, South Africa.

Baldwin-Ragave, Laurel, Jeanelle de Gruchy, and Leslie London, eds. 1999. *An Ambulance of the Wrong Colour: Health Professionals, Human Rights and Ethics in South Africa.* Rondebosch, South Africa: University of Cape Town Press.

Ballard, Richard. 2005. "Social Movements in Post-Apartheid South Africa: An Introduction." In *Democratising Development: The Politics of Socio-Economic Rights in South Africa,* ed. Peris Jones and Kristian Stokke, 77–100. Leiden, The Netherlands: Martinus Nijhoff.

Berger, Jonathan. 2008. "Litigating for Social Justice in Post-Apartheid South Africa: A Focus on Health and Education." In *Courting Social Justice: Judicial Enforcement of Social and Economic Rights in the Developing World,* ed. Varun Gauri and Daniel M. Brinks, 38–99. Cambridge, U.K.: Cambridge University Press.

Bilchitz, David. 2003. "Towards a Reasonable Approach to the Minimum Core: Laying the Foundations for Future Socio-Economic Rights Jurisprudence." *South African Journal on Human Rights* 19 (1): 1–26.

Chenwi, Lilian. 2006. "Giving Effect to the Right to Adequate Housing: The Need for a Coherent [National] Policy on Special Needs Housing." *ESR Review* 7 (4): 10–14.

Citizen. 2008. "Housing Activist Grootboom Dies in Cape Shack." August 5.

Corder, Hugh. 1992. "A Charter for Social Justice: A Contribution to the South African Bill of Rights Debate." Department of Public Law, University of Cape Town and Legal Resources Centre, Bellville, Western Cape, South Africa.

Davis, Dennis. 2004. "Socio-Economic Rights in South Africa: The Record of the Constitutional Court after Ten Years." *ESR Review* 5 (5): 3–7.

de Villiers, Bertus. 1994. "Social and Economic Rights." In *Rights and Constitutionalism: The New South African Legal Order,* ed. David van Wyk, John Dugard, Bertus de Villiers, and Dennis Davis, 499–628. Oxford, U.K.: Oxford University Press.

de Vos, Pierre. 2006. "Housing." In *Reflections on Democracy and Human Rights: A Decade of the South African Constitution (Act 108 of 1996),* ed. Nasila Rembe, 73–77. Johannesburg, South Africa: South African Human Rights Commission.

Dugard, Jackie. 2006. "Court of First Instance? Towards a Pro-Poor Jurisdiction for the South African Constitutional Court." *South African Journal on Human Rights* 22 (2): 261–82.

Friedman, Steven, and Shauna Mottiar. 2006. "Seeking the High Ground: The Treatment Action Campaign and the Politics of Morality." In *Voices of Protest: Social Movements in Post Apartheid South Africa*, ed. Richard Ballard, Adam Habib, and Imraan Valodia, 23–44. Pretoria, South Africa: HSRC Press.

Gloppen, Siri. 2005. "Social Rights Litigation as Transformation: South African Perspectives." In *Democratising Development: The Politics of Socio-Economic Rights in South Africa,* ed. Peris Jones and Kristian Stokke, 153–80. Leiden, The Netherlands: Martinus Nijhoff.

Harthon, Moray, Lauren Royston, and Stuart Wilson. 2008. "Victory for Engagement in Relocation from San Jose." *Business Day* September 9.

Heywood, Mark. 2003. "Contempt or Compliance? The *TAC* Case after the Constitutional Court Judgment." *ESR Review* 4 (1): 7–10.

———. 2005. "Shaping, Making and Breaking the Law in the Campaign for a National HIV/AIDS Treatment Plan." In *Democratising Development: The Politics of Socio-Economic Rights in South Africa,* ed. Peris Jones and Kristian Stokke, 181–212. Leiden, The Netherlands: Martinus Nijhoff.

Khoza, Sibonile, ed. 2007. *Socio-Economic Rights in South Africa: A Resource Book.* 2nd ed. Bellville: Socio-Economic Rights Project of the Community Law Centre, University of the Western Cape.

Landsberg, Chris, and Shaun Mackay. 2006. "South Africa 1994–2004." In *Reflections on Democracy and Human Rights: A Decade of the South African Constitution (Act 108 of 1996),* ed. Nasila Rembe, 1–14. Johannesburg, South Africa: South African Human Rights Commission.

Liebenberg, Sandra. 1995. "Social and Economic Rights: A Critical Challenge." In *The Constitution of South Africa from a Gender Perspective,* ed. Sandra Liebenberg, 79–96. Cape Town, South Africa: David Philip.

———. 2002. "South Africa's Evolving Jurisprudence on Socio-Economic Rights: An Effective Tool in Challenging Poverty?" *Law Democracy and Development* 6 (November): 159–91.

———. 2004. "Social Rights Claims: How Responsive Is 'Reasonableness Review'?" *ESR Review* 5 (5): 7–11.

———. 2006. "The Interpretation of Socio-Economic Rights." In *Constitutional Law of South Africa, Part II,* ed. Stu Woolman, Theunis Roux, and Michael Bishop, 33–66. Johannesburg, South Africa: Juta.

Mbali, Mandisa. 2005. "The Treatment Action Campaign and the History of Rights-Based, Patient-Driven HIV/AIDS Activism in South Africa." In *Democratising Development: The Politics of Socio-Economic Rights in South Africa,* ed. Peris Jones and Kristian Stokke, 213–44. Leiden, The Netherlands: Martinus Nijhoff.

Mbazira, Christopher. 2008. "You Are the 'Weakest Link' in Realizing Socio-Economic Rights: Goodbye—Strategies for Effective Implementation of Court Orders in South Africa." Community Law Centre, University of the Western Cape, Bellville, South Africa.

Mureinik, Etienne. 1992. "Beyond a Charter of Luxuries: Economic Rights in the Constitution." *South African Journal on Human Rights* 8: 464.

Rust, Kecia. 2006. "Analysis of South Africa's Housing Sector Performance." FinMark Trust, Johannesburg, South Africa.

Sachs, Albie. 1992. *Advancing Human Rights in South Africa.* Oxford, U.K.: Oxford University Press.

Schneider, Helen, Peter Barron, and Sharon Fonn. 2007. "The Promise and the Practice of Transformation in South Africa." In *State of the Nation, South Africa 2007,* ed. Sakhela Buhlungu, John Daniel, Roger Southall, and Jessica Lutchman, 289–311. Pretoria, South Africa: HSRC Press.

South Africa. 1994. "Free Health Services for Pregnant Women and Children under the Age of 6." South African Government Notice 657, Government Gazette 15817.

South Africa, Department of Health. 1997. "White Paper on the Transformation of the Health System in South Africa." Pretoria, South Africa.

South African Human Rights Commission. 2003. "Fifth Economic and Social Rights Report, 2002–03." Johannesburg, South Africa.

South African Institute of Race Relations. 1997. "South Africa Survey, 1996/1997." Johannesburg, South Africa.

South African Law Commission. 1994. "Final Report on Group and Human Rights (Project 58)." Pretoria, South Africa.

24News.Com. 2008. "76% Rise in Prisoners on ARVs." July 29. http://www.news24
.com/News24/South_Africa/Aids_Focus/0,,2-7-659_2366195,00.html
(accessed March 9, 2009).

van den Heever, Alex M., and Vishal Brijlal. 1997. "Financing and Expenditure."
In *South African Health Review,* 81–89. Durban, South Africa: Health Systems
Trust.

van Rensburg, H. C. J. 2004. "The History of Health Care in South Africa." In
Health and Health Care in South Africa: Structures and Dynamids, ed. H. C. J.
van Rensburg, 52–103. Pretoria, South Africa: Van Schaik.

Wegerif, Marc, 2006. "Farm Evictions: A Failure of Rights." *ESR Review* 7
(33): 8–11.

CHAPTER 7

Establishing Social Equity:
Bolivia, Ecuador, and Peru

Sophia V. Georgieva, Enrique Vásquez, Gover Barja,
Fernando García Serrano, and Ramiro Larrea Flores

Poverty and inequality are two of the most persistent challenges in developing countries, increasingly proving that concerns for social justice, economic growth, and sustainable development are indivisible and require simultaneous and holistic attention. The high inequality in the Andean states[1] is especially challenging because it is reinforced not only by income disparities, but also by ethnic and cultural diversity and geographic obstacles that prevent a high proportion of the population from actively influencing social, economic, or political processes. This is apparent from the especially high incidence of poverty among indigenous populations, most of whom reside in rural and mountainous areas. In Peru, 59 percent of Quechua and Amazonic groups and 57 percent of Aymara people are in the bottom income quintile, compared with only 29 percent of nonindigenous people (Vásquez 2007).[2] In Ecuador, poverty among indigenous people reaches 80.2 percent, compared with 57.9 among nonindigenous groups. In Bolivia, 73.9 percent of indigenous people and 52.5 percent of nonindigenous people live in poverty (Hall and Patrinos 2006).

Vulnerable populations in the Andean subregion are defined not only by their lower income and lack of access to a market economy, but also by their restricted access to basic services such as good-quality education, health care, and information on adequate nutrition. Over the past half-century, the Andean states have achieved tangible results in expanding public services and granting basic opportunities to more citizens. For instance, illiteracy in Ecuador decreased from 44.2 percent to 9.0 percent between 1950 and 2001;[3] less than 3 percent of Peruvian youth ages 5–24 were illiterate in 2005, compared with 22 percent of the older generations;[4] and in Bolivia, 67 percent of mothers today receive medical attention at delivery, compared with only 47 percent 10 years ago (UNDP 1998, 2007). Still, serious disparities in access and in the quality of basic services remain in those three states, and they contribute to perpetuating the inequality and poverty traps there.

Since the mid-20th century, the following three major stages in social policy (roughly comparable across the three states) can be discerned in Bolivia, Ecuador, and Peru:

1. an expansion of the public service sector in the 1970s and early 1980s that led to creation of major social security institutions and succeeded in insuring most formally employed citizens [5]
2. a retreat of public funds from social services during the structural adjustment period in the late-1980s and early 1990s resulting from the belief that economic growth and market forces would be sufficient to eliminate persistent inequalities
3. a proliferation of targeted and conditional cash transfer programs, initiated since the late 1990s, emphasizing universal opportunities for basic education, health care, adequate housing, and nutrition and aiming to provide those opportunities to the most vulnerable groups, regardless of formal affiliation with the institutions of social security.

The notion of social policy based on fundamental rights and explicit entitlements relatively similar to the Chilean health model of 2004 (Regime of Explicit Guarantees in Health) has gathered strength in social policy analysis throughout Latin America. Instead of seeking to define "vulnerable groups" and target their access to basic services, the social guarantees approach tested in Chile seeks to define basic universal entitlements and to eliminate obstacles that could prevent *any* group from receiving them. So far, none of the Andean states has adopted explicitly rights-based or social guarantees programs. However, the progressive attention on economic, social, and cultural rights in legislation, policy strategies, and concrete programs in those countries gives reason to believe that a rights-based model may have grounds in the Andean context. Budget constraints as well as contrasting governance approaches—of the Ministry of Social Development on the one hand and the Finance Ministry and financial institutions on the other—are some of the primary challenges to reaching a social contract and gaining approval of policies based on rights principles. This chapter examines primary and secondary education and selected health policy experiences in Bolivia, Ecuador, and Peru to illustrate the progress made toward defining and meeting universal entitlements in these policy areas, and it highlights ways in which a social guarantees focus may help improve the effectiveness of these programs. The chapter uses the social guarantees and subguarantees concept (see chapter 2) as a framework for analysis.

A fundamental principle of the social guarantees framework is that entitlements to basic services and the mechanisms put in place to fulfill them should be defined clearly; reflected in the country's legal, institutional, and policy frameworks; and protected over the long term by relevant budget arrangements. Another key feature of this framework is that it envisions mechanisms not only for access to and quality of services, but also for their affordability and opportunity for redress, among other factors, making sure that people encounter no obstacles to receiving the defined services.

Since the ratifications of the countries' constitutions in the 1990s and, more recently, ratification of the 2008 Constitution of Ecuador and approval of a new Constitution in Bolivia in January 2009, the normative frameworks in the three countries have become increasingly explicit in acknowledging social and economic rights for all citizens, including language of both "rights" and "guarantees" in the social and economic realm. The constitutions establish, for instance, that primary and secondary education is obligatory and free of charge. (In Bolivia, only primary education was obligatory prior to the 2009 Constitution.) The provision of bilingual education is stipulated in all three constitutions, as is the responsibility of the state to monitor and supervise educational quality.

Traditional medicine also is respected in the three states. The new Constitution of Bolivia has advanced significantly with regard to the use of traditional medical services, declaring that the state will promote respect for and research into traditional medicine, will register natural medicaments, and will regulate the quality of traditional medical practices (art. 42). The duties of the state regarding health—at least according to the Constitution—are generally less clear than those in education, and they pertain mostly to promoting a healthy lifestyle and awareness-raising on public health issues. Concrete entitlements to medical care, as an expression of the right to health, are not specified in the constitutions of any of the three states. More explicit language on the state's responsibility regarding health rights has been added recently: the 2008 National Constitution of Ecuador declares that the state will "guarantee this right . . . through permanent, opportune, and non-discriminatory access to integral health services and services in reproductive health" (art. 32); and the Bolivian Constitution of 2009 guarantees access of citizens to all needed medications, prioritizing the use of generic ones (art. 41).

Apart from constitutional entitlements, the effective fulfillment of rights relies on the existence of coherent supporting legislation that elaborates in detail the services, standards, and division of responsibilities related to their provision. The purpose of this legislation is to clarify the role of all respective stakeholders—state agencies, the private sector, civil and community institutions—allowing citizens to seek accountability from the respective institution when entitlements are being denied. In this respect, the Andean subregion can benefit greatly from a social guarantees framework. Progressive reforms in the constitution or in national policy strategies often are not followed up with effective supporting norms and mechanisms, nor are those reforms always allotted sufficient budgets. Legal commitments related to bilingual education, for example, rely almost exclusively on international aid, and they lack a steady and adequate source of funding. As a result, the advances made on the high policy level do not reach their full potential impact on the lives of poor people.

Overall, the protection and fulfillment of economic and social rights in the Andean states and throughout the Americas still lag behind those of civil and political rights. Civil and political freedoms—such as universal suffrage, the right to identity, and indigenous groups' rights to consult with and/or be represented directly in political decisions—largely have been achieved; but disparities in education, health, and housing persist. The realization of economic, social, and cultural rights in the Andean subregion has been addressed mainly with regard to the protection of cultural identity—for example, the right to receive education in one's native language or to practice or seek health care in traditional medicine. In this manner, states in the region generally have ensured that economic, social, and cultural rights will be *respected*. To ensure that these rights are not only respected but in fact *fulfilled* would require a more proactive approach by policy makers and society as a whole. The existence of coherent legislation on social and economic entitlements, and clear institutional responsibilities in all stages of service delivery, are key steps in this direction.

Another essential feature of a rights-based social policy is that policy priorities are determined as a result of a balanced dialogue within a society. The rights-based approach implies obligations both on the state and on its citizens; hence, citizens' engagement in determining entitlements, implementing and monitoring programs to fulfill them, and raising awareness about them is an absolute prerequisite for the success of this policy approach.

The notions of national dialogue and consultations with diverse social groups are not new in the Andean states. In Peru during the early 2000s, President Alejandro Toledo broke new ground by opening up dialogue on a renewed social agenda to government, civil society, the private sector, and international donor agencies. That dialogue resulted in the 2002 signing of the National Accords aimed at improving equity and social justice, and it led to the creation of a long-term Roundtable for Poverty Reduction, responsible for maintaining dialogue on the social agenda and protecting the neutrality and transparency of new social programs. Some civil society organizations already are being instrumental in raising awareness of and monitoring health and nutrition rights, education rights, and children's rights. Nevertheless, the National Accords do not grant citizens' organizations regular participation and voice in decision making.

Similarly in Ecuador, civil society groups—such as the Observatory for the Rights of Children and Adolescents, the Fiscal Policy Observatory, and the Social Contract for Education—have taken on planning and monitoring functions regarding social services, on setting up concrete indicators on children's education and health rights, and on informing the public on their performance.

In Bolivia, the Participation Act of 1994, the National Dialogue process of 2000, and the subsequent legal Act of 2001, based on municipal and regional discussions, have redefined social policy planning procedures and established a "social control mechanism" whereby citizens carry out participatory planning to prioritize spending in their municipalities (MacLean-Abaroa 2001). The Dialogue Act (which resulted from the National Dialogue process) also identified at the national level policy priorities related to social and economic rights and established concrete mechanisms to address them—for example, the Universal Maternal and Child Insurance (UMCI) system, which will be discussed in more detail below.

In summary, participatory practices and civil participation have advanced markedly over the past decade, setting a possible foundation for the success of rights-based policies in the Andean subregion. Nevertheless, to achieve a balanced dialogue at the national, municipal, or neighborhood level, all citizens need to possess adequate information. Raising awareness on rights and entitlements among the most vulnerable groups and in the most remote locations in the Andean states is a remaining challenge that civil society, the private sector, and other nongovernmental groups ideally would help the state overcome. Currently, a number of donor-driven projects in the region are focusing precisely on local mechanisms for raising awareness of social standards (for example, nutrition and quality of basic education).

Finally, a successful rights-based policy requires a stable fiscal commitment to reflect the legal, institutional, and policy advances in the social agenda. Until 2005, public spending in health and education as a percentage of gross domestic product (GDP) in the three states discussed here was among the lowest in the world.[6] Spending on education as a percentage of GDP even declined in Peru and Ecuador between 1991 and 2005.[7] That decline has been reversed in the past couple of years, but it is too soon to assess how stable this recent trend will remain over the long run. In 2006, after a consultation with various representatives of the public and civil society, the government of Ecuador approved a regular annual increase in the education budget that amounted to 0.5 percent of GDP until the budget allocation reaches a proportion of 6.0 percent. The same consultation approved a mandatory increase of 0.5 percent of GDP for the health sector until the allocation reaches 4.0 percent (García, Larrea, and Enríquez 2007; UNESCO 2007). The 2008 Constitution of Ecuador declares health, education, and justice to be priority sectors in terms of state expenditure (art. 286), for which consistent funding should be guaranteed. In Bolivia, the government's commitment to the funding of public services is expressed in its commitment to the Millennium Development Goals and beyond—to an expanded set of objectives defined in Bolivia's National Development Plan—and it is those objectives that determine minimum spending. Thus, in all three states there is a pronounced commitment on the part of the government to the adequate financing of social policy. Yet, even if a fiscal agreement is reached on the national level, states still face the challenging possibility that finance authorities ultimately may not allocate the money to complete the budget for the agreed goals.

Redistribution of resources is necessary in most cases to make the social guarantees approach feasible and affordable. To be fully aware of the challenges before implementing rights-based social policy in any state, regardless of its level of development, one needs to look not only into the absolute and relative social budget allocations and the quality of the economic and social management, but also into the overall patterns of resource distribution in the state. In Ecuador, for example, part of the debate over social spending in recent years was concerned with the difference between allocations for public service, which benefit primarily the poor and the middle classes (5.7 percent of GDP in 2005, with 1.8 percent of GDP going to basic education and 1.2 percent going to health), and allocations for universal subsidies in electricity, gas, gasoline, and diesel (7.0 percent of GDP), which benefit mostly the middle and wealthy classes (García, Larrea, and Enríquez 2007). In Peru, the discussion was focused on the leaks and insufficient coverage of the social programs, which revealed that the very poor were not necessarily the main program beneficiaries.

Uneven tax systems, along with limited capacity for tax collection, also have been cited as a reason behind persistent inequality in Latin America. Low revenue collection is characteristic of the region, owing largely to macroeconomic crises, high inflation, and sustained political opposition. It has been claimed that taxing high-income classes directly is difficult in the region, mainly because a large fraction of the state's income comes from capital and high taxation may cause capital flight. Some progressive tax reforms to benefit the poor have been introduced in the region—such as the tax on bank debits to replace income taxes in Ecuador—but these initiatives are scarce (see Justino and Acharya 2003).

Even in the context of limited public resources, governments have demonstrated some positive examples of effective prioritization and protection of defined entitlements in social policy. Bolivia's recent program of maternal and infant health care is one example. During the 1990s, health policy allocations in Bolivia rose steadily, on the basis of the expectation that the government would collect increasingly higher revenues from the private sector to sustain the enlarged social spending. In practice, a series of external shocks after 1999 hampered the country's economic growth, leading the public sector into substantial fiscal deficit (a situation that improved substantially after 2004). Because social spending could not be lowered easily, given the widespread poverty in the country, it was necessary to define priorities in spending. Thus, the UMCI was born. The context in which this program arose is comparable in many ways to that in Bolivia's neighboring states.

Political instability throughout the Andean subregion historically has undermined the sustainability of social policies. To be successful, any current or future initiative toward a more equitable social contract needs to consider—to the extent possible—measures that allow for the progressive improvement of programs—institutions, and financial agreements, while protecting them from being discontinued or reversed.

The following sections employ a social guarantees framework of analysis to (1) illustrate the progress that Bolivia, Ecuador, and Peru have achieved toward the fulfillment of selected entitlements in education and health; and (2) highlight areas in which the policies and programs in question can be improved to better protect citizens' rights to education and health.

Universal Entitlements in Basic Education

Rights-based principles can be identified clearly in the education policies of Bolivia, Ecuador, and Peru. All three states constitutionally have declared the right to universal and free education (12 years in Bolivia,[8] 10 years in Ecuador, and 12 years in Peru), and the states assume responsibility for making education during those periods accessible to all. The Ecuador Constitution of 2008 states that education is free and obligatory until the end of high school (*bachillerato*) or an equivalent level, that public education is free until the university level inclusive, and that bilingual education should be provided. It also declares the responsibility of the state to guarantee— according to the principles of social, territorial, and regional equity—that all people have access to the public education system. Bolivia's Constitution prior to 2009 declared only primary education as free and obligatory, although the period of primary education formally was extended from 5 years to 8 years. According to the new Bolivian Constitution (2009), education is obligatory through the secondary (*bachillerato*) level and free of charge up to the tertiary level (art. 81). In Peru, the Constitution of 1993 states that education is obligatory and free at the preschool (*inicial*), primary, and secondary levels and that access to university education at public institutions for anyone who demonstrates sufficient academic ability should not be impeded for financial reasons. It also declares the state's responsibility to regulate and supervise quality in the education sector.

Opportunities for access to basic education have been augmented significantly since the mid-20th century. The infrastructure and enrollment rates for primary and secondary education have grown in rural and urban areas alike, and bilingual education programs now are operating (albeit with very limited resources) throughout the region. Decentralization and participatory approaches to the delivery of education also have increased, drawing parents' associations and local nongovernmental organizations (NGOs) into the decision-making process. Nevertheless, important challenges remain, namely in maintaining the quality of basic education and in bringing bilingual programs up to par with Hispanic education. First, the lower priority placed on quality and quality monitoring makes it difficult for policy makers fully to assess the outcomes of educational reforms. Creating and enforcing clear quality standards need to go hand in hand with efforts to raise enrollment and prevent children from dropping out of school early. Second, serious disparities remain between bilingual education and Hispanic education in terms of access, quality, financial protection, and overall spending, thus putting indigenous groups at a disadvantage.

Through some basic questions and answers, table 7.1 highlights the basic education areas of progress and lag according to a universal, rights-based perspective. It uses the concept of social guarantees and subguarantees to assess whether mechanisms have been put in place to address a number of essential aspects of educational delivery—access, quality, financial protection (affordability), redress, continuous revision, and civil participation.

Although expanded, access to education remains limited particularly for low-income groups and students in rural areas, who face stronger financial constraints and longer commutes. Even if the opportunities for enrollment are provided, dropout rates remain high. In Bolivia in 2005, only about 77.8 percent of children completed the mandatory 8 years (Barja and Leyton 2007:27). In Ecuador, it was reported that approximately 10.6 percent of school-age children work and study at the same time and that 16.0 percent only work and do not attend school.[9] Adult illiteracy rates on the national scale are 13 percent in Bolivia, 12 percent in Peru, and 9 percent in Ecuador (UNDP 2007). There are virtually no mechanisms within the education system to ensure the continuous provision of basic education that takes into account financial, geographic, or other barriers to access, so a high disparity exists between enrollment and completion. Access is limited, particularly for indigenous groups, despite the long-term existence of bilingual education systems. In Peru, where national-level school completion rates are the highest of the three states (94 percent for primary and 88 percent for secondary school), no more than 10 percent of indigenous children gain access to bilingual education. Bilingual education there is provided only up to the primary level, and it is very limited in both resources and outcomes. In Ecuador, access to bilingual education is limited to 66 percent at the elementary level, and to 86 percent in primary and 22 percent in secondary grades. The fact that a number of indigenous children have no birth certificates further complicates their access to school (García, Larrea, and Enríquez 2007:55).

Despite the fact that basic education at the levels described above is guaranteed free of charge, students must contribute financially to attend school. In Ecuador until April 2007, an annual enrollment fee of $25 was in place,

Table 7.1. The Social Guarantees Matrix for Basic Education Programs in Bolivia, Ecuador, and Peru

Subguarantee	Bolivia	Ecuador	Peru
Access			
Are the beneficiaries and services clearly defined?	Yes—universal, free, and mandatory primary and secondary education (12 years, ages 6–18; extended in January 2009, under the new Constitution, from 8 years of primary education only)	Yes—universal, free, and mandatory elementary, primary, and secondary education (10 years, ages 6–15)	Yes—universal, free, and mandatory preschool, primary, and secondary education (12 years, ages 4–16)
Are there institutional procedures for monitoring access?	No; by law, the Ministry of Education is responsible.	Yes; monitoring for bilingual education is realized through the National System of Nationalities and Peoples of Ecuador.	No concrete mechanism exists. By law, parents' associations are responsible.
Are there legal or institutional mechanisms that ensure nondiscrimination in access to services?	Bilingual programs are available for indigenous people.	Bilingual programs are available.	A bilingual and intercultural program is available for indigenous people.
Are services guaranteed for the amount of time needed?	Yes; the Bono Juancito Pinto cash transfer, given out at the end of the school year, has been introduced to prevent students from dropping out.	No	Yes; but dropout rates are high, especially among rural girls and indigenous people.
Is there a maximum waiting period for receiving a service?	No	No	No
If the service is unavailable within the prescribed waiting period, what is a guaranteed alternative (in the same time period)?	None; when the problem is age or a physical restriction, alternative education helps complete or complement.	None	None; alternative education programs exist for adults, but they are not a replacement for timely education.

Quality			
Are there clear quality standards?	No	Yes, as defined in the curricular reform of 1996.	No; they currently are being developed by the Ministry of Education.
Are programs being evaluated on a regular basis?	No	No	No regular mechanism is established. The Ministry of Education conducted evaluations in 1996, 1998, 2001, and 2004.
Are standards and evaluation results communicated effectively to the public?	No	No	No, but the results of teachers' evaluations have been published by the press since 2008.
Financial protection			
Do beneficiaries need to contribute to the cost of service?	They need not contribute to tuition. They incur related costs (such as transportation and books) that are not covered by the government. The government provides school breakfast.	No	Yes; they contribute about one-third of the cost: transportation, uniforms, and some school materials as well as parents' association fees.
Are services accessible to beneficiaries who cannot contribute to the cost?	They are believed to be accessible through supplementary programs (school breakfast and family cash transfers). However, costs for transportation books, uniforms, or other supplies are not covered.	Access is limited because of related costs—transportation and lack of school infrastructure or resources to hire teachers (especially in bilingual programs).	Yes; financial assistance is available.
Is this information communicated effectively to the public?	All laws and norms regarding the education sector are public.	No	Parents' associations and the Ombudsman are responsible. The consistency of information varies across communities.

(continued)

Table 7.1. The Social Guarantees Matrix for Basic Education Programs in Bolivia, Ecuador, and Peru (continued)

Subguarantee	Bolivia	Ecuador	Peru
Redress and enforcement			
Are there mechanisms allowing citizens to claim adequate provision of the services guaranteed?	Yes; SD 25273 of January 1999 specifies the channels.	Yes; but some are difficult to access, and others do not operate throughout the country.	Mechanisms to make claims and/or seek redress are available through parents' associations and the Ombudsman.
Continuous revision and participation			
Are there mechanisms that allow for continuous improvement of services?	No, not at the national level.	The Children's Rights Index has been applied since 2003 by the Observatory for the Rights of Children and Adolescents.	Programs exist to this end, but there is no guaranteed mechanism.
Do civil, parent, or community organizations have a concrete role in the design, implementation, and monitoring of the program?	Yes; a network of local, departmental, and national councils is the primary decision maker in education delivery.	The Observatory for the Rights of Children and Adolescents has produced a report every three years since 2002; the Social Contract for Education; national, regional, and local indigenous organizations.	Yes; parents' associations and different NGO networks have roles.
Which law or institution guarantees citizens' involvement?	SD 25273 of January 1999	National Council for Children and Adolescents and its executive secretariat, created in 2004	Law 28628 regulates the participation of parents' associations.

Source: Authors' compilation.
Note: NGO = nongovernmental organization; SD = Supreme Decree.

and registration costs were covered for only 63 percent of students. In Peru, students and their families are expected to cover approximately one-third of educational expenses. Partial financial protection mechanisms have been introduced to curb the high dropout rates. Family cash transfers conditional on school attendance, such as the Juntos program in Peru and Bono Juancito Pinto in Bolivia, have been popular measures of financial protection throughout the region. These conditional benefits contain additional incentives to attend school, and they strengthen the monitoring of attendance. But it is unclear whether they actually reduce attendance barriers for children. School feeding programs, introduced in Bolivia and Peru, and distribution of textbooks and uniforms have been other methods of financial protection, showing good results if applied consistently across communities.[10] The new national Constitution of Bolivia declares that support for students at all education levels will be made available through financial aid, feeding programs, clothing, transportation, and school materials as well as through merit-based scholarships (art. 82). The relevant policies, programs, and budget channels need to be established to fulfill and monitor this guarantee. Overall, the three states have demonstrated both willingness and flexibility in introducing programs to lower financial constraints for basic education. All of these financial protection programs, however, operate as separate forms of assistance that do not effectively ensure the affordability of basic education for all. They address some related costs (such as food and clothing), but not others (such as transportation). Rural youth still exhibit higher dropout rates and lower secondary school enrollment rates, largely because of transportation costs. In Peru, 48.9 percent of rural youth are able to go to secondary school, compared with 76.2 percent of urban youth (Ramirez 2004). A consistent mechanism for financial protection with adequate attention to secondary as well as primary education has been proposed by civil society in Peru, but it is yet to be developed and approved by the government (Vásquez and Monge 2007).

Some discrepancies in educational spending also have been observed. For example, only 35 percent of Ecuador's education spending in 1999 reached the poorest two quintiles. In addition, annual spending in the bilingual education system ($154 per student in 2006) was considerably lower than that in Hispanic education ($300 per student in 2006) (García, Larrea, and Enríquez 2007:33). Spending in bilingual education increased by 30 percent in 2007, but there is still a large gap. Peru, despite impressive enrollment statistics, exhibits low education spending for the region, 90 percent of which is channeled toward payroll. In Bolivia, the fact that only primary education was guaranteed until recently accounted for a significant discrepancy between primary and secondary education spending. Primary education spending grew from $201.4 million to $263.6 million between 2000 and 2004, whereas spending in secondary education in 2004 was only $74.5 million (Barja and Leyton 2007:25).

Perhaps the greatest challenge to the delivery of education from a rights perspective is the lack of consistent attention to quality. Although mechanisms to expand access and citizens' participation have improved consistently in recent decades, none of the three countries yet counts with a regular mechanism to measure and improve quality. On the one hand, this results in low learning levels on a national scale. In a country with very high enrollment rates, such as Peru, a 2004 evaluation showed that fewer than 24 percent of students exhibited satisfactory language skills and fewer than 5 percent had sufficient math skills, thus leading to the conclusion that Peruvians are "very well schooled but very poorly educated" (Guigale, Fretes-Cibils, and Newman 2006:21). On the other hand, weak attention to universal quality contributes to deepening the gaps between high- and low-income classes, rural and urban areas, and indigenous and nonindigenous students. In all three countries, a policy pattern of decentralizing education transferred greater monitoring responsibility onto community groups and parents' associations. Because low-income, rural, and indigenous groups generally lack access and possess less information on what constitutes "good-quality" education, they are not as likely to demand improvements.

To prevent disparities in quality and to raise the quality of basic education nationwide, governments may consider establishing clear national standards and a monitoring system. These can be applied at the local level with the help of parents and community associations. Such a unified monitoring system is still incipient in each of the three states. An educational quality measurement system was created in Bolivia in 1995 and subsequently abolished in 2004. Currently, the Constitution of 2009 indicates that monitoring, measurement, evaluation, and accreditation of educational quality will be managed by a technical government entity independent of the Ministry of Education (art. 89). In addition, an ad hoc national educational conference can be called every 5 years to provide orientation to education policy. In Ecuador, a national testing system (*Aprendo*) was used in 1996, 1997, and 2000, and a different one was used in 2001. A consensual curricular reform was approved in 1996, establishing goals for teachers and students, but there is no mechanism for monitoring it. Peru's

General Law on Education states that norms and standards for each level of the education system should be established, but the country does not count with a unified quality standard. Instead, the Ministry of Education gives education centers the autonomy to disseminate indicators, criteria, and other instruments to measure learning, but it does not *oblige* them to do so. A National System for Evaluation, Accreditation, and Certification of the Quality of Education was conceived in Peru to serve as a comprehensive mechanism for regulating quality, but at the time of this writing, it was not operational.

The lack of information on quality standards and the lack of established financial protection channels have impeded the ability of students and parents to claim entitlements to basic education. Formal mechanisms of redress in the three states exist on the regional and national levels; however, they are not always linked to concrete entitlements, and the information and incentives for using them are scarce. In Ecuador, a Constitutional Tribunal and an Ombudsman are available but are hard to access. Councils and cantonal boards for the protection of the rights of children and adolescents may serve as redress and enforcement institutions, but they are available only in Quito and Cuenca. Community councils for the protection of children and adolescents are being created. In Peru, the primary mechanisms for redress are the parents' associations and the Ombudsman (created in 1993, with offices in each region). Parents' associations give citizens ample right to pursue grievances, but they have not been very effective in addressing quality concerns. That ineffectiveness occurs mostly because they lack information about quality standards; however, it also is reinforced by the scarcity of resources and the low availability of teachers in more remote locations. In addition, the students who face greatest risk of dropping out often are not ones whose parents actively participate in parents' associations, so those bodies are an insufficient channel to guarantee access and nondiscrimination.

Channels for civil participation are developing progressively in the Andean states and already have shown results in education reforms. Civil society organizations and the Catholic Church, for instance, played a key role in the Bolivian educational reform of 1994 that called for greater gender equity and for modernization of the administrative system and the curriculum, among other improvements. In this process, NGOs filled a gap between the government and the population. Currently, networks of local, departmental, and national councils comprising civic and public representatives continue to exist in Bolivia and are involved heavily in decision making in the education sector. Their role is codified within the country's Popular Participation Law. Bolivia's new Constitution formally recognizes and guarantees social, community, and parental participation (art. 83). In Ecuador, the Observatory for the Rights of Children and Adolescents and the citizen movement Social Contract for Education provide much-needed feedback on the state of basic education services. The former entity monitors basic education as part of a composite Children's Rights Index that measures nine rights on a scale of 0–10 (where 10 means full respect for rights). In 2007, Ecuador scored 4.3 on this scale (UNICEF 2007:9). The participation of parents' associations in Peru is established by law (No. 28628), but there is room for improvement in their effectiveness, as noted above. Different networks of NGOs also are active at the local level.

Thus, the analysis from a rights-based perspective, using the matrix of guarantees and subguarantees in five basic areas, enables one to identify important advances in basic education policy, as well as aspects that still fall short of realizing citizens' entitlements to which states have committed themselves. It demonstrates a marked increase in access in contrast to a lack of clear quality standards and quality supervision. And the analysis brings attention to the lack of consistent financial protection mechanisms to prevent children from low-income groups, rural areas, and indigenous populations from dropping out of school early.[11] When such mechanisms are established, information channels and local-level institutions—now existing only in some areas—may enable citizens to claim and redress their entitlements. On the national level, Bolivia, Ecuador, and Peru have developed elaborate and concrete legislation that highlights entitlements related to basic education and delegates specific institutional responsibility for their realization. However, weak institutional capacity at the local level and low or disproportionate financing of education programs continue to favor higher-income, urban, and nonindigenous groups and to compromise the universal rights-based commitments established by law.

Universal Entitlements in Health Care

In the 1980s, the Pan-American Health Organization established health as a fundamental right of every human being (PAHO 1989; Hilburg Catter 2003). Unlike the right to education, however, the interpretation of the right to health is less well defined in the Andean subregion and in the

Americas as a whole. Constitutionally, each of the three states discussed in this chapter recognizes every human being's right to a healthy life. In Ecuador, the 2008 Constitution also speaks of free access to medical care (without guaranteeing concrete services) and of the state's duty to monitor health services.

In Ecuador, the Constitution guarantees the promotion and protection of health for all people (meaning potable water, decent housing, developing nutritional security, and soforth. It further declares that public health care services will be universal and free of charge at all levels of attention (diagnostic, treatment, medications, and rehabilitation [art. 362]) and that emergency care may not be denied for any reason (art. 365). In the former Bolivian Constitution, with its amendments of 2005, the duties of the state regarding health care were framed in the context of social security. The state assumed an obligation to "protect the human capital and health of the population and ensure that the livelihoods of persons with disability are protected" (art. 158). The new Bolivian Constitution of 2009 is more explicit in declaring that "the state in all its levels will protect the right to health by promoting public policies directed to the . . . free access of the population to health services" (art. 35) and will "guarantee access to universal health insurance" (art. 36). It prioritizes the promotion and prevention services (art. 37). The Peruvian Constitution of 1993, which establishes the right of each person "to maintain a healthy life free of discrimination," limits the duties of the state to health promotion, and leaves treatment, recovery, and rehabilitation services to the individual responsibility of citizens.

More explicit language on the right to health can be seen, however, in national laws and policy strategies in the health sector that are updated regularly in an increasingly participatory manner. The General Law on Health in Peru and the strategy of its Ministry of Health are examples of that. However, national strategies and the legislation regulating the major institutions in the sector are too general to be considered an effective rights-based policy.

It is only in the past decade that a normative framework on health programs with concrete and universal entitlements and institutional obligations has become effective in the subregion. Three such programs will be discussed here—Universal Maternal and Child Insurance in Bolivia,[12] the Free Maternal and Child Health Care Program in Ecuador,[13] and the Integral Health Insurance (IHI) system in Peru.[14] These programs set an example for policy instruments through which specific entitlements may be fulfilled, even though challenges of legal, policy, and institutional coordination prevent them from fully realizing their stated objectives. Making these programs sustainable is essential to securing their ability to protect established health entitlements.

Despite the lack of clarity on its normative duties, the state is still the largest provider of health services in Bolivia, Ecuador, and Peru when measured by the percentage of public health infrastructure. In Peru as of 2005, the Ministry of Health owned 96.5 percent of all health posts (small health centers), 62.3 percent of health centers, and 32.2 percent of hospitals in the country. All three states have undertaken some degree of decentralization of health services, giving more financial and management independence to regional health authorities and municipalities. Even so, health care remains primarily concentrated in major urban centers—for example, in Peru, 48 percent of all physicians are based in Lima (Vásquez 2007:28). This centralized infrastructure and concentration of professionals in urban centers is another major challenge to realizing universal health programs.

In the past 10 years, creative initiatives involving local and international NGOs have emerged in the three states. They have contributed strongly to overcoming geographic and socioeconomic barriers and to raising awareness of medical and nutrition entitlements in urban and rural communities alike. In Peru, ForoSalud (Foro de la Sociedad Civil en Salud; Network of Health NGOs) has partnered with CARE-Peru to train a number of women volunteers in the most remote areas to monitor nutrition and health standards within their communities and to be involved in demanding better health services. Governments also have taken steps to encourage citizen participation by decentralizing health authority to the municipal level and engaging communities in determining policy priorities. Thus, the social control mechanisms in Bolivian municipalities (National Dialogue Law) and the local committees for health administration in Peru were established. The latter provides a good example of community leaders playing an active role in local health management. Peruvian Law 27657 (art. 3) states that the local committees "constitute a contract between the government and the population for a shared provision of basic health services."

Financial constraints and an inadequate distribution of health spending across population groups are additional serious impediments to a rights-based approach to health policy in the region. In Peru, the poorest quintile of the population absorbs 7 percent of all health spending (public and private), whereas the richest quintile absorbs 44 percent (Vásquez, Cortéz, and Riesco 2000). This disparity results in large part from the fact that higher-income groups use more (and more expensive) health services. With respect to public spending only, the state supports 32 percent of the expenditures of the poorest quintile and 40 percent of those of the richest quintile. But even with this difference, the amount of public funds allocated to the richest quintile is approximately nine times higher than the amount spent on the poorest one.

The analysis of the selected health programs shows that resource constraints often are *not* a significant cause of programs' suboptimal performance. Bolivia's UMCI is financed by the National Treasury and by 10 percent tax transfers from municipalities. When funds do not suffice, the municipalities may request additional funding from a special account set up during the 2000 National Dialogue process. In 2003, only 47 of Bolivia's 314 municipalities (and 28, as of 2004) requested additional financing, and most of the municipalities enjoyed positive balances. Contrasting these figures with the fact that 28.7 percent of mothers and 42.6 percent of children did not have access to UMCI during that period proves that the availability of funding cannot compensate for other barriers in the program's design and implementation (Bolivia, Ministry of Health and Sports 2005:5). In 2006, the public sector in Bolivia had an overall fiscal surplus of 4.6 percent (Bolivia Information Forum 2007), which motivated some district governments to propose even more ambitious health insurance schemes within their districts than the one provided by the national government. Expanded insurance programs in Peru can be considered in districts that enjoy higher tax revenues from the mining industry, but these resources generally have been invested in infrastructure.

The consistent funding of these health programs has been ensured through special measures in all three states, as shown above for Bolivia's UMCI. The Free Maternity and Infant Health Care Program in Ecuador is financed through the Ecuadorean Solidarity Fund and 3 percent of tax revenues from such consumer goods as cigarettes and alcohol (García, Larrea, and Enríquez 2007:21). Funding for Peru's IHI system is guaranteed, and an Intangible Fund for Health Solidarity was created specifically to facilitate excluded groups gaining access to health services.

Table 7.2 and the analysis that follows employ the social guarantees framework to demonstrate the extent to which the selected programs in Bolivia, Ecuador, and Peru succeed in protecting entitlements to health. From the perspective of rights, they represent some of the most progressive health policies within each state. Nevertheless, they give unequal attention to some of the key features of a rights-based policy—they emphasize access

Table 7.2. The Social Guarantees Matrix for Selected Health Programs in Bolivia, Ecuador, and Peru

Subguarantee	Bolivia (UMCI)	Ecuador (FMCHC)	Peru (IHI)
Access			
Are the beneficiaries and services clearly defined?	Yes; both are defined by law.	Yes; both are defined by law.	Yes; they are defined by law for a list of services giving priority to maternal and infant care. IHI does not include rehabilitation services.
Are there institutional procedures for monitoring access?	No	Yes	No
Are there legal or institutional mecha-nisms that ensure nondiscrimination in access to services?	Yes, for indigenous people.	No	None are clearly specified.
Are services guaranteed for the amount of time needed?	Yes, clearly specified.	Not specified	Yes, for some services, such as hospitalization.
Is there a maximum waiting period for receiving a service?	No	No	For tertiary-level (specialized) hospital services, the maximum waiting period is 18 days (SD 006-2005-SA, Art. 3).
If the service is unavailable within the prescribed waiting period, what is a guaranteed alternative (in the same time period)?	None is guaranteed.	None is guaranteed.	None is guaranteed.
Quality			
Are there clear quality standards?	No; the law only mentions recommendations on quality.	Yes; quality standards are based on international standards.	No
Are programs being evaluated on a regular basis?	No	Not at the national level	No, despite existing institutions (Food and Nutrition Program for High-Risk Families, National Institute of Health)

Are standards and evaluation results communicated effectively to the public?	No	No	No
Financial protection			
Do beneficiaries need to contribute to the cost of service?	No	Not by law, but in practice many do contribute.	Yes; by law but, the service should be subsidized for the poorest people.
Are services accessible to beneficiaries who cannot contribute to the cost?	Yes	Access is limited for many women.	There is no clear information.
Is this information communicated effectively to the public?	No	No	Some information is communicated through NGOs.
Redress and enforcement			
Are there mechanisms allowing citizens to claim adequate provision of the services guaranteed?	Yes, at both local and national levels.	Yes, but not in all provinces and municipalities.	No; there are no clearly specified mechanisms.
Continuous revision and participation			
Are there mechanisms that allow for continuous improvement of services?	Yes, but the mechanisms are not functioning.	No regular mechanisms are available.	None is guaranteed on the national level.
Do civil, parent, and community organizations have a concrete role in the design, implementation, and monitoring of the program?	Yes; they have a role in design and implementation, but not a significant role in monitoring.	Not concretely, though there are designated mechanisms.	The NGO ForoSalud
Which law or institution guarantees citizens' involvement?	Popular Participation Law	Users' Committees of the Law on Free Maternity and Infant Health Care	General Law on Health 26842

Source: Authors' compilation.

Note: FMCHC = Free Maternal and Child Health Care Program; IHI = Integral Health Insurance; NGO = nongovernmental organization; UMCI = Universal Maternal and Child Insurance.

and financial protection while lagging behind in the protection of quality, citizens' participation, and citizens' ability to claim and redress services.

The three programs discussed in this section incorporate a progressive design if analyzed from a rights-based perspective. First, they provide services to clearly identified groups with regard to universally established health standards. Second, they describe a set of minimum and well-defined medical benefits required by those groups. Third, they are entrenched in specific laws and regulations that guarantee equitable and nondiscriminatory provision and financing. Last but not least, their legal framework establishes mechanisms of continuous revision and redress. In practice, however, they fall short of achieving their goals of universal access and quality, and do not enable citizens to easily demand the services to which they are entitled through these programs.

The Bolivian UMCI defines a list of 585 benefits to be provided free of charge to all mothers from the gestation period until 6 months after childbirth and to all children up to 5 years of age. The services are to be provided in a decentralized manner, with the budget and administrative procedures necessary to complete them defined within each district and municipality. These benefits are obligatory and granted in all health establishments. Since January 2007, new benefits have been added to the program, including preventive health tests for women, and the program was extended to all women under 21 years of age. In 2004, it was estimated that 28.7 percent of mothers and 42.6 percent of children did not have access to UMCI (Bolivia, National Institute of Statistics 2005).

The IHI[15] system in Peru ensures free health care for people in extreme poverty. As of December 2008, a total of 10,358,793 Peruvian citizens were affiliated with the system that covers maternal, child, and other essential health services, representing a 48.3 percent increase from December 2007. Currently, the program operates in all 25 regions of the country with the objective of covering all settlements where 65 percent or more of residents live in poverty or extreme poverty. For the rest of the settlements, it aims to apply a user identification system that estimates the payment capacity of each registered person (Peru, Ministry of Health).[16] Although the government publishes extensive statistics on the program's coverage,[17] it does not specifically monitor the percentage of that population who is eligible but does not access the program's services. Breaches in access nevertheless can be inferred from the differences in some statistics.

The Free Maternal and Child Health Care Program in Ecuador defines 54 benefits that include services during pregnancy, natal and postnatal care, family planning, detection of cancer and HIV/AIDS, and so forth. However, it excludes treatment of sexually transmitted diseases and some common childhood pathologies, even ones that require hospitalization.

The large degree of informality—that is, lack of formal insurance—in the Andean subregion calls for more creative methods to ensure universal access. This is especially noted in Bolivia where a large part of the population does not have health insurance or seeks care in the informal sector. According to the Bolivian Household Survey for 2003–04, 76 percent of people who got sick or had an accident searched for medical attention and 24 percent did not. Out of the former group, 54.3 percent did so in the formal health care system, and the remaining 45.7 percent received attention in the informal sector. From those who did not seek medical care, 40.9 percent pointed out a lack of money as the main reason; 30.1 percent considered that their condition was not serious enough to warrant attention; and 29.0 percent alluded to other reasons, including distance from a medical center, bad quality of service, and lack of insurance (Bolivia, National Institute of Statistics 2005).

Breaches of access to the three programs often result from cultural or language barriers or geographic obstacles affecting indigenous people and other ethnic minorities, such as Afro-Peruvians or Afro-Ecuadoreans. Rather than launching separate programs targeted to the needs of indigenous or rural populations, governments can make the existing universal health programs more inclusive by looking into questions such as: Which groups will face the greatest barriers or discrimination to access services? and What instruments can be put in place to facilitate their access? This aspect has been addressed only partially in the three health programs analyzed here. Protocols of attention to indigenous and Afro-Ecuadorean communities were not included in the maternity and child health program, contributing to the exclusion of these groups from services.

Universal access to the three programs also is heavily compromised by nonexistent or ineffective public information mechanisms. The 2005–06 Life Conditions poll in Ecuador revealed that only 34 percent of women knew of their entitlements under the maternity and infant health program (García, Larrea, and Enríquez 2007:24). Peru's National Communication Policy on Health (1994) and subsequent creation of the Institutes for Health Education (2003) have taken some steps to address the issue of scarce public information.[18] Even more effective have been donor and civil society efforts in training local women as educators in health and nutrition (see Cotlear 2006; DFID/CARE-Peru 2006).

Given that these programs offer a set of universal and free services, they did not include complex financial protection mechanisms—such as levels of contribution depending on income or contribution ceilings. This puts rural and marginalized groups at a disadvantage. Even though formally they do not need to pay for the services, they often incur related transportation costs or fees. A 2004 Ecuador survey showed that 28.0 percent of pregnant women had to pay for medical services during delivery and pre-/postnatal care, and 26.1 percent had to pay for supplies in public health centers (CEPAR 2005:33). A more differentiated system of financial protection within the program would help even out access to the program for all income groups.

One of the greatest weaknesses, common to all three programs, is the lack of embedded mechanisms to ensure quality. Instead, quality assurance for the programs derives from general health system norms[19] or from sporadic initiatives outside of the program or outside of the health sector (driven by donors or civil society) that aim to upgrade quality.[20] Of even more concern is the fact that health professionals show very little awareness on issues of quality, management, and enforcement of standards. In a 2000 demographic and health survey by Peru's Instituto Nacional de Estadística e Informática, about 45 percent of respondents did not know about or did not take into consideration existing management and enforcement mechanisms. More than 30 percent considered nontransparent contracting and supply practices in the health centers to be frequent or very frequent. Moreover, 22 percent of the physicians interviewed reported they were not willing to take any measures if it were discovered that medical supplies were procured in a dubious manner, and 25 percent were indifferent on the transparency of staff selection (Alcazar and Andrade 2000).

With regard to opportunities for redress, only the UMCI in Bolivia contains structured procedures consistent with the decentralized nature of the program. At the local level, any citizen is entitled to bring claims and allegations before his or her local health directorate. The latter registers the claim or allegation and sends it to the network manager, who has a maximum of 10 days to initiate appropriate investigations and deliver a report that includes corrective recommendations. The local health directorate is responsible for acting on these recommendations and communicating its actions to the claimant. A fraud and control system under the Ministry of Health was developed to monitor the functioning of the redress framework. However, it is impossible to assess how effective this mechanism is because statistics on the number of registered claims by type and their corrective recommendations are not available publicly. In Ecuador and Peru, various civil and governmental organizations—such as the users' committees in Ecuador and both Infosalud and ForoSalud in Peru—have the potential to act as agencies of redress. That is not their explicit mandate, however, and they contribute more to raising public information on health entitlements and mobilizing collective demand for service improvement. Two cases of judicial redress based on articles 3 and 7 of the Constitution were recorded in Peru: two people demanding access to HIV medication; and a group of women, supported by civil society groups, demanding access to contraception drugs.

The Popular Participation Law in Bolivia enabled sizable community participation in designing and implementing the UMCI program. Social networks, composed of grassroots organizations and civil society representatives, were created with well-outlined functions to (1) exert social control so that the beneficiaries of UMCI receive quality services and denounce all cases of mistreatment and discrimination before the local health directorates; (2) identify and help overcome the barriers that keep people from accessing UMCI services; (3) participate in all negotiations within the local health directorates and in their planning process; and (4) promote social mobilization in support of the health sector. Furthermore, the social networks have the responsibility to develop continuous and well-articulated social management within the health system to guarantee the exercise of the right to health. As mentioned above, no statistics or evaluation is available to document how well the social networks ensure program accountability. The new Constitution of Bolivia indicates that the state will regulate quality through medical reviews that evaluate personnel, infrastructure, and equipment; will sanction malpractice; and will guarantee organized participation of citizens in making decisions about the health system (arts. 39 and 40).

In Peru, the Local Committees for Health Administration provide some good examples of community participation in health administration (for example, in the construction of new health infrastructure). Where local committees have been implemented, it has resulted in a more responsive and accountable service delivery model (World Bank 1999:31). This model, however, is not active in all parts of the country. A consultation mechanism was created to collect indigenous people's perspectives on health priorities and health policy methods.[21] In summary, Peru exhibits a lot of positive promotion of citizen participation, but the mechanisms are not functioning in a coordinated manner, and that undermines their potential to provide feedback and directly influence specific state programs.

Similarly, with regard to revision and improvement mechanisms in the three states, a number of channels exist and possess the necessary powers to influence health authorities. But they are not always linked to concrete policies and programs with the explicit mandate to monitor and improve them, and often are operating in limited geographic areas.[22] The office of the Ombudsman (*Defensor del Pueblo*) in Bolivia shows one positive example. In its 2005 report, the Ombudsman acknowledged that some services essential to women's health are not included in the UMCI (Bolivia, Defensor del Pueblo 2005). It showed that many conceiving-age women are at risk because of the lack of measures to prevent uterine cancer. The Ombudsman tracked down an old regulation that extended the program's coverage to some additional services, including annual Pap tests for all women. Linking monitoring mechanisms and agencies to a regular process of revising policies and programs would result in more efficient interventions in the health sector.

The analysis above enables us to draw two fundamental conclusions regarding the programs' potential to fulfill established health entitlements and promote a rights-based approach. First, the analysis from a social guarantees perspective illustrates that sole attention to free and universal access, without considerations for quality and other important indicators, compromises the overall effectiveness of the programs. Universal design has helped expand coverage and eliminate some usual breaches of access. At the same time, insufficient attention to quality standards and their monitoring, and to mechanisms of redress, are not addressed. The list of entitlements and benefits generally is provided free of charge on a universal basis rather than through differentiated financial protection mechanisms. A majority of patients still incur personal expenses because of related costs or insufficient resources and supplies at their medical centers.

Second, the analysis suggests that the institutional potential for rights-based policies in Bolivia, Ecuador, and Peru is much stronger than what can be inferred if one looks strictly at the agencies formally associated with the three programs. A broader look at agents and activities in the health sector reveals a variety of creative approaches by civil society, community organizations, donor institutions, and Ombudsman offices that contribute—each in its own way—to reducing gaps in access, information, quality, or other areas. Taking advantage of this existing potential and linking it directly to the implementation and monitoring of policies and programs can result in a more coordinated and effective framework to fulfill health entitlements.

Conclusion

An analysis from the perspective of social guarantees highlights some essential lessons for increasing equity and inclusion through social policy. On a broader scale, it shows the importance of giving equal and adequate weight to the four basic domains of policy planning—legal, institutional, instrumental/programmatic, and financial.[23] When legal commitments are made but resources are not allocated to complete them or a sustainable institutional structure is not established to fulfill them, state commitments have no potential to influence inclusion. This seemingly self-evident statement is especially important when rights of vulnerable groups are at stake— low-income groups, ethnic minorities, or others—given their low potential for mobilization and weak representation in decision-making channels. Even though indigenous groups, women, youth, people with disabilities, and other marginalized populations now have more channels to express their views than they had in the past, and there are more state institutions and civil organizations to represent them at national and local levels, the relative influence of these channels on universal policy design and resource allocation remains weak. Thus, most bilingual education programs in the region consistently are underfunded, regardless of constitutional commitments to provide bilingual options in basic education. To respond to the needs of vulnerable groups in practice as well as in law, governments' commitments need to be reflected in all policy domains—legal, institutional, programmatic, and financial. This point can be strengthened by establishing ongoing mechanisms to incorporate civil feedback in policy making instead of or in addition to one-time nationwide consultations.

With regard to the planning of concrete programs, the social guarantees and subguarantees perspective demonstrates the value of a holistic vision in service delivery. In both education and health programs, the analysis reveals that progressive attention has been given to expanding coverage and access while quality norms and their monitoring consistently have been neglected. Beyond the access and quality disparity, which already has been acknowledged and well documented in social policy literature of the region, the subguarantees analysis points to a number of areas that affect program performance but are not given explicit consideration. These areas include mechanisms of financial protection (that is, the need to look at all related costs and the affordability of the services for all citizen groups) and accessible and affordable channels for redress, among others. Considering these aspects in program design is equally important as considering access and quality. School dropout rates, for instance, largely are the result of households' inability to afford related costs (food, uniforms, textbooks, and transportation), and the same is true for basic health services. In addition, the social guarantees analysis shows that progress in subguarantee areas (access, quality, and financial protection) is strongly interrelated. One cannot establish an effective mechanism for redress if quality or financial protection standards on the basis of which beneficiaries may claim services do not exist. Nor can continuous revision be realized if there are no norms on which to base an evaluation. Certainly, the list of subguarantees can be expanded and made more precise. The analysis in this chapter has included some of the most essential components.

This chapter has highlighted the need for policy planning that gives as much consideration to the process of service delivery as it does to broad targets. National strategies and policies in basic services largely are driven and shaped by such targets—for example, in the case of Peru, reducing the incidence of malaria by 40 percent and of tuberculosis by 30 percent and establishing an autonomous social security system by 2011, and, in the case of Bolivia, reducing infant mortality to 30 per 1,000 live births between 2003 and 2015. On the one hand, such broad national commitments in the framework of the Millennium Development Goals have stimulated the expansion of coverage to protect vulnerable populations and to sustain budgetary commitments for related programs. On the other hand, if taken as an ultimate goal of social policy, these broad commitments also should motivate governments to look beyond targets and ensure sustainable policy designs. More sustainable designs would address a range of criteria, including but not limited to universal access, quality, financial protection, redress, and regular revision. In other words, achieving targets and improving the process and effectiveness of policies should go hand in hand.

The social guarantees framework suggests one route toward such inclusive and sustainable social policy design. The content of citizens' entitlements or benefits as well as the concrete mechanisms for their delivery are to be developed, discussed, and approved within each society's unique context.

Notes

1. According to the United Nations Development Programme's 2007/08 Human Development Index (UNDP 2007), Bolivia, Ecuador, and Peru have Gini coefficients of 0.60, 0.54, and 0.52, respectively.

2. According to Peru's 2007 population census, the indigenous population is only 14.82 percent, measured by the number of people whose mother tongue is indigenous.

3. Figures are from Ecuador's Population and Housing Census, series 1950–2001, produced by the Integrated System of Social Indicators.

4. These figures were published by Peru's Ministry of Education, Office of Education Statistics, in 2005.

5. During this period, health and education infrastructure was extended to most remote areas, and access to these services increased radically.

6. Public expenditures on health as a percentage of GDP in 2004 were 1.9, 2.2, and 4.1 for Peru, Ecuador, and Bolivia, respectively, according to the 2007/08 *Human Development Report 2007/2008*(UNDP 2007).

7. It declined from 2.8 percent to 2.4 percent of GDP in Peru, and from 2.5 percent to 1.0 percent in Ecuador. In Bolivia, it rose from 2.4 percent to 6.4 percent (UNDP 2007).

8. Prior to January 2009, the Bolivian Constitution considered only primary education (8 years) to be mandatory.

9. The figures are from Ecuador's National Institute for Statistics and Census. The Center for Development and Self-Management (DyA–Ecuador), a leading NGO that seeks to improve quality and coverage of health and education services and to influence public policy, gives a worse picture—69.9 percent work and study simultaneously, 15.0 percent exclusively work, and 13.3 percent only study (cited in García, Larrea, and Enríquez 2007:38).

10. A program begun in Peru in 2008 has committed to delivering laptop computers (one per child) in rural areas.

11. A new proposal that tries to provide a monetary subsidy to rural girls and adolescents as well as indigenous children in Peru has been suggested by Vásquez and Monge (2008; also see Vásquez 2008).

12. The program's normative basis is Law 2426, in force since January 2003.

13. Its normative basis is Law 14, October 2005.

14. Its normative basis is found in the General Law on Health (modified through Law 27604), Ministerial Resolution 725-2005/MINSA, Supreme Decree 004-2007-SA.

15. Information about the system is available at http://www.sis.gob.pe/a_quien_antec.html (accessed March 12, 2009).

16. Information is available at http://www.sis.gob.pe/a_estad_cuadr.html [accessed March 31, 2009].

17. Coverage statistics are available at http://www.sis.gob.pe/estad_indic_070723_2.htm (accessed March 17, 2009).

18. By 2006, the Institutes for Health Education had grown to 699 educational centers, 300,000 students, and 13,308 trained educators; currently, there are more than 762 accredited centers and 585,381 students (Peru, Ministry of Health 2006, cited in Vásquez 2007:49).

19. For example, Peru's Law on the Ministry of Health (Law 27657, art. 8) states that "all health establishments and health services should be appropriate from a scientific and medical point of view and should be of good quality."
20. These initiatives include the Ombudsmen, the Observatory for the Rights of Children and Adolescents in Ecuador, and the programs Coverage with Quality and Project 2000 in Peru.
21. The mechanism for consultation was created through an agreement (a ministerial resolution) between the Ministry of Health and the Interethnic Association for the Development of the Peruvian Selva.
22. For example, Peru's Support to Modernize the Health Sector program is active only in the regions of Apurimac, Ayacucho, and Huancavelica.
23. See chapter 2 for a more detailed discussion of the policy domains and the social guarantees model.

References

Alcázar, Lorena, and Raúl Andrade. 2000. "Transparencia y rendición de cuentas en los hospitales públicos: El caso peruano." Working Document 1, Instituto Apoyo, Lima, Peru.

Barja, Gover, and Jorge Leyton. 2007. "Derechos, asignaciones garantizadas y política social. Caso de estudio: Bolivia." Unpublished manuscript, Social Development Department, World Bank, Washington, DC.

Bolivia, Defensor del Pueblo (Office of the Ombudsman). 2005. "Octavo informe del defensor del pueblo al congreso." La Paz, Bolivia.

Bolivia Information Forum. 2007. "Bolivia's Economy—An Update." http://www.boliviainfoforum.org.uk/news-detail.asp?id=22 [accessed March 17, 2009].

Bolivia, Ministry of Health and Sports. 2005. "Seguro Universal Materno Infantil, SUMI." La Paz, Bolivia. http://www.sns.gov.bo/direcciones/seguros/seguro/texto%20completo.pdf (accessed March 17, 2009).

Bolivia, National Institute of Statistics. 2005. "Encuesta continua de hogares 2003–2004." La Paz, Bolivia.

CEPAR (Centro de Estudios de Población y Desarrollo Social). 2005. "Encuesta demografica y de salud materna e infantil 2004. Final Report." http://www.cepar.org.ec/endemain_04/nuevo05/pdf/texto/01_introduccion.pdf(accessed March 17, 2009).

Cotlear, Daniel, ed. 2006. *A New Social Contract for Peru: An Agenda for Improving Education, Health Care, and the Social Safety Net.* Washington, DC: World Bank.

DFID (U.K. Department for International Development)/CARE-Peru. 2006. *Derechos en salud: De pobladores a ciudadanos.* Lima, Peru: CARE-Peru.

García, Fernando, Ramiro Larrea, and Marcela Enríquez. 2007. "Derechos, garantías y políticas sociales en el Ecuador." Unpublished manuscript, Social Development Department, World Bank, Washington, DC.

Guigale, Marcelo M., Vicente Fretes-Cibils, and John L. Newman. 2006. *An Opportunity for a Different Peru: Prosperous, Equitable, and Governable.* Washington, DC: World Bank.

Hall, Gillette, and Harry Anthony Patrinos, eds. 2006. *Indigenous Peoples, Poverty and Human Development in Latin America.* New York: Palgrave Macmillan.

Hilburg Catter, Carlos J. 2003. "Análisis del contexto socio-económico 1902–2002." Pan-American Health Organization, Washington, DC.

Justino, Patricia, and Arnab Acharya. 2003. "Inequality in Latin America: Processes and Inputs." Working Paper 22, Poverty Research Unit, University of Sussex, Brighton, England.

MacLean-Abaroa, Ronald. 2001. "Bolivia: Mechanisms for Involving Civil Society in Decision-Making in Order to Promote Transparency, Government Accountability and Social Equity." Paper presented at the Second Meeting of the Inter-American Development Bank's Social Equity Forum, Washington, DC, November 1–2.

PAHO (Pan-American Health Organization). 1989. *The Right to Health in the Americas: A Comparative Constitutional Study.* Washington, DC: PAHO.

Peru, Ministry of Health. 2006. "Información situacional. Dirección General de la Promoción de la Salud." Lima, Peru.

Ramirez, Elliana. 2004. "Estudio sobre la educación para la población rural en Peru." In *Educación para la población rural en Brasil, Chile, Colombia, Honduras, Mexico, Paraguay y Peru,* 329–90. Rome, Italy: Food and Agriculture Organization.

UNDP (United Nations Development Programme). *1998 Human Development Report.* New York: UNDP. http://hdr.undp.org/en/media/hdr_1998_en_indica tors1.pdf (accessed April 4, 2009).

———. 2007. *Human Development Report 2007/2008: Fighting Climate Change: Human Solidarity in a Divided World.* New York: UNDP. http://hdrstats.undp .org/indicators/57.html (accessed April 4, 2009).

UNESCO (United Nations Educational, Scientific, and Cultural Organization). 2007. "Raul Vallejo Corral: Remove Obstacles Limiting Access to Education." *UNESCO Courier* 10. http://portal.unesco.org/en/ev.php-URL_ID=41201& URL_DO=DO_TOPIC&URL_SECTION=201.html (accessed April 4, 2009).

UNICEF (United Nations Chldren's Fund). 2007. "Indigenous Children: Double Exclusion." *Observatorio Alerta* May. http://www.odna.org/ ODNA-PDF/alerta1.pdf (accessed April 4, 2009).

Vásquez, Enrique. 2007. "Análisis de las garantías sociales en educación, salud, alimentación y pueblos indígenas en el Perú." Unpublished manuscript, Social Development Department, World Bank, Washington, DC.

————. 2008. "Niñez indígena y educación intercultural bilingüe en el Perú." Unpublished manuscript, Grupo Impulsor de la Educación Rural, Lima, Peru.

Vásquez, Enrique, Rafael Cortéz, and Gustavo Riesco. 2000. *Inversión Social para un Buen Gobierno en el Perú*. Lima, Peru: Centro de Investigación, Universidad del Pacífico.

Vásquez, Enrique, and Álvaro Monge. 2007. "Por qué y cómo reducir la brecha de género de las niñas y adolescentes rurales en el Perú?" Unpublished manuscript, Manuela Ramos Movement, Universidad del Pacífico, Lima, Peru.

————. 2008. "Políticas públicas contra la persistente desigualdad de género de educación de las niñas y adolescentes rurales en el Perú." Unpublished manuscript, Manuela Ramos Movement, Universidad del Pacífico, Lima, Peru.

World Bank. 1999. *Peru: Improving Health Care for the Poor*. World Bank Country Study. Washington, DC: World Bank.

CHAPTER 8

Achieving Equitable and Inclusive Citizenship through Social Policy: The Cases of Jamaica and St. Kitts and Nevis

Rachel Hannah Nadelman, Lavern Louard-Greaves, and Carol Watson Williams

A shared heritage of slavery, colonialism, and racism across the independent Anglophone islands of the Caribbean[1] has informed these nations' conditions of poverty and inequality as well as their institutionalized social policy. Caribbean social service systems have been categorized by some as "distinctly curative in nature," based on the prevalence of programs designed to mitigate the residual effects of economic policy (OAS 2008: 1). At the same time, current social policy regimes have evolved to offer sophisticated legal protection and enunciation of rights, demonstrating the influence of rights-based global norms and standards. Respectively the largest and the smallest of the Anglophone Caribbean's independent islands, Jamaica and St. Kitts and Nevis provide two representative examples of how current practices in social service delivery in the region do or do not contribute to the realization of citizens' rights. Given these two island nations' shared historical and contemporary influences, what role does the fulfillment of rights and the promotion of equal and inclusive citizenship play in how government carries out its social contract with its citizenry? How could applying the social guarantees framework strengthen the current systems?

The extent to which the state equitably and inclusively meets citizen demands for social service entitlements can be viewed as an indicator of its capacity to realize basic human rights. Social guarantees (see chapter 2) are tools for designing and monitoring social policy and service delivery to address challenges of injustice, inequity, and exclusion. Through legal, administrative, programmatic, or financial mechanisms, social guarantees aim to clearly specify individuals' entitlements to public provision and to ensure the fulfillment of those obligations by the state. Disaggregated across the dimensions of access, quality, financial protection, redress and enforcement, and continuous revision and participation, social guarantees provide an effective way to move beyond a declarative framework of universal rights by defining rights as a set of guaranteed services that makes those rights tangible and contributes to their being achieved. This chapter therefore uses the social guarantees framework of analysis to

- explore Jamaica's and St. Kitts and Nevis's progress in realizing citizen rights and promoting inclusive citizenship through social policy
- draw attention to the normative, policy, and programmatic obstacles that prevent such realization
- highlight the ways in which a system of social guarantees could help improve the equitable provision of such services.

Both country discussions will examine the education and health sectors, and the Jamaica section will include an analysis of the housing sector.

Institutionalized social policy in the Anglophone Caribbean has its roots in the British colonial response to the fierce rioting that spread across many of the islands during the 1930s. A century after Great Britain had abolished slavery in its colonies, the majority of islanders continued to be treated as subjects instead of citizens, living in poor conditions with minimal opportunities. The riots marked a turning point in Caribbean imperial history. Individual frustration and despair ignited in public protest and violence, forcing colonial authorities for the first time to accept responsibility for meeting the populace's needs. Modeled after England's common-law tradition, the first colonial social service systems followed a top-down, welfarist approach with implementation shaped by political patronage. With independence or ascendancy to statehood status in the 1960s and 1970s, most newly autonomous Caribbean governments expanded their social policies. Although movements to more equitably share social and economic benefits between citizens did take hold in some nations—most notably in Jamaica during the 1970s—such interventions were not necessarily grounded in a rights philosophy. During subsequent periods of fiscal austerity or political conservatism, many of the gains were reversed. Today throughout the Caribbean, as represented in Jamaica and St. Kitts and Nevis, government and popular attitudes toward social assistance and public services remain heavily top-down and exhibit vestiges of political patronage.

By and large, the Anglophone Caribbean states have become contracting parties to the universal system of human rights (ECLAC 2007). With this accession, these nations have obligated themselves to integrate the basic tenets of these conventions into legislation and to implement policies and programs that support the realization of such rights. With few exceptions, the Anglophone Caribbean islands have included in their constitutions the necessary provisions and guarantees to preserve civil and political freedoms. Overall, these obligations are respected and upheld. Regarding social and economic rights, however, there is a notable discrepancy between commitment and practice. At best, these rights have been codified minimally in legislation or made effective through practical implementation. From policy makers to development planners to the media to the general public, there is little understanding of human rights as tools to advance development processes or enhance equity in social service provision. In this context, assistance to the poor, even when supporting access to basic services, is still conceived in the framework of a patron-client relationship and, hence, does not contribute to the formation of a rights consciousness.

The Caribbean nations—exemplified by Jamaica and St. Kitts and Nevis—have realized policies and programs that contribute to inclusive citizenship although not necessarily conceiving them from a human rights perspective. Basic examples can be seen across the social service sectors. In education, primary and secondary school are mandatory for all children and free of charge. As a result of this open access and financial protection, both countries have achieved universal enrollment at the primary level. In health, the primary care systems are designed and delivered so that citizens will not face geographic obstacles to accessing services, providing care facilities even in the most remote rural areas. Increasing regionalization through organizations such as the Caribbean Community (CARICOM) and the Organization of Eastern Caribbean States (OECS) has enabled member-states to benefit from economies of scale and a larger pool of technical expertise to strengthen social service provision. For example, CARICOM sponsored the Declaration of the Port of Spain to commit members to improve access to and quality of treatment for noncommunicable diseases by 2012, providing strategies to facilitate the likelihood of reaching the goal. The OECS has established a central medication purchasing mechanism that procures costly drugs in bulk, thereby lowering drug costs for individual countries so that the drugs can be distributed at no or low cost to citizens. Although one may not discount the significant barriers to the realization of citizen rights that currently exist in Jamaica and St. Kitts and Nevis, the significant national and regional investments that these island nations have made to provide social services equitably suggest that there may be a basis for the implementation of a social guarantees approach to advance the fulfillment of universal entitlements.

The Case of Jamaica:
Rights and Politics in the Delivery of Social Service

From slavery to emancipation, Crown colony government to independence, Jamaica[2] has experienced the complete absence of rights, the limited acknowledgment of rights, and the explicit recognition of equal rights. A signatory to the two basic human rights covenants and three of the four major human rights conventions (ECLAC 2007), the country has achieved universal enrollment for primary-school-age children; high levels of immunization; and annually increasing rates of access to electricity, potable water, sanitary facilities, and communication technologies.[3] While exhibiting low and disappointing rates of economic growth and high public debt, Jamaica also has demonstrated significant improvements in critical social indicators (for example, access to basic amenities and life expectancy) and substantial decreases in overall poverty.[4] Over the last four decades, particularly the 1970s and in the first decade of the 21st century, Jamaica has invested substantially in social services, passing legislation, designing programs, and promulgating policies to improve the lives of ordinary citizens. A recent innovation in social policy is the social protection reform that merged previous welfare initiatives into the Programme for Advancement through Health and Education, the Caribbean's first conditional cash transfer program.

Nonetheless, the enduring effects of a society deliberately shaped by inequity remain. Birth registration, the gateway to full participation and rights protection in Jamaican society, still is inaccessible for at least 5 percent of births annually (Fox and Gordon-Strachan 2004). Violent crime—arguably Jamaica's largest social challenge—continues to increase each year, soaring from 1,076 per 100,000 people in 2006 to 1,244 per 100,000 in 2007 (Planning Institute of Jamaica 2006a, 2007). Even among the poor there are distinctions to be made in terms of the realization of rights: children in rural areas have access to lower-quality schools than do urban poor children; women have more difficulty accessing state housing benefits than do men because they participate in the labor market at lower, more informal levels; and the rural poor have more limited access to health care than do the urban poor because of the geographic distribution of specialty hospitals. Although efforts have been made over the past 50 years to meet the basic needs of all Jamaicans, the opportunity to experience and realize these benefits has been mixed for the population. This layered approach is reflected today in the provision of social services, especially in education and housing.

Efforts toward the fulfillment of rights in Jamaica therefore must be analyzed against the backdrop of disappointing economic progress and elevated levels of crime, coupled with high public investment in social services and marked improvements in key social indicators. The matrix in table 8.1 captures key elements of existing social guarantees and sub-guarantees in Jamaica relating to education, housing, and health care. The analysis to follow explores how rights-based norms and procedures have or have not been integrated into the delivery of social services in each of these areas.

Education

Since its beginnings, Jamaica's educational system has had a two-tiered structure. At inception, elementary education was designed to "civilize" the general population. This elementary education, which became synonymous with the "All Age" schools (largely considered to be the poorest quality in the system), was provided together with a classical and broader academic education for middle- and upper-class children. With political independence, access to education and guaranteed primary education widened. Since 2001, the system has included universal secondary education through grade 11. Yet the two-tiered system has remained. Poorer students are more likely to qualify to attend the lower-status All Age primary and junior high schools and the new secondary schools currently referred to as "upgraded high schools." Middle- and upper-class students largely continue to attend private schools for primary education and, after grade 6, go to the prestigious secondary high schools patterned on the British system. The Grade Six Achievement Test is the major determinant of how students are tracked into the two tiers. Until the early 1990s, these two school types encompassed different curricula and examinations, divergent governance structures, and unequal resources.[5] Although the overt structural differences have been removed, the disparities between the schools remain.

Table 8.1. The Social Guarantees Matrix for Education, Housing, and Health Care in Jamaica

Subguarantee	Education	Housing	Health care
Access			
Are the beneficiaries and services clearly defined?	Yes—compulsory for children ages 6–16, and changing to age 18	NHT, with all contributors to the trust; certain income and geographic groups are eligible for social housing, such as the Inner City Housing Project.	Yes; in some cases, there are legal provisions: Immunization Act, Public Health Act, and NHF for prescribed illnesses.
Are there institutional procedures for monitoring access?	Yes; there is a major monitoring tool to see if children of school age are not going—JSLC; also Ministry of Education Census.	No	No; but the Ministry of Health has a health information system that indicates types and number of cases; JSLC.
Are there legal or institutional mechanisms that ensure nondiscrimination in access to services?	Education Act, Ministry of Education, education regions	No; access to housing benefit is still discretionary in many cases. NHT is the most developed selection process. Access to financing is discriminatory by definition (that is, on the basis of income).	There is no overarching nondiscrimination legislation, but there are the original rights-based principles from the 1970s; decentralization is through regional health authorities.
Are services guaranteed for the amount of time needed?	Universal coverage up to grade 9	No; beneficiary can lose home for nonpayment.	Not clearly guaranteed, and not for all treatments
Is there a maximum waiting period for receiving a service?	Available on demand	No	No
If the service is unavailable within the prescribed waiting period, what is a guaranteed alternative (in the same time period)?	No; but there are proposals for entrance to extension schools; building classrooms	No	None

Quality			
Are there clear quality standards?	Yes; standard testing is used to measure learning at primary and secondary levels. The teacher-to-student ratio is defined. Teachers at both secondary and primary (especially at primary and early childhood) levels need special certification. National grade level curriculum standard are used. Grade 4 literacy and numeracy assessments are made.	Clear housing standards have been established by legislation for housing in the formal sector.	Not sure if there are standards for all aspects; there are service-level agreements that set standards for health facilities at different levels; international standards are used.
Are programs being evaluated on a regular basis?	Quality is measured by the Ministry of Education; there are plans for an inspectorate through the Education Transformation project, with regional branches. It is not clear how regularly measurement takes place.	No	Only some clearly defined programs, such as HIV/AIDS and malaria; not sectorwide.
Are standards and evaluation results communicated effectively to the public?	Yes; standardized test scores are available and evaluation results are published in the media.	No	Very often not to the general public; may be available to those who can access them.
Financial protection			
Do beneficiaries need to contribute to the cost of service?	There are no tuition fees; families meet other costs related to education, transportation, lunch, books at secondary level, and uniforms.	NHT, contributory scheme	There are no user fees; but the client bears other costs, such as those for medication and some diagnostic services.
Are services accessible to beneficiaries who cannot contribute to the cost?	Yes; there is a book rental scheme and there are school feeding programs. Fees for secondary school were abolished in September 2007.	Yes; most social housing programs do not require contribution; some require mortgage payment, such as the Inner City Housing Project.	Yes; NHF covers the cost of some medication.

(continued)

Table 8.1. The Social Guarantees Matrix for Education, Housing, and Health Care in Jamaica (*continued*)

Subguarantee	Education	Housing	Health Care
Is this information communicated effectively to the public?	Yes	Not sure	Yes
Redress and enforcement			
Are there mechanisms allowing citizens to claim adequate provision of the services guaranteed?	Yes—parent-teacher associations, school boards and Ministry of Education; new inspectorate is planned.	No	Without assuming guarantees, there are mechanisms for people to express their concerns and then to have those concerns addressed.
Continuous revision and participation			
Are there mechanisms that allow for continuous improvement of services?	Yes	Yes	Yes—monitoring and evaluation mechanism.
Do civil, parent, or community organizations have a concrete role in the design, implementation, and monitoring of the program?	Yes—the parent-teacher association	For some social housing, such as site and service	Often "closed shop," but participating in specific projects, such as HIV/AIDS awareness and violence prevention.
Which law or institution guarantees citizens' involvement?	Consultation code in the public sector; consultation is mandated for every new policy and law being developed. Code sets out process of consultation that must take place.	Consultation code in the public sector; consultation is mandated for every new policy and law being developed. Code sets out process of consultation that must take place.	Not a guarantee; consultation code in the public sector; consultation is mandated for every new policy and law being developed. Code sets out process of consultation that must take place.

Source: Authors' compilation.

Note: JSLC = Jamaica Survey of Living Conditions; NHF = National Health Fund; NHT = National Housing Trust.

As of 2009, Jamaica is four years into a process of "Education Transformation." Despite a strong legal framework,[6] high enrollment rates, significant curriculum reform, and other educational improvement efforts, a 2004 report by the Task Force on Educational Reform concluded that the educational system at all levels had performed well below target, as measured by national and regional student assessment scores. The systemwide reform that followed addresses issues of equity, quality, access, outcomes, and performance by undertaking sweeping changes, such as modernizing the Ministry of Education to be smaller and more efficient, augmenting facilities and upgrading infrastructure, and introducing new instructional strategies to deal with students' literacy and numeracy weaknesses. These policy, legislative, and institutional initiatives are being pursued in a national climate that fiercely advocates improvements to the education system. At the same time, the decision to absorb the Education Transformation project into the Ministry of Education, coupled with a lowering of performance targets because of slow realization of results, does bring into question the ultimate effectiveness of the reforms (Wynter 2009).

The 2006 Jamaica Survey of Living Conditions (JSLC) shows that from preprimary through grade 9, Jamaica provides high levels of access to education. Although school fees were abolished only in 2007, since the early 1980s children ages 3–5 have had almost universal enrollment (Planning Institute of Jamaica 2005). At the secondary level, there is near-universal access by the younger cohort (ages 12–14), but that access drops to 88.3 percent among the group ages 15–16 and to 45.9 percent among the older cohort (ages 17–18) for whom there is no guaranteed policy provision. Although education is intended to be guaranteed through 11th grade, a shortage of physical spaces in 10th and 11th grades has created the biggest barrier to fulfillment. The most notable disparities in educational access occur across geographic location and gender. In rural areas, 85.8 percent of the children complete their secondary education, whereas in urban and suburban areas, 91.7 percent of the children do so. That gap is largely the result of the rural shortages of space in grades 10 and 11. High enrollment for girls (92 percent) is offset by lower levels for boys (85 percent). Statistically, boys are more likely to be enrolled at schools that terminate at grade 9 and, hence, are affected more adversely by the shortage of room in the subsequent grades. Recognizing this major barrier to access, the Ministry of Education—under the Education Transformation project—has constructed new high schools, creating more than 6,250 additional places for grades 10 and 11, with a special focus on rural areas.[7]

Although enrollment levels are high in Jamaica, attendance continues to be a challenge (Planning Institute of Jamaica 2007). All Age schools have the lowest attendance rates. Students outside the metropolitan center and particularly in rural areas are especially challenged by high transportation costs because public systems that offer students subsidized travel opportunities are available only in the capital and other principal cities on the western end of the island. Furthermore, a feeling of insecurity from general fear or specific violent incidents is increasingly responsible for school closure and children's inability to leave their communities to attend school. Although there are no empirical data available on the number of school days lost to violence, anecdotal evidence suggests that this is an emerging issue that needs to be monitored carefully. Therefore, although schooling is guaranteed for Jamaican youth through grade 11, the existing barriers to daily attendance potentially reduce overall access to the education system.

Although it is clear that barriers to access and attendance require constant monitoring and improvement, the education sector in Jamaica struggles most with issues of quality. This struggle is directly related to Jamaica's two-tiered system, with its traditional high schools renowned for rigor and academic performance and the nontraditional and All Age schools infamous for their poor results. When evaluating education outcomes on the aggregate level, it generally is conceded in Jamaica that the results are well below socially acceptable standards. As a means to assess students' academic readiness and competence, since 1999 the National Assessment Program has instituted four examinations at the primary level to test academic readiness, literacy, and overall achievement. It has also instituted the Grade Six Achievement Test, which is used for secondary-level placement. Perhaps the most significant quality challenges can be found in secondary education provisions, which, as discussed above, are fraught with the most extreme problems of selectivity and elitism. The traditional high schools always have included grades 12 and 13, during which they offer the General Cambridge Advanced-Level Examination and the Caribbean Advanced Proficiency Examination. Even today, many of the upgraded high schools—the former new secondary schools—do not offer these additional years of schooling and, therefore, do not enable their students to take the examinations that are crucial for advancement. Available results data from the Caribbean Secondary Education Certificate (CSEC) examinations, collated by the National Council of Education, show that the upgraded high schools generally are the poor performers. Given the existing situation, it is no surprise that youth reported the main obstacles to finding suitable jobs to be "no suitable training opportunities," "unsuitable general education," "no education," "unsuitable vocational education," and "not enough jobs available" (Planning Institute of Jamaica 2006b).

Jamaica currently has in place several mechanisms that offer financial protection to students and prevent their exclusion on the basis of financial need. Although primary and secondary education is free, schools request that parents provide a voluntary contribution to defray some school-related expenses. Based on the Education Act, the Ministry of Education provides some financial support programs, such as subsidized school meals, a secondary schools book rental scheme, and reduced-fare transportation for students in the Kingston Metropolitan Area (KMA) and Montego Bay. The largest percentages of family contributions come not from direct school costs, but from related expenditures such as lunch and snacks, transportation, and extracurricular academic support.

An integral part of the design and execution of the Education Transformation project has been citizen/stakeholder participation. Active citizen engagement is emphasized as integral to successful reforms, demonstrated through two of the six new work streams—student behavior change and community-school relations. The initiative's objectives were derived from results of islandwide consultations with education professionals and the broader public, undertaken in fiscal 2003/04. Education Transformation organizes town hall–type meetings in major towns to apprise the public of the developments, solicit feedback and suggestions, and address any concerns. Among the innovations to encourage parental involvement are the establishment of the National Parent Teachers' Association of Jamaica and the development of a National Parenting Policy led by the Early Childhood Commission. The main role of the National Parent Teachers' Association is to improve the school-home relationship and bring parents into the system as key rightsholders. However, the association is severely underresourced and underfunded. In addition to structured opportunities to participate in the design of educational policy, there is an active civil society lobby that is responsible for putting the inadequacies of the current education system squarely in focus, particularly in public debates around crime and economic development in Jamaica. This lobby, which includes stakeholders from across Jamaican society, has begun a process of continual revision, using performance data to advocate for the reassessment of the education system that led to the Education Transformation project.

According to the Education Act and the Early Childhood Act, as well as under general common law governing administrative actions, parents and guardians can seek redress for grievances by bringing legal claims. Although they are few, there have been instances of successful court challenges to the educational system. The well-established and accessible governance structures in the education system—school board, principal, Ministry of Education regional office, and Ministry of Education head office—offer some limited redress measures for families. In addition, on a local level, parents and caregivers directly may seek the intervention of the ministry to mediate problems; and it is not uncommon for parents to seek the removal of principals, teachers, or board members for alleged underperformance.

Housing

The need for affordable, decent housing is a long-standing challenge to improved living conditions in Jamaica. Although the Constitution provides no explicit right to housing, Jamaica has recognized the human need for shelter. As a signatory to the United Nations' Universal Declaration of Human Rights, Jamaica implicitly recognizes housing as a right. Since Jamaica's independence in 1962, successive governments have focused on housing and land tenure; but this social service, more than any other, has been the source of political patronage. Most blatant during the immediate pre- and post-independence period were the homogenous "garrison communities" created to secure political support for the party in power. This deliberate geographic distortion for political purposes is no longer a feature of housing provision in Jamaica, although the society continues to spend significant sums to address the remnants of its negative social consequences. Despite a steady growth rate below 1.0 percent since 1998, and 0.5 percent since 2000, the demand for housing has continued to outpace supply; thus, the housing needs of thousands of Jamaican families remain unmet. Therefore, according to Jamaica's 2007 Population and Housing Census, informal shelter[8] has developed as a low-income solution.

Jamaica has substantial legislative and institutional frameworks for housing provision. In the absence of updated legislation or well-defined policy and institutional structures, housing financing, affordability, delivery, access, and security are dysfunctional and cumbersome. The Housing Act of 1955 is the cornerstone of the legislative framework, authorizing the Minister of Housing to decide the areas suited to development and to allow or disallow any proposed housing construction. Developed in 1996, the National Land Policy addresses some of the more complex and critical issues related to land management and development, including access and ownership rights.[9] The National Housing Trust is the country's most important and sustained effort to provide housing. Established in 1976, the trust's mission at the outset was to increase and enhance the existing housing stock and provide financial assistance to the neediest contributors with funds collected through a compulsory payroll deduction (2 percent from workers and 3 percent from employers).

Access to and distribution of land, supported by local tenure arrangements,[10] historically have affected housing affordability and security. Land ownership is proved through a registered title (superior to a common-law title) and is considered to be conclusive evidence of ownership. Whereas 78 percent of land in Jamaica is considered to be privately owned (Mycoo n.d.), the 1996 National Land Policy revealed that less than 45 percent of such land had registered titles. The 2006 JSLC indicates that approximately 21 percent of the population lives on rented or leased land, a percentage that has been declining steadily since 1997 when it stood at 27 percent. This decline may be interpreted very cautiously as reflecting the outcome of consistent efforts to regularize ownership and land tenure in Jamaica. According to regional housing statistics, security through housing ownership is greatest in rural areas.[11] With housing security higher in the poorest consumption quintile than in the wealthiest (2006 JSLC), questions remain regarding the conditions and formality of such housing. Despite the steady increase in housing security among households, many do not have formal land tenure status and so are classified as squatters.[12] Other households do have property tenure (meaning they have registered titles for their strata homes), but do not have land tenure in the strictest application.[13] Given this context, it is clear that levels of access in the housing sector are far more complex to interpret than they are in the education sector. Ownership seems to be an ambiguous concept: among Jamaicans with access to shelter, about 40 percent live in conditions not considered legally secure (2004 and 2007 JSLC)—a figure that has remained relatively unchanged for more than a decade. This legal uncertainty means that current access to shelter may be in peril over the long term.

Housing quality can be assessed on the basis of access to such fundamental amenities as potable water, type of toilet facility, and electricity. Many homes considered legally tenured, particularly in rural areas, are of poor quality and do not have private access to water and toilet facilities (2006 JSLC). In 2006, one-half of Jamaican households had one or more person(s) per habitable room. Based on the international standard for persons per habitable room (1.00 to 1.01), a considerable proportion of Jamaica's households (50 percent) live in overcrowded conditions.[14] The proportion of such households was highest in rural areas (52 percent), followed by the KMA (48 percent) and other towns (47.8 percent). The percentage of dwellings with access to piped drinking water remained fairly constant from 1996 to 2006; however, the proportion of households relying on public standpipes declined from 14.9 percent in 1995 to 6.7 percent in 2006, in large part because of public policy. Slightly less than two-thirds of households in 2006 had access to a flush toilet, an increase since 1996 when the proportion was 53.6 percent. As of that same year, one-third of households relied on pit latrines, although this figure has declined from its 1996 level of 46.1 percent. Although conditions in housing seem to be improving—as demonstrated by increased access to plumbing—the extent of rural housing that lacked private access to water and in which families live in overcrowded conditions leads to the conclusion that the overall quality of available housing is not high (2006 JSLC).

Financial protection in the form of loans and mortgages to buy or build houses is a critical area of concern in Jamaica's housing market. Increased housing costs and inequitable wealth distribution have made it difficult for most Jamaicans to buy or build homes. As the principal housing financier, the National Housing Trust has provided more than J$ (Jamaica dollars) 41.5 billion[15] in mortgages since 1990. Additional support has come from Jamaica's credit unions, building societies, and the private sector in the form of loans, and from local government through subsidies. Despite these large sums dedicated to housing finance, the majority of the poor remain unable to benefit. The National Housing Trust has not met low-income groups' needs, even though they originally were conceived as the main target of the trust. One of the principal reasons is the inability of such individuals to meet the requirements to qualify for a mortgage. Indications are that less than 10 percent of Jamaicans has sufficient income to qualify for private sector mortgages to purchase the cheapest units available (Klak and Smith 1999). This situation is compounded for those low-income women who work in the informal sector and, therefore, are not registered with the trust. These financial constraints that the poor face increase the likelihood that they will purchase property in areas that pose an environmental hazard (for example, areas prone to flood damage).

There is a considerable lack of community participation in planning for housing and in mechanisms for continuous revision of housing policy and programs in Jamaica. Despite several attempts at interagency cooperation, land and housing development programs and plans of action have not made provisions for community involvement in local development initiatives. The 1957 Town and Country Planning Act mandates community involvement within the land development process, but this has not been enforced at national, local, or community levels. The absence of updated planning legislation has resulted in a fragmented approach to sustainable land-use planning. Without changes in the legislative and institutional frameworks guiding land management, particularly at the policy level, community involvement will never translate into social and economic benefits for all communities.

As with participation and continuous revision, the redress mechanisms in the housing sector remain underdeveloped. Concerns about lack of housing provision and poor-quality housing are raised either directly with the housing provider or with a political representative. There is no formal mechanism through which citizens may redress grievances. In instances where there has been a breach of contract in delivery of housing (usually between private developers and citizens), individuals have the option of bringing the matter before the courts for settlement. Expensive and slow, this mechanism does not recommend itself to many Jamaicans.

Health Care

Since 1962, the Jamaican health system has operated on the principle that every citizen is entitled to a basic level of care. Although not officially stated in the Constitution, the legislative framework for the health sector mandates protection of several key areas in health: children's health, maintenance of vital statistics (Immunization Act and Registration [Births and Deaths] Act), and general public health (Public Health Act). Outside of these national laws, the health system is driven by the international agreements to which Jamaica is a signatory. Policy shifts since independence have resulted in significant changes to health care: expansion of the sector in the 1970s; severe contraction in the 1980s that forced many Jamaicans to turn to private care; reform in the 1990s, including cost sharing in public hospitals; and today, the removal of user fees for primary and some secondary health services.[16] Examined closely, however, largely economic and political positions—rather than a rights mandate or objective assessments of the population's health—have driven these macrolevel shifts.

Based on a primary health care model and the principle that no citizen should have to travel far for health services, Jamaica's extensive network of hospitals and health centers, nongovernmental organizations, and private providers is designed and delivered to ensure that all Jamaicans have access to basic care. Although it is largely a public sector system, private providers play a considerable role in health care delivery. In contrast to primary care, significant access challenges remain for secondary and tertiary care. With only two specialty hospitals serving the needs of the 2.6 million Jamaicans, there are obvious concerns about capability to provide effective care beyond basic levels. Access is affected not only by institutional capacity, but also by affordability. Since 2007, user fees at public hospitals have been removed in two phases, first for children and then for adults.

Notwithstanding system improvements, increased use of public health provision, and removal of user fees, the health system continues to function below the level of demand. Although visits to private facilities cost an average of 40 percent more than visits to public facilities and only 18.4 percent of Jamaicans had private insurance, data from 2006 reveal that among those who sought medical care, 52.8 percent received private care and 41.3 percent received care in the public system. In addition, because the public system chronically suffers from drug shortages, most Jamaicans must seek their medications from the private system (data from various years of the JSLC). Moreover, fee removal for children in 2007 led to a sharp increase in the number of children coming into the public system and showed the inability of hospitals to handle increased demand with existing resources. The fact that the government did not support fee restructuring with measures to manage the expected influx of patients or cultivate new funding sources to replace previous user fees demonstrates that the system changes more likely were undertaken to increase political capital and popular support than to improve service access to promote equitable citizenship.

The quality of health care in Jamaica can be assessed broadly by the health status of the population. Measured in accordance with several international indicators, that status generally is regarded as good. Like many developing countries, Jamaica has made the epidemiologic transition from infectious and communicable diseases to chronic lifestyle diseases. Although macroeconomic indicators appear satisfactory, they mask a story of limited capacity; insufficient medical personnel; and chronic shortages of pharmaceuticals, diagnostic instruments, and treatment equipment in the public system.[17] These quality concerns contribute to Jamaicans' decisions to use private rather than public providers when feasible. In addition, violence, other preventable injuries (motor vehicle and domestic accidents), and HIV/AIDS place significant pressure on the already severely burdened public system. The J$2.2 billion annual cost to treat violence-related injuries (Jamaica, Ministry of Health 2002) imposes a severe burden on the system because resources that could have been used for other types of care

are diverted to treat these injuries. The health system has yet to adjust to the HIV/AIDS challenge; however, because of outside assistance, this has not hindered service provision. Currently, the Global Fund to Fight AIDS, Tuberculosis, and Malaria largely administers and finances HIV/AIDS prevention and care in Jamaica, so the Ministry of Health neither has been forced to adjust its annual budget to cover the substantial costs nor has developed mechanisms to recruit and oversee appropriately skilled staff. Eventually, these services are expected to be integrated into the Jamaica-managed system. But because the Global Fund operates parallel with (not under) the auspices of the Ministry of Health budget, the full financial and resource impact of the HIV response has not been felt by the public health system. When this funding arrangement changes, Jamaica will have to find its own resources to support current programs. In addition, the ministry is not gaining the requisite experience to take over management of these services when Global Fund support ends.

Jamaica currently offers measures for financial protection in the health system to facilitate access to direct medical care and supplementary services, such as medication. User-fee removal, as discussed above, has reduced monetary obstacles to public care. Given that capacity has not been augmented and the lost revenue has not been replaced, however, it is likely that the care itself will suffer, material shortages will increase, and even financial protection will have a reduced impact if citizens continue to patronize the private system. In response to the shortage of pharmaceuticals in the public system and their high cost in the private system, in 2003 the government developed the National Health Fund. Institutionalized by the National Health Fund Act and financed through an excise tax on locally produced cigarettes and an annual contribution of J$500 million from the consolidated fund, the National Health Fund provides subsidized medication from participating private pharmacies to registered beneficiaries diagnosed with conditions covered by the program. This is an example of the health system using a strategy advocated by the social guarantees approach. With increasing enrollment levels, however, the fund also has suffered from a decline of almost 50 percent in revenue because of falling cigarette production and sales. If the country is to continue providing such financial protection and to maintain the level of benefits over the long run, the government must find additional ways to sustain resource inflows.

The Jamaican health system has demonstrated its flexibility for community participation and continuous revision, responding to a changing health profile and the occasional outbreak of infectious diseases. This flexibility reflects the system's ability to respond continuously to its environment and to revise its operations accordingly. Initiatives centered on relatively new health concerns, such as HIV/AIDS and violence, have reflected well on the system's continuous revision practices. In response to changing demand over the past several decades, the sector has shifted significant resources into preventive—rather than only curative—aspects of health and well-being. At the same time, the scope for citizen participation in health care design and delivery remains limited in Jamaica. Design largely is seen as an "expert" activity with little input from the general population. Most citizen engagement takes place as part of behavior change programming centered on HIV/AIDS prevention, healthy lifestyle promotion, child health, and violence prevention.

Although driven by the principle of health care as a citizen's right, Jamaica's health system does not have clearly defined institutional and administrative mechanisms to offer opportunities for redress if the right is not fulfilled or is abused. Jamaica has no specific legislation to protect citizens from medical negligence, and all challenges must be pursued under the regular common-law provisions dealing with the tort of negligence. With no constitutional provisions establishing a right to health care, citizens lack legal recourse for care denied in public health facilities. Medical negligence cases brought to court are notorious for their low rate of success because the health sector is perceived as a "closed shop" in which medical professionals are unwilling to give evidence against colleagues. Where such action has been pursued successfully, it is at considerable expense and usually requires the expert testimony of medical professionals from outside Jamaica.

The Social Guarantees Framework Applied to Jamaica

The most groundbreaking changes have taken place within the education system through the current Education Transformation process, which has launched unprecedented citizen participation in sector reform. In health, fee restructuring that began in 2007 offers the possibility of eliminating exclusion based on financial resources, and the pharmaceutical program offers great possibilities for implementing a system of social guarantees. In the housing sector, the existence of the National Housing Trust, although not yet accessible to all Jamaicans, represents a unique government investment in citizens' shelter. Although the country is demonstrating adherence to some of the cornerstone principles of the social guarantees approach, there remain severe challenges that must be addressed decisively if universal entitlements are to be fulfilled. Therefore, the education, housing, and health sectors remain solidly at a preguarantee stage.

In education, the guarantee of access may be most clear cut and closest to realization. Supported both by policy and legislation, the government has signaled in concrete terms its commitment to protecting and upholding the right of every child to go to school. Where there were inadequate provisions for the cohort of youth ages 17–18, the government is taking steps to provide places for them, and it is working to extend the compulsory education provision from age 16 to age 18. Quality undoubtedly is the area in need of most reform if the right to quality basic education is to be realized in Jamaica. The inequity in the quality of education is demonstrated by the disproportionate failure rates on the secondary-level terminal examinations of students from upgraded high schools versus rates from the traditional high schools. To make advancements achieving inclusive citizenship, this is one area of the education system that requires immediate attention. In terms of redress, a key mechanism by which to achieve social guarantees—the Education Transformation accountability framework—is the first step to providing citizens with accountability mechanisms. The facts that it does not appear to have advanced beyond the preliminary stages and that, even when fully implemented, it would not offer a path for families to redress poor performance show that redress mechanisms remain underdeveloped. Ultimately, the final outcomes of this transformative initiative remain to be seen, and the current uncertainties about its future management increase the uncertainty of the final achievements.

In housing, although there is no explicit right established in the Constitution, Jamaica has recognized the human need for shelter. Even with a range of programs developed over 50 years, huge deficits remain and much of the population is in need of social housing intervention. The state's and private providers' patent shortage of capacity to meet shelter and financing demands, and the limited capacity of the population to carry mortgages, have been barriers to any movement beyond the preguarantee stage. A lack of creative approaches to increasing the accessibility of mortgage financing also prevents expansion of this sector. The poor most of all remain vulnerable to informal and unlicensed schemes because of their lack of success in participating in the formal market. The lack of affordable options leaves the poor more prone to purchase property in environmentally hazardous regions. Housing requires a long-term commitment, and if a right to shelter is to be realized, the sector must no longer be treated as separate from an overall sustainable development framework.

Instead, it must be examined in the context of overall economic factors, such as employment and income-earning opportunities.

Finally, the current capacity of the health care system falls short of satisfying the overall demand for care. As a result, almost half of the population seeks ambulatory care and pharmaceuticals from the private sector. With the elimination of user fees, Jamaica took an important step toward removing obstacles to care and guaranteeing access. However, using a social guarantees lens shows that when provisions for universal access are implemented without attention to their impact on capacity or effectiveness, such provisions may have the unintended result of reducing real access and overall service quality. The health system's lack of mechanisms for redress means that patrons of the system have no official way to resolve problems if service quality truly has diminished. Therefore, unless there is significant expansion in public sector capacity in critical areas, health policy makers cannot contemplate guaranteeing health service delivery. Moving to a level of guarantees would entail attention to expanding capacity and establishing effective mechanisms for redress.

In all three sectors, changes in fee structures for accessing services have been linked with economic and political shifts. Social guarantees require that social service delivery be guided objectively by the rights of citizens, not subjected to political manipulation. In Jamaica, changes such as removing fees for health and education and providing social housing often are announced as part of political campaigns rather than being grounded in and guided by data and rigorous policy analysis. In the health and education sectors, cost-sharing regimes have been introduced and subsequently removed, on the basis of a confluence of economics and political expediency. To the credit of the delivery system, providers have shown the flexibility to respond to these changes and continue to provide the general population with a menu of basic services.

High levels of crime and violence undermine the prospect of realizing social guarantees in Jamaica. Violence contributes to uncertainty and prompts reluctance to invest in and grow the economy, thus perpetuating dismal economic performance and the flight of human resources. Social capital, critical to vibrant citizen participation and pursuit of redress, also is crippled in an environment of fear and violence. Although Jamaica has shown its ability and willingness at legislative, policy, and institutional levels to uphold the basic rights of its citizens, it has much work to do to provide a stable social and economic environment in which it can pursue a system of guarantees.

The Case of St. Kitts and Nevis:
Improving Quality through Regional Policy Coordination

St. Kitts and Nevis is a relatively new democracy in its 25th year of independence from British colonial rule. A twin island state located in the eastern Caribbean, the country has a combined territory of 104 square miles, and a population of 49,393 (circa 2005), approximately 75 percent on St. Kitts and 25 percent on Nevis. The year 2005 was a turning point for the country: shifts in the global sugar trade, falling market prices, and increased production costs compelled the country to abandon its centuries-old sugar monoculture, therefore closing its state-run sugar industry and laying off 12 percent of the country's workforce (OECS Secretariat 2005). This transition to economic diversification and nontraditional economic development mainly focused on services changed the country's cultural, economic, and social landscapes.

Facing deteriorating fiscal performance, failed countercyclical fiscal policies, and devastating physical hurricane damage incurred between 1995 and 1999, St. Kitts and Nevis embarked on a fiscal adjustment program in the late 1990s. Although the reforms realized tangible successes in 2003 and 2005,[18] the fiscal situation has remained unstable because of the continued high ratio of debt to gross domestic product (GDP).[19] This weak fiscal position threatens macroeconomic stability and hinders the country's ability to improve resource allocation for such essential services as education and health care as it seeks to meet national, regional, and international economic and social development imperatives. In addition, as has been the case for many of the smallest island nations, globalization has placed unprecedented strain on St. Kitts and Nevis's economic infrastructure and, therefore, on the services it can provide to its citizens. By participating in regional approaches through CARICOM, the Caribbean Examination Council, and the OECS, St. Kitts and Nevis has had access to innovative strategies that have enabled the country to adapt to these challenges and to benefit from new collaborative opportunities.

Despite guaranteed access to primary, secondary, and tertiary education and to basic health care, and despite high levels of income per capita, poverty remains a persistent problem in St. Kitts and Nevis. A fiscal 1999/2000 poverty assessment, funded by the Caribbean Development Bank and conducted by the regional firm Kairi Consultants Ltd., indicated that approximately 30.5 percent of the population on St. Kitts and 32 percent on Nevis are poor, with more than half on both islands under

25 years of age. In addition, it was found that more than 94 percent of poor people were employed and working, indicating an issue not so much of unemployment as of a discrepancy between wages and the cost of living (Kairi Consultants 2001).

To assess the degree to which current practices in education and health provision contribute to realizing citizens' rights in St. Kitts and Nevis, the matrix in table 8.2 encapsulates the advances and lags that exist in those two sectors.

Education

With its introduction of universal access to secondary education in 1967, St. Kitts and Nevis was one of the region's earliest pioneers in education at that level. The federal government guarantees primary through secondary education, with strong measures of financial protection at the tertiary level. Modeled after the British structure, education in St. Kitts and Nevis primarily is provided through the public system and is based on a governing philosophy of "Education for All" (St. Kitts and Nevis, Ministry of Education 2007). The Education Act, first enacted in 1967, provides the normative foundation for both public and private education in the nation. The act guarantees free, mandatory primary and secondary education to all children between the ages of 5 and 16, and it has been subject to multiple revisions to manage breaches in access, quality, financial protection, and citizen participation. The revised Education Act of 2005 explicitly establishes a rights-based mandate to provide education for all children across the Federation. This act provides the legal and operational frameworks for rights-based developments and policies in education and outlines the general goals and objectives of the system in this new context. These actions have come close to guaranteeing full access, financial protection, and continuous revision of basic education, but issues of equitable quality—especially in the secondary education system—are still to be resolved.

Since the inception of the universal system of education in 1967, access to both primary and secondary education has expanded significantly. Whereas near-perfect completion rates (99 percent)[20] have been demonstrated at the primary level, the greatest obstacle to the continuous provision of basic education has been the lack of mechanisms to retain students in secondary school. All students automatically are transferred from primary to secondary levels, with placement determined by students' individual achievement data. Despite this automatic transfer, absolute enrollment in public secondary schools dropped by 10.8 percent between

Table 8.2. The Social Guarantees Matrix for Education and Health Care in St. Kitts and Nevis

Subguarantee	Education (primary and secondary)	Health care
Access		
Are the beneficiaries and services clearly defined?	Yes; the Education Act of 2005 guarantees free and mandatory education for children aged 5–16. Tertiary education—free but not obligatory—is part of the public system.	Yes; definition is through the National Policy on Health and Cabinet policy decisions.
Are there institutional procedures for monitoring access?	Parents are responsible for attendance of the students. In addition, each school has a school attendance officer appointed by the Child Welfare Board.	Community health nurses make weekly visits to elderly or disabled people and new mothers; the School Health Program ensures immunizations and medical and dental checkups.
Are there legal or institutional mechanisms that ensure nondiscrimination in access to services?	The Education Act	Human Rights Desk for HIV/AIDS ensures nondiscrimination for HIV/AIDS patients.
Are services guaranteed for the amount of time needed?	Yes; there is universal coverage until age 16.	No; medication is guaranteed to patients with HIV/AIDS and other chronic diseases.
Is there a maximum waiting period for receiving a service?	Basic education services should be made available between the specified ages (5–16).	No
If the service is unavailable within the prescribed waiting period, what is a guaranteed alternative (in the same time period)?	There is no guarantee in the same time period. However, an alternative vocational curriculum has been developed for high school students.	There is no guarantee in a specific time frame.
Quality		
Are there clear quality standards?	Yes; standards are established by the national CDU and the Ministry of Education, in accordance with subregional standards set by the OECS.	No; processes are under way: community health operations manual being revised; main hospital in a process of accreditation.

(continued)

Table 8.2. The Social Guarantees Matrix for Education and Health Care in St. Kitts and Nevis (continued)

Subguarantee	Education (primary and secondary)	Health care
Are programs being evaluated on a regular basis?	For primary school, the CDU administers end-of-year exams. System is being initiated in some secondary schools, but generally there is no secondary school monitoring other than final CXC and CCSLC exams.	No; prior to the accreditation process, little attention has been paid to evaluation.
Are standards and evaluation results communicated effectively to the public?	Yes; CXC results data on the national level are presented in the media by the Minister of Education.	No, because there is no regular mechanism for evaluation of services.
Financial protection		
Do beneficiaries need to contribute to the cost of service?	There are no tuition fees. Public child care/preschool centers charge a fee. Parents are responsible for purchase of uniforms, textbooks, and food and for some transportation costs.	They are responsible for some fees (as outlined under the "Access" subguarantee). User fees are charged for specialist care.
Are services accessible to beneficiaries who cannot contribute to the cost?	Yes; but accessibility is not guaranteed. The Ministry of Education provides some assistance, and private scholarships are available for uniforms and school supplies.	Yes; accessibility is through exemptions and fee waivers on request through the Ministry of Social Development. Elderly people and school-age children are exempt from fees.
Is this information communicated effectively to the public?	Yes; communication is through community social workers or requested from the Social Assistance Department and the Ministry of Education.	Criteria for fee exemptions can be unclear and may depend on a Social Assistance Department referral.
Redress and enforcement		
Are there mechanisms allowing citizens to claim adequate provision of the services guaranteed?	Yes; but they are not implemented fully. The Education Act asserts appeals can be made to the Education Appeal Tribunal, which is not yet operational. Judicial channels fare is available but rarely used.	The Human Rights Desk for HIV/AIDS is the only formal mechanism. However, its effectiveness has not been evaluated.

(continued)

Table 8.2. The Social Guarantees Matrix for Education and Health Care in St. Kitts and Nevis (*continued*)

Subguarantee	Education (primary and secondary)	Health care
Continuous revision and participation		
Are there mechanisms that allow for continuous improvement of services?	Yes; review is provided for every 5 years.	No; the National Health Plan (set for the period 2007–11) likely will be revised in or prior to 2011.
Do civil, parent, or community organizations have a concrete role in the design, implementation, and monitoring of programs?	Yes; the Education Act of 2005, Division 2. However, parents and civil society have not had an active role in designing and monitoring quality standards.	There are no defined guidelines for participation. A multisectoral and multidisciplinary group was formed to produce the National Health Plan for 2007–11.
Which law or institution guarantees citizens' involvement?	The Education Act of 2005 outlines the roles and responsibilities of parent-teacher associations, parents, NGOs, and civil society.	None

Source: Authors' compilation.
Note: CCSLC = Caribbean Certificate of Secondary Level Competence; CDU = curriculum development unit; CXC = Caribbean Examination Council; NGO = nongovernmental organization.

2001 and 2006, and completion rates are recognized anecdotally as significantly lower than enrollment (although there is no official tracking system for secondary completion or dropout rates). If policy design is to improve dropout rates, particularly among low-income youth, careful consideration should be given to issues of distance, social factors, curriculum, teacher training, and student learning.

The lack of any official recognition for graduating from secondary school, regardless of whether one passes the CSEC examination, has been blamed for diminished secondary enrollment and completion rates. Annually, 25 percent of secondary students—the majority of whom are those students streamed into lower achievement bands—are not permitted to sit for the CSEC exam, and that reflects the influences of a system based mainly on student academic abilities and a curriculum not geared to prepare them sufficiently. With no other means to recognize their investment in secondary education, these students have had little incentive to complete their studies. Therefore, although the government has guaranteed all students access to education through the secondary level for the greater part of four decades, the reality has been one in which a fourth of students cannot access the secondary-level certification required to secure postschooling employment. To begin addressing this inequity, the Ministry of Education, with the assistance of regional institutions such as the Caribbean Examination Council and Jamaica's Human Employment and Resource Training (HEART) Trust/National Training Agency, introduced a new program—the Caribbean Certificate of Secondary-Level Competence—and a Caribbean Vocational Qualification. Although their impact is still unknown because the first class graduated only in June 2008, these initiatives potentially could better guarantee educational access for all citizens.

Historically, gender and cultural biases bred into the education system have truncated teen mothers' education and have contributed to increasing secondary-level dropout rates. In the Federation, teens make up 20 percent of new mothers. Before a 1997 Cabinet decision established every young woman's right to return to school after a pregnancy, many young women would not have had the opportunity to complete their education. This policy underscores the rights enshrined in the United Nations' Convention on the Rights of the Child, to which St. Kitts and Nevis is a signatory. Although this has been operational in St. Kitts for years, it was not implemented in Nevis until 2007. The resistance that Nevis still experiences at all levels of the education system has forced the Nevis Island Administration to revisit this decision. Notwithstanding, anecdotal evidence from St. Kitts indicates that this policy has helped remove a significant barrier that previously stymied young women wishing to finish their schooling.

The government of St. Kitts and Nevis has acknowledged that, although the system offers high levels of access to education, quality remains a fundamental challenge. At the secondary level, quality of instruction is far more uneven than at the primary level, and the unevenness is exacerbated by the early streaming of students into higher- or lower-ability bands. Other than creating alternative certifications for secondary education, the Ministry of Education has not undertaken a concerted effort to address instructional inequality. Poor academic instruction is one of the main causes of overall quality weaknesses in St. Kitts and Nevis's educational system. The demand for teachers outstrips the rate of training, so untrained teachers continue to be recruited. Probably because of the government's strained finances and the level of remuneration offered to teachers, regional recruitment has not emerged as a solution. Employing skilled and qualified instructors remains a challenge, but over the past three years the country has been trying to address this dearth of teachers by instituting new training programs and expanding training opportunities. In addition, regional and subregional collaboration has provided needed assistance to the small island nation—particularly initiatives that mitigate the high costs associated with any large-scale reform. With the adoption of the OECS Education Reform Strategy (2000–11), St. Kitts and Nevis has new strategic tools to sharpen its focus on key education development requirements and better carve out its own road map for its educational system's progress.

Financial protection for education is offered through a variety of public and private programs. There are no tuition fees required for enrollment in the Federation's 24 primary and nine secondary public schools, and textbooks for primary and secondary school are free of charge. Through the Social Assistance Act, the state must provide uniforms to indigent students. There are many supporting programs that together succeed in reaching a large number of children who need financial assistance to remain in school. Information about government-sponsored assistance programs is disseminated to the public regularly. Although there are various financial assistance programs for education, there is not a single, unified, state-regulated system of financial protection for education that takes into account all component costs. The advantages of such a unified system would be more transparency and, therefore, more public confidence that each student's costs would be covered, even if he or she is not among the very top academic achievers.

The Federation's 2005 Education Act and the OECS's subregional Education Reform Strategy 2010 ("Pillars for Partnership and Progress") encourage participation in the education system by parents, students, civil society, and other relevant stakeholders. The Education Act underscores continuous revision, which requires that the education system be reviewed every 5 years to ensure ongoing development and to assess progress in policy areas. The Curriculum Development Unit also commits to revising the curriculum every 5 years by gathering input from teachers, parents, and employers through national consultations. The process by which the government developed the revised Education Act (2005) and the Green Paper on Education Development and Policy (2007) incorporated feedback from citizens, even though the framework for such participation was not defined clearly. Students' and parents' main forums for involvement are through parent-teacher associations (PTAs), the National Council of Parent-Teacher Associations, and student councils.

A mechanism for redress in the form of an education appeals tribunal has been envisioned in the Education Act of 2005 to hear and decide appeals or to act as a mediator. Several years after the proposal, however, the tribunal is not operational. In reality, citizens may submit formal complaints directly only to school principals, the Chief Education Officer of St. Kitts or of Nevis, and the Minister of Education. There is, however, no established mechanism for following up these claims. There is a strong emphasis on quality in the policy discourse, but the mechanisms for redress focus mainly on disputes over disciplinary issues or dissatisfaction over issues related to homeschooling or to children with special needs. The latter areas are important, but it is jarring that no mention is made of a formalized system of redress that addresses shortcomings affecting learning outcomes, especially for the 25 percent of students who are placed in lower streams and are at high risk of dropping out.

Health Care

Regional and global norms have increased St. Kitts and Nevis's attention to the realization of social and economic rights in the health sector. Although neither the 1976 Health Act nor the 1983 Constitution explicitly guarantees a right to health care, Article 24 of the United Nations' Convention on the Rights of the Child—to which St. Kitts and Nevis is a signatory—mandates that the state provide children with basic health care, combat disease, and ensure appropriate prenatal and postnatal care for mothers. Until recently, St. Kitts and Nevis's normative framework for health had not kept pace with changes within the country's epidemiologic profile. Through regional efforts and the development of a new St. Kitts and Nevis Strategic Plan for Health (2008–12), St. Kitts and Nevis is adapting to better reflect current health priorities. The financial framework for public health care has remained relatively constant over the past decade—at 7 percent of total expenditures between 2005 and 2008 and at 6 percent of GDP since 2002.

The cornerstone of St. Kitts and Nevis's health care system is primary health care delivery. The principle of inclusive access is made operational through a decentralized network of primary health centers that provides facilities within easy reach of all communities. Nurses make up the main medical staff, with general practitioners consulting between two or three different centers. Therefore, the twin islands' citizens are considered to have full access to basic care. This claim cannot be substantiated by hard evidence because there are no mechanisms to track service usage or the number of people who attempted to but could not receive care. In contrast to primary care, secondary health services remain highly concentrated in urban settings. Hospitals and private care practitioners function as the key providers of secondary health services. Medical specialists are limited at health centers. For example, each island has only one obstetrician/gynecologist available to pregnant women seeking care. Although the government is credited with providing universal access to medical care, the limited numbers of primary care physicians at health centers and of available specialists are themselves a potential breach of access.

St. Kitts and Nevis has invested in improving quality as well as quality standards in recent years, both independently and through regional collaboration. As its first comprehensive approach to health care, in 2008 the Federation launched the Strategic Plan for Health (2008–12), the main thrust of which is to secure improvements in the quality of care by reorganizing the health sector's structures and financing mechanisms. In addition, the country is involved in the first accreditation of one of St. Kitts and Nevis's major hospitals (Joseph N. Francis Hospital) and a revision of an *Operations and Procedures Manual for Community Health*. St. Kitts and Nevis's health care has been bolstered further by participation in regional initiatives—most notably, CARICOM's Caribbean Cooperation in Health Initiative and 2007 Summit of Ministers of Health, and the Pan Caribbean Partnership Against HIV/AIDS. These regional efforts have served to highlight weaknesses in domestic health policies and practices and to provide a platform for uniform action to address them, helping St. Kitts and Nevis strive for better articulated services and systems of delivery. Even with these important improvements, St. Kitts and Nevis faces a lingering weakness: the system lacks uniform service standards and mechanisms for monitoring compliance. As a result, there is no consistent way to evaluate the current reforms.

Service in all community health centers is free, irrespective of insurance. Through regional cooperation within the OECS, St. Kitts and Nevis has been able to guarantee free medications and better care for patients with HIV/AIDS and other chronic diseases. Realizing this guarantee has become possible with the establishment of a new central purchasing mechanism based in the OECS Secretariat, which procures costly drugs (such as antiretrovirals) in bulk. Assisted by the Clinton Foundation, this initiative has lowered drug costs for individual countries, thereby enabling the smallest member-countries—such as St. Kitts and Nevis—to provide these life-sustaining medications to patients at no or low cost. Although strong financial protection mechanisms are in place for basic care, chronic noncommunicable diseases, and HIV/AIDS-related specialty care, it remains unclear if other secondary-level treatment is financially accessible to the population, especially those who are poor but not deemed indigent by the

Ministry of Social Development. Given the government's commitment to leaving no one behind with respect to quality health care, further research on epidemiologic priorities and reasonable annual ceilings for out-of-pocket expenses per individual or household would diminish the risk of citizens' exclusion from the system. The financial protection system in education and health is not uniform for both St. Kitts and Nevis. Some policies and programs in place for St. Kitts may not be in place for Nevis, and vice versa. Therefore, there is a need for greater synchronization between the islands.

The only formal mechanism for redress in the health sector is the Human Rights Desk for HIV/AIDS, which was created to address and report discrimination and breaches in services. At the community level, the mechanism appears to be underused, largely because of a perceived lack of confidentiality. The likelihood that patients will use the Human Rights Desk is diminished further because of cultural issues (such as fear of consequences associated with admitting to HIV/AIDS-positive status) and administrative issues (such as the existence of minimal regulations that would make effective the decisions issued by the Human Rights Desk). Overall, the current lack of concrete service standards or regular monitoring mechanisms for compliance means that citizens and service providers do not have an objective, agreed standard by which to measure the adequacy of service provision and, therefore, determine the need for redress. The Patient Charter now being written outlines the rights and responsibilities of patients and has the potential to become an efficient basis for redress. But the charter will be effective as such only if the institutional channels and responsibilities for making and resolving claims, and for enforcing decisions, are made explicit and are communicated widely to the public.

The diverse actors involved in the committee responsible for St. Kitts and Nevis' Strategic Plan for Health, including representatives from the ministries of health, sustainable development, and finance; from nongovernmental organizations; and from faith-based groups demonstrates the government's interest in and commitment to principles of civic participation in health services. At the same time, there has been no direct citizen participation in health policy formulation. Continuous revision is underdeveloped in the health sector. The primary piece of legislation on health policy—the Public Health Act of 1976—has not been revised since its creation. That lack of revision has undermined the legitimacy of progressive institutional and programmatic arrangements, such as the Human Rights Desk for HIV/AIDS, the enhanced protection for patients with chronic noncommunicable and communicable diseases, the financial assistance to the elderly, and other reforms that have reflected either changes in the epidemiologic profile of the population or a move toward a rights-based discourse on health policy.

The Social Guarantees Framework Applied to St. Kitts and Nevis

Over the past years, St. Kitts and Nevis has adopted key programmatic and policy reforms to improve access, quality, and financial protection in education and health—some developed within the country and others facilitated by regional and subregional collaboration. In education, the country has instituted reforms to reduce early school abandonment and increase the likelihood that school graduates will transition successfully to tertiary education and have greater labor mobility. In the health sector, bulk drug purchasing at the subregional level has allowed increased access and financial protection by enabling free, universal provision of medications for chronic and noncommunicable diseases and HIV/AIDS.

Even in the context of such pioneering policies and programs, however, the continued deterioration of the country's fiscal performance has created challenges that could threaten St. Kitts and Nevis's ability to consolidate gains and address emergent needs. In addition, social sector decisions largely have been Cabinet policy decisions rather than legislated initiatives and, therefore, can be reversed from government to government. The current lack of coordinated service standards and monitoring and evaluation systems for the health sector has weakened the country's capacity to provide quality services equitably. All of these factors may contribute to the present environment in which recipients of free medical care or educational scholarships commonly are chosen at the discretion of individual government officials. Social guarantees necessitate that citizens have access to vehicles through which they can seek redress for rights and entitlements not sufficiently fulfilled. In St. Kitts and Nevis, although limited mechanisms for redress are in place, the current use of piecemeal standards (of which many service providers and beneficiaries are unaware), combined with the accepted practice of discretionary decision making, mean that citizens now lack an established standard on which to base their grievances. To the country's credit, St. Kitts and Nevis is in the midst of addressing this systemic deficiency by working to align national standards and procedures with those established at the regional level. St. Kitts and Nevis now has the platform from which to establish and abide by clear quality standards in all areas of public services.

The Social Guarantees Approach:
Prospects for Jamaica and for St. Kitts and Nevis

The social guarantees framework of analysis shows Jamaica and St. Kitts and Nevis to have implemented advantageously social policies and programs that foster inclusion and equity. The analysis by subguarantee for the education, housing, and health sectors shows that the greatest strengths are in the access subguarantee. Opportunities for participation appear to be improving, particularly in education. Although redress still is not standardized in the social sectors, over the past decade both countries have introduced new accountability mechanisms through which citizens may seek to rectify wrongs in service delivery.

Even with these important achievements, however, Jamaica and St. Kitts and Nevis continue to face systemic obstacles to guaranteeing the overall fulfillment of citizens' social and economic rights. A significant hurdle results from the countries' not equally emphasizing legal, institutional, programmatic, and financial commitments when developing or reforming policy. As discussed in the introduction, just as the social guarantees perspective gives equivalent weight to the five subguarantees to determine overall fulfillment of rights, it is essential to attend equally to the four fundamental spheres that constitute policy planning. In Jamaica, for example, the government's programmatic decision to remove health care user fees now threatens the quality of services because measures were not taken at the same time either to replace lost resources or to increase capacity to manage new patients previously unable to patronize the system. In St. Kitts and Nevis, financial allocation without official programmatic commitments has had the reverse effect because educational scholarships and other financial assistance can be distributed on the basis of administrators' discretion rather than according to firmly established criteria.

Social guarantees require that citizens have access to vehicles through which they may seek redress for rights and entitlements not sufficiently fulfilled. In recent years, both Jamaica and St. Kitts and Nevis have introduced redress mechanisms for specific programs, but generally there are no concrete ways for citizens to hold service providers accountable. And the concern goes beyond the limited availability. What is more serious is that one finds evidence of minimal citizen demand for such mechanisms. This low demand may be attributed, in part, to the overall lack of awareness of human rights in Caribbean societies. Citizens who are not aware of their economic and social rights also are not likely to expect there will be ways to address impediments to the fulfillment of those rights. From a social guarantees perspective, therefore, it would be important not only to implement redress mechanisms systematically, but also to build capacity and raise citizens' awareness about their rights and the delivery of inclusive social policy.

Given current realities, social policy in Jamaica and in St. Kitts and Nevis can be understood as follows: in Jamaica, even with strong normative underpinnings, social service provisioning has proved susceptible to the vicissitudes of the economic and political environment, expanding in times of growth and contracting in leaner times; in St. Kitts and Nevis, a social welfare strategy prevails above a universal, rights-based approach in the legal and institutional design of social service provision. Therefore, carrying out a social guarantees approach to social policy in Jamaica and St. Kitts and Nevis would imply

- the articulation of rights and entitlements in the legal and institutional framework and coordination of these commitments with the programmatic and instrumental and the financial frameworks
- coordination of existing programs so as not only to promote and support the goals of universal access, quality, financial protection, redress, revision, and participation, but also to ensure that these aspects of service delivery are available and protected for all citizens
- wide public initiatives to raise citizens' awareness of their rights and entitlements
- the development and operationalizing of channels for redress.

Both Jamaica and St. Kitts and Nevis have considerable work to do to provide a stable social and economic environment in which to pursue a system of social guarantees. At the same time, the fact that both countries continue to prioritize promoting greater inclusion and equity in social policy delivery through national and regional reforms reveals key first steps being taken in this direction.

Notes

1. These nations include Antigua and Barbuda, The Bahamas, Barbados, Belize, Dominica, Grenada, Jamaica, St. Kitts and Nevis, St. Lucia, St. Vincent and the Grenadines, and Trinidad and Tobago.
2. At the time of the 2000 population census, Jamaica's population was 2.68 million (Statistical Institute of Jamaica 2001).

3. Findings are from various years of the Jamaica Survey of Living Conditions (hereafter, JSLC).

4. The level of poverty in Jamaica has fallen substantially since 1995. In 2006, it was at 14.3 percent, the lowest in more than a decade and down significantly from levels in excess of 25 percent in the early 1990s (2006 JSLC).

5. The 1994 Reform of Secondary Education program established a common curriculum between grades 7 and 9 to ensure that all students across the secondary system were following the same curriculum at the first cycle of the secondary system (Davis 2004).

6. The foundation of the process comprises the Education Act (1965), the National Education Policy (2001), and an extensive legal and instrumental framework for early childhood education, including a draft National Plan of Action for Early Childhood, an Early Childhood Commission, and an Early Childhood Policy. The legislative framework comprises the Early Childhood Commission Act of 2004 and the Early Childhood Act and Regulations enforced in 2005. These laws are bolstered by the broader Child Care and Protection Act of March 2004.

7. Ruth Morris, senior director, Modernization Unit, Jamaica Ministry of Education, in discussion with the author, February 15, 2008, Kingston, Jamaica. In 2007, Portia Simpson Miller, then prime minister, announced that eight high schools were constructed, resulting in 7,685 spaces in addition to 15,000 spaces created in 2006. An additional four new high schools were introduced in the 2007/08 academic year. This construction was financed in part with funds taken from the National Housing Trust. That funding was not applauded by all because it was argued that the trust's funds never should be used for anything other than providing housing benefits to contributors.

8. These are developments that have not met established planning standards, such as required building setbacks, height, and minimum floor area ratio. Examples include squatter settlements and nonconforming built developments.

9. As it relates to shelter delivery, the policy specifies that measures and programs be formulated and implemented (1) to offer affordable access to land and legal security of tenure as strategic prerequisites for a variety of uses by the majority of people; (2) to develop sustainable human settlements and increase the provision of adequate shelter for all, in both urban and rural areas; and (3) to rationalize property taxation and expenditure measures to enhance greater efficiency in the provision of necessary services.

10. Land tenure arrangements in Jamaica operate at two levels: a legal system of both freehold and leasehold, which often conflicts with what is considered to be a traditional system based on the categories of family land, bought land, and inherited land (McHardy 2007).

11. In 2006, approximately 68.0 percent of rural households owned their houses, compared with 47.7 percent of households in the KMA (2006 JSLC).

12. According to the 2001 population census, Jamaica had close to 20,000 squatters living in more than 500 squatter communities. Squatting usually is defined as living in residential areas that have developed outside the legal planning system.

13. For example, in the KMA where household ownership is 47.7 percent, formal land tenure status among these households is far below 10 percent because of increasing housing densities and limited land space in the region (2006 JSLC).

14. Habitable rooms include those used for general living purposes such as sleeping and eating. Excluded are garages, kitchens, bathrooms, toilets, verandas, passageways, and the like (2006 JSLC).

15. A billion is 1,000 millions.

16. The financial framework for health care is funded through a combination of public and private resources, with the government providing the largest share—for example, approximately J$20 billion in 2006, with almost J$15 billion going directly to health service delivery. The overall public expenditure on health fell from 6 percent in the 1990s to less than 4 percent in 2003 (Planning Institute of Jamaica 2005).

17. Dr. Karen Lewis Bell, senior director, Jamaica Ministry of Health, in discussion with the author, February 12, 2008, Kingston, Jamaica.

18. The positive changes include increased government revenue collection, control of noninterest expenditures, and a notable reduction in capital expenditure.

19. See chapter 2 of St. Kitts and Nevis, Ministry of Sustainable Development (2006).

20. Osmond Petty, permanent secretary of education, St. Kitts and Nevis, in discussion with the author, February 13, 2008, Basseterre, St. Kitts.

References

Davis, Rae. 2004. "A Transformed Education System." Final Report of the Task Force on Education Reform, Kingston, Jamaica.

ECLAC (Economic Commission for Latin America and the Caribbean). 2007. "Sustainable Development from a Human Rights Perspective and the Challenge It Represents for the Caribbean SIDS." Discussion Paper for the First Meeting of Ministers and High Authorities of Social Development of the OAS, Reñaca, Chile, July 8–10.

Fox, K., and G. Gordon-Strachan. 2004. "Assessing the Level of Birth and Birth Registration in Jamaica." Unpublished manuscript, Planning Institute of Jamaica, Kingston, Jamaica.

Jamaica, Ministry of Health. 2002. "HIV/AIDS/STI National Strategic Plan 2006–2009." Kingston, Jamaica.

Kairi Consultants. 2001. "Country Poverty Assessment Report, St. Kitts and Nevis, Volumes 1 and 2." Tunapuna, Trinidad and Tobago.

Klak, Thomas, and Marlene Smith. 1999. "The Political Economy of Formal Sector Housing Finance in Jamaica." In *Housing and Finance in Developing Countries,* ed. Kavitta Datta and Gareth A. Jones, 59–74. London: Routledge.

McHardy, Pauline. 2007. "Squatting in the Context of Low-Income Housing Delivery." Unpublished manuscript, Kingston, Jamaica.

Mycoo, C. n.d. "Urbanisation and Housing in the Caribbean." Unpublished manuscript, University of the West Indies, Kingston, Jamaica.

OAS (Organization of American States). 2008. "Institutionalization of Social Policy in the Caribbean." Presentation prepared for the First Meeting of Ministers and High Authorities of Social Development of the OAS, Reñaca, Chile, July 8–10.

OECS (Organization of Eastern Caribbean States). 2002. *OECS Human Development Report 2002: Building Competitiveness in the Face of Vulnerability.* Castries, St. Lucia: OECS.

OECS Secretariat. 2005. "St. Kitts and Nevis: Retraining the Sugar Workers." Castries, St. Lucia.

Planning Institute of Jamaica. 2005. "Jamaica Human Development Report 2005: Global Challenges, a World of Opportunities." Kingston, Jamaica.

———. 2006a. "Economic and Social Survey of Jamaica." Kingston, Jamaica.

———. 2006b. "Transition of Jamaican Youth to the World of Work." Kingston, Jamaica.

———. 2007. "Economic and Social Survey of Jamaica." Kingston, Jamaica.

Statistical Institute of Jamaica. 2001. "Jamaica Household Census." Kingston, Jamaica.

St. Kitts and Nevis, Ministry of Education. 2007. "Green Paper on Education Development and Policy: Raising the Standard, Maximizing Resources, Aligning with Regional and Best Practices—Promoting Success for all (2007–2017)." Basseterre, St. kitts.

———. Ministry of Sustainable Development. 2006. "Adaptation Strategy in Response to the New EU Sugar Regime—2006–2017." Basseterre, St. Kitts.

Wynter, Robert. 2009. "Education Transformation Going Nowhere." *The Jamaica Gleaner,* January 18.

CHAPTER 9

Moving toward Comprehensive Social Policy: The Case of Uruguay

Fernando Filgueira, Sophia V. Georgieva, and Sergio Lijtenstein

Uruguay is the country with both the greatest political stability and the strongest welfare tradition in the Latin American and Caribbean region. It has been committed to achieving universal access to basic social services, while actively pursuing goals of economic growth. Uruguay has the lowest inequality in the region (with a Gini coefficient of 0.43), and one of the highest rates of social cohesion as measured by the number of citizens who perceive a high degree of solidarity in the society—76 percent, according to the opinion survey Latinobarómetro in 1996–98. An active society and strong middle class contribute to its high rates of social and human development. Latinobarómetro also shows that Uruguayans have the highest percentage of citizens (39 percent) who express trust in the way government resources are spent. Uruguay's society is relatively ethnically homogeneous, compared with other countries in the Latin American region—88 percent white, 8 percent mestizo, 4 percent Afro-Uruguayan, and a practically nonexistent Amerindian population.[1]

In the early 1900s, Uruguay made significant progress with regard to labor rights (for example, children under the age of 13 were not eligible to work, and those under 19 years of age worked a shorter number of hours) and limited the maximum number of working hours per week. By the 1930s, Uruguay was considered a modern country, with a well-established middle class and a high level of literacy. Uruguay's political institutions have enjoyed support and legitimacy from its citizenry, with the exception of a 12-year military regime (1973–85) that was ended by the financial and economic crises of the 1980s (World Bank 2008b).

Social policy in Uruguay traditionally has reflected a system of entitlements based on an old corporatist welfare model. Under this model, all social security provisions (old-age pension, unemployment benefits, or others) were associated with the salary of a formally employed head of household. The rest of the population, generally women and children, received social benefits through their affiliation with the breadwinner of the family. Thus, from the 1930s[2] until the late 1990s, social protection in Uruguay evolved to respond to the needs of an industrial society with a stable family structure. In this society, the benefits associated with employees in the formal sector were able to reach the majority of the population.

In the past decade, however, because of a combination of factors—globalization, more flexible labor markets, and less stable family structure—new social risks have emerged. These risks include income instability, polarized fertility trends (much higher fertility rates in the low-income strata compared with those in the high-income class), residential segmentation, and increasing inequality in the quality of services and opportunities for accessing them. This new reality has called for reforms in social policy to reestablish equity among various groups.

Three main socioeconomic groups can be distinguished in Uruguay's current fragmented society, from the point of view of income opportunities and social protection: (1) retired citizens and some public sector employees who rely on benefits from the state (approximately 32 percent of the population); (2) a high-income group of young and middle-aged citizens, many of whom are employed in the private sector and have few or no children (roughly 28 percent of the population); and (3) a vulnerable group with fewer two-parent families than those in the other two groups, many minors, and few opportunities for formal employment with accompanying state benefits (about 40 percent of the population). A marked generational discrepancy in poverty also has emerged. The likelihood of children under age 5 being poor is about 10 times greater than that for seniors above the age of 65 (Filgueira et al. 2007).

The much greater likelihood for youth to be in a situation of poverty than for elderly citizens to be in such situation is partly a result of the new social realities described above—namely, globalization, more flexible labor markets, higher degree of informality, and growing segmentation among socioeconomic groups. In addition, however, it can be attributed partly to an obsolete social protection "contract" that, on the one hand, allows for organized participation and contains strict guarantees for formal employees and pensioners, and, on the other hand, has a weaker structure and allows almost no participation in decision making for vulnerable families with children. Civil agency and the capacity to organize and claim rights generally are high in Uruguay, but only for certain segments of the population. Middle-class groups—mainly formal employees and the retired—traditionally are the most mobilized and exert the most pressure on social policy decisions. Given the new social challenges in the country, brought about by external and internal factors, it is necessary to redesign the existing social contract and social programs to consider the interests of the more vulnerable and less organized groups.

With the election of President Tabaré Vázquez in 2005, the government renewed its emphasis on social issues and looked for innovative alternatives to improve social policy, mainly as a result of the deep economic recession of 1999–2002 during which 30 percent of the population fell into poverty, unemployment rose to 20 percent, and real wages declined sharply (IMF 2005). The Ministry of Social Development was created in March 2005 to develop and implement cross-sectoral policies for youth, women, the elderly, people with disabilities, and families living in poverty and extreme poverty. A central part of the ministry's assigned mandate was to coordinate the executive branch's actions in the areas of nutrition, education, health, housing, work, social security, nondiscrimination, and the enjoyment of a healthy environment with a focus on vulnerable groups. It also was responsible for implementing the National Social Emergency Program (PANES, by its Spanish acronym). The Ministry of Social Development chairs the Social Cabinet, which comprises the ministers of economy and finance, education and culture, labor and social security, public health, housing, territorial mapping, and environment. The Social Cabinet's main functions are to develop integrated social policies, define priorities, and ensure their funding.

Prior to 2005, a system of family allowances was the primary social protection mechanism in place, implemented by the Social Insurance Bank of Uruguay. From its creation in the first half of the 20th century until 1999, the family allowances system was limited to formal employees and to an amount equivalent to 8 or 16 percent of the minimum wage.[3] Between 1999 and 2004, the program was extended to all families living in poverty, regardless of their affiliation with the formal labor market. Expanding coverage by law, however, did not expand it in practice because the implementing institution, the Social Insurance Bank, had relied exclusively on formal labor registries to identify eligible families. Its capacity to reach out to poor households involved in the informal sector or those who lacked proper identity documents was low.

In 2005, the government established the 2-year National Social Emergency Program to respond more successfully to the emerging social risks. Without being explicitly rights based, PANES contributed to fundamental rights principles of nondiscrimination, enhanced equity, increased access, and public awareness of entitlements. It created a separate registry of beneficiaries and began a community outreach campaign to identify eligible households; incorporated an employment program (Trabajo por Uruguay) and a "poverty-exit" program (Rutas de Salida); and established food, education, and health assistance. It also increased the base amount of the family cash allowance to the equivalent of the minimum wage. PANES was one of the few programs in the world that incorporated poverty-exit strategies in its design by trying to increase opportunities for the poor in many aspects, including the enhancement of their social capital (World Bank 2008a). With its new approach of reaching out to more poor families and combining cash transfers with other social benefits, PANES served as a pilot project for a comprehensive social policy model in Uruguay. After the program ended in 2007, this approach was continued and expanded under the current Plan for Social Equity, which has been in force since January 2008.

The Move toward a Comprehensive Model of Social Policy

Since 2005, with the creation of the Ministry of Social Development and the beginning of PANES, the Uruguayan government has clearly indicated its intent to transition to a more integral model of social policy that goes beyond income support and reaches out to all vulnerable citizens.

Using a social guarantees template as a framework of analysis, table 9.1 summarizes some of Uruguay's evolutionary advances in social protection policies—from a system of family allowances and the 2-year social emergency program to the integrated Plan for Social Equity. The social guarantees-based analysis examines more closely four basic components of this policy evolution: access, quality, opportunities for redress, and civil participation and potential for continuous revision.[4]

The notion of social guarantees (described in detail in chapter 2) refers to a set of policy mechanisms that determines specific entitlements and obligations related to fundamental rights and ensures the fulfillment of

Table 9.1. The Social Guarantees Matrix for Social Protection Policies in Uruguay

Subguarantee	Family allowance program	PANES	Plan for social equity
Access			
Are the beneficiaries and services clearly defined?	Yes—all families in poverty and extreme poverty with minors under 18 years of age; defined conditional cash transfers	Yes—all families in poverty and extreme poverty; cash transfers plus six more services (food, education, housing, and health assistance, professional training, and basic skills training in language and math)	Yes—all families in poverty and extreme poverty; a wider variety of services offered to different groups of beneficiaries, depending on their projected needs[a]
Are there institutional procedures for monitoring access?	Yes; procedures are through the Social Insurance Bank, but they are designed only for formal employees.	Yes; procedures include the former family allowances system mechanism, civil society, and door-to-door visits.	Yes; procedures are based on the PANES experience.
Are there legal or institutional mechanisms that ensure nondiscrimination in access to services?	No	Yes; there are mechanisms in the sense that the program reaches out to more households who previously were unaware of these benefits or who lacked the proper documents.	Yes; mechanisms are based on the PANES experience.
Are services guaranteed for the amount of time needed?	Yes; they are guaranteed as long as the family continues to meet eligibility criteria.	Yes; they are guaranteed within the two years of program operation.	It depends on the program. The employment assistance program is a one-time assistance. Income support continues as long as the person or household remains eligible.
Is there a maximum waiting period for receiving a service?	No	No	No

(continued)

Table 9.1. The Social Guarantees Matrix for Social Protection Policies in Uruguay (continued)

Subguarantee	Family allowance program	PANES	Plan for social equity
If the service is unavailable within the prescribed waiting period, what is a guaranteed alternative (in the same time period)?	None	None	None
Quality			
Are there clear quality standards?	The cash transfer amount is clearly established,[b] but it is set at a level that does not allow for any tangible impact on poverty or extreme poverty.	The cash transfer amount is set at a higher level.	Quality indicators have been elaborated, but not concrete guidelines/standards for each program.
Are programs being evaluated on a regular basis?	No	An evaluation was conducted at the end of the program.	A system of social indicators recently was created and is maintained and updated by MIDES.[c]
Are standards and evaluation results communicated effectively to the public?	No	Yes	The MIDES social indicators and results are available to the public through the Internet.[c]
Redress and enforcement			
Are there mechanisms allowing citizens to claim adequate provision of the services guaranteed?	Yes; they are available through the Social Insurance Bank; they are limited to formal sector employees.	Yes; they are available through MIDES.	Yes; they are available through MIDES.
Continuous revision and participation			
Are there mechanisms that allow for continuous improvement of services	No; but the laws that regulate the program were revised in 1995, 1999, and 2004.	No; it was only a 2-year program.	No

Do civil, parent, or community organizations have a concrete role in the design, implementation, and monitoring of the program?	No	The role is not in the design, but in the implementation of PANES.	A social council of civil society representatives has been established in each province. However, the role of these councils in relation to the plan's programs is still to be defined.
Which law or institution guarantees citizens' involvement?	None	None	Guidelines for civil participation exist, but they are not strictly linked to particular roles and programs of the plan.

Source: Authors' compilation.

Note: MIDES = Ministry of Social Development; PANES = National Social Emergency Program.

a. For example, the National Youth Institute, together with civil society and local governments, coordinate programs for vulnerable youth (Arrimate—Espacio Joven, Rutas de Salida Adolescente, and Amplifica Tu Voz).

b. Decree-Law 15.084 of 1980, modified by Law 16.697 of 1995, Law 17.139 of 1999, and Law 17.758 of 2004.

c. The Social Observatory of Programs and Indicators is available at http://mides.redirectme.net/mides/portalMides/portalMides/portal.php (accessed March 19, 2009).

those obligations on the part of the state. The four subguarantees examined in table 9.1 (access, quality, redress, and participation/continuous revision) refer to policy mechanisms created to realize each of these respective areas. They have been supplemented by a set of questions to describe more precisely the policies or instruments sought with regard to each subguarantee. In this way, the social guarantees matrix gives a basic overview of the progress and shortcomings of each subsequent social protection policy in Uruguay with regard to reaching the stated goal of enhancing opportunities for all.

Two overarching characteristics of the evolution of social protection policy that have affected all four subguarantee areas are (1) the comprehensive nature of PANES and the Plan for Social Equity, going beyond conditional income support; and (2) the institutional arrangements that enable the Ministry of Social Development to coordinate a truly multisectoral policy for social inclusion.

With the introduction of PANES, the Ministry of Social Development aimed to complement and upgrade the system of family allowances by incorporating many elements of a rights-based perspective—namely, a commitment to monitoring access for all eligible families, the engagement of civil society, and a mixed basket of transfers and services to ensure more effective assistance than that granted by the traditional family allowances program.

In terms of access, PANES has been highly effective, reaching out to 80–90 percent of its target population. This success relates strongly to the mechanisms of ensuring access that the program adopted (Rofman 2007). The formal process of collecting application forms from eligible beneficiaries was accompanied by house-to-house visits to verify the information and, most important, to increase awareness about social security options and identify eligible families who had not applied. Many eligible families who had not registered in the regular family allowances system were identified as a result of PANES. Creating an institutional mechanism to be responsible for outreach and promotion of the program (through the Ministry of Social Development), in addition to the Social Insurance Bank, incorporated new methods of outreach to citizens and, thus, opened more opportunities for inclusion. Even though PANES was highly successful in terms of targeting, its eligibility criteria excluded a number of extremely poor citizens: 30.2 percent of the extreme poor who applied for the program did not receive the cash transfer benefits (Reuben, Miodosky, and Watanabe 2008:2).

The Plan for Social Equity offers an even more decentralized model with more services and more institutions responsible for their delivery; hence, it has added flexibility to increase access to the services offered. However, if the various programs within the plan fail to define and promote their services clearly in line with the needs of their targeted population, there is a risk that many citizens will be excluded from the plan's benefits. For instance, it was difficult for men who had to decline higher-paid temporary work to attend the PANES employment program training classes. To ensure better access, the Plan for Social Equity needs to look into more flexible access requirements to prevent the exclusion of temporary workers.

The quality of social protection mechanisms—understood as their adequacy in terms of reducing poverty and enhancing equal opportunities—has improved progressively between the family allowances and PANES models. On the one hand, this increase in quality is inherent in the way in which beneficiaries were selected and the amount of cash transfers was determined under PANES. Beneficiaries were identified as those whose income fell below the average value of the basic food basket as of March 1, 2005, and families below the minimum value of the poverty line. This group included all families in the poorest quintile of the population. Beneficiaries received a monthly transfer of Ur$1,360 (approximately US$55) for the 2 years of the program, adjusted every 4 months according to the Consumer Price Index (Filgueira et al. 2007). The Plan for Social Equity envisions yet another increase in the amount of family allowances, including a higher allowance for families with high school students to encourage their retention in the school system.

On the other hand, the quality of the social protection system is raised by the multisectoral nature of PANES and the Plan for Social Equity. PANES was designed as a social emergency plan integrating seven assistance programs—for income, food, housing, education, health, and employment support, as well as a program to overcome poverty (Rutas de Salida). The current plan encompasses an even wider network of programs and services, including a set of structural reforms and long-term strategies outside the realm of social programs (such as tax reforms that aim to address social inequality). This trend toward a comprehensive social protection model suggests a new vision for measuring quality and impact as well—one that includes increases in self-esteem, personal and professional skills, and the social network of citizens, in addition to income variation.

According to a World Bank evaluation in 2007, PANES's cash transfer component proved to have a significant impact on extreme poverty.

The rate of extreme poverty in 2006 was 2.87 percent; estimates suggest it would have been 4.87 percent without the program. The impact on poverty, however, was lower: 27.4 percent of the population was living in poverty in 2006, compared with an estimated 27.8 percent if the program had not existed. The employment component of PANES registered impacts in areas such as self-esteem, language and teamwork skills, increased social capital, and citizens' awareness of their rights—all factors that augment one's chances for reintegration into the labor market and that cannot be recorded by means of traditional indicators as number of people trained or number of training courses delivered (World Bank 2008a:4).

Defining innovative indicators for the quality and impact of the various components of the social equity plan and setting up a regular monitoring and evaluation mechanism would be two of the greatest challenges for Uruguay's progressive social policy scheme. In a recent evaluation of PANES, the Ministry of Social Development conducted a special study on a sample of low-income families to complement the national household survey. The study recommended that the sample for all household surveys be modified to include more households in poverty than normally would be represented in a national survey (World Bank 2008a). Incorporating these lessons in the monitoring and evaluation of the Plan for Social Equity will make it more likely to achieve its goal of enhancing equity between the poor and the rest of society, and will allow for adequate supervision of the quality of the plan's programs.

As of November 2008, the Ministry of Social Development has launched a publicly accessible database of social indicators (Social Observatory of Programs and Indicators), consisting of a system of social indicators and a repository of social programs.[5] The first contains more than 100 indicators relating to poverty, nutrition, health, education, livelihood security, gender, and demographics, among others. The second is an information system on the performance of social services. The Observatory was created and will be maintained jointly by the Ministry of Social Development and the Social Sciences Department of Uruguay's state university, Universidad de la República.[6] These measures, however, relate more to the transparency and accountability of social policies than to the quality of service provision. The enforcement of clear quality guidelines for each program of the social equity plan is still pending.

The ability to claim and redress one's entitlements is a key element of any policy aiming to protect and fulfill citizens' rights, such as the new social equity plan. Administrative channels for redress were present both under the old family allowances system and under PANES through the Social Insurance Bank and the Ministry of Social Development, respectively. In PANES, concrete actions and time periods were specified for resolving claims related to its cash transfer program: citizens had 10 business days to file their claims with the Ministry of Social Development and the ministry had 30 business days to issue a decision; if the decision was favorable, benefits were to be restored to the claimant automatically. The Plan for Social Equity would require a more sophisticated system of redress, or a redesign of the ministry's responsibilities to act as a channel of redress for various programs. Redress under the social equity plan can be advanced further by considering an independent administrative body or branch of the Ministry of Social Development to carry this mandate.

PANES also was progressive in terms of civil participation. Various nongovernmental organizations assisted in its implementation, even though civil society was not involved in the initial design of the program. When the Ministry of Social Development was created, local social councils were established as well, in recognition of the importance of local government and civil society involvement in the functioning of the new ministry. Their objectives were to ensure that social programs such as PANES incorporate more feedback from citizens and to establish a civil mechanism for monitoring the programs.

The analysis from a social guarantees perspective demonstrates that adopting an integrated approach to social policy has the potential to enhance equity and inclusion by enabling greater access for the poor and providing more adequate benefits to contribute toward overcoming poverty. At the same time, integral social policies require more sophisticated mechanisms to ensure that all of their programs take into account appropriate access mechanisms, that all citizens have the necessary information and resources to claim their benefits, and that the relevant impact indicators are being monitored.

Institutional Arrangements:
Role of the Ministry of Social Development

A comprehensive social policy model presupposes a more integrated institutional structure as well. Because of the large number of institutions that administer various social services within the Plan for Social Equity—from income transfers to food, health, education, labor, and housing support—the coordinating role of Uruguay's Ministry of Social Development has grown in significance. On the one hand, the ministry serves as a coordinating body for programs whose functioning requires a network of actors. Income transfer programs, for example, are administered primarily by the Social Insurance Bank of Uruguay, but they also involve the Ministry of Labor and Social Security, the Budget and Planning Office, the Ministry of the Economy and Finance, and the Central Bank of Uruguay. On the other hand, creation of the Ministry of Social Development and of the multisectoral Social Cabinet signals the government's commitment to guarantee adequate coordination of all institutions and programs, with the goal of creating an effective policy for social equity (Rofman 2007).

Through PANES, the Ministry of Social Development has begun to assert itself as a key player in defining new and more effective approaches to reducing poverty. The analysis of the different subguarantees presented above shows that the main areas of progress realized from the beginning of the family allowances system through the Plan for Social Equity—advancing access, increasing the menu of services, introducing better monitoring and evaluation methods and indicators, and serving as a channel for redress—largely may be attributed to the role of the Ministry of Social Development. The existence of a coordinating institution allows for creating links with civil society and the private sector. During PANES, those links have had a direct impact on expanding access and quality. The ministry's mandate and efficiency in serving as a hub for an integrated social policy are still to be perfected, and the consideration of a social guarantees and subguarantees matrix can provide a useful framework to that end.

Under the Plan for Social Equity, the Ministry of Social Development will be solely responsible for such programs and institutions as the Encouraging Universal Basic Education Program, Infamilia (offering services for vulnerable youth), the Institute for the Blind, and rehabilitation centers for people with disabilities. In other programs and institutions, the ministry will have shared responsibility—for example, in the food assistance program that provides to households in extreme poverty a magnetic card with which to purchase food in local stores.

The ministry has the potential not only to coordinate among all relevant sectors for a positive impact on welfare, but also to ensure cost efficiency of social policies by trying to eliminate overlap in program functions and beneficiaries. Between 2005 and 2007, for example, some families benefited from a double cash transfer—one under the family allowances program and another through the cash transfer component of PANES (the Citizen Income Program). The Plan for Social Equity will revert to a unified family allowances program that builds on the PANES experience. Although the Ministry of Social Development will assume some coordinating functions in the new plan, allowances will continue to be disbursed by the Social Insurance Bank. A similar overlap had occurred with employment promotion programs. The National Employment Union and National Employment Directorate administered programs in addition to PANES's employment initiative. The employment component of the Plan for Social Equity (Uruguay Trabaja) will link to the existing programs—for example, it will use their training services, their links with the private sector, and their accumulated research on labor market options.

In sum, a decentralized network of governmental and nongovernmental agencies—each specialized in the delivery of certain social services—is a possible institutional structure for a comprehensive social policy model, and it has many advantages in terms of the quality of services and impact on welfare. However, it is equally important to be able to set cross-sectoral priorities and to guide, monitor, and regularly revise social policies to ensure that they work toward the overall objective of a more inclusive and equitable society. The Ministry of Social Development is well positioned to perform such a coordinating function; however, its effectiveness depends on the availability of clear standards and mechanisms through which each component of the social equity plan can be monitored and assessed. These clear standards may include quality standards and standards for the selection of beneficiaries, service priorities, and channels for redress.

Finally, for an integrated social policy model to be successful, the adequate institutional arrangements have to go hand in hand with relevant fiscal commitments and with a legal framework to uphold both the institutional and financial arrangements. In the case of Uruguay, this would imply revision of an established fiscal pact that responds to the needs of vulnerable households and youth in poverty, together with the needs of former and current state employees for whom the social protection system traditionally was designed.

Fiscal Arrangements: Revising an Established Social Contract

As mentioned in the beginning of this chapter, the Uruguayan social security system is one of the oldest in Latin America and in the world. In the

1960s, it had achieved the highest level of coverage in the region. Traditionally it has consisted of a pension system and a family allowances system. However, there have been important gaps in the way norms and guarantees are structured in the two systems. Because the social protection system was built to reflect a society of predominantly formal employees, it continues to respond to the needs of the pensioners' group and public sector employees; but it has less impact on society's growing vulnerable group that includes a large percentage of Uruguay's youth. PANES and the Plan for Social Equity have sought to redesign the existing social contract in favor of vulnerable groups, and so far have been successful in bringing the state's institutional framework and content of social benefits more in line with the needs of the poor. Through the Plan for Social Equity, the government has yet to negotiate a new fiscal pact that substantiates its new commitments to the country's most vulnerable groups. This section of the chapter outlines some of the major differences in the ways in which the pension system and the family allowances system have evolved, showing a persistent discrepancy between the two in their shaping of entitlements and financial commitments.

One of the biggest differences in the ways the pension system and policies assisting vulnerable groups have evolved is the level of participation and representation achieved by each. It has had a marked impact on the effectiveness of each policy. Strong representation and political pressure by pensioners' networks brought about important and permanent improvements in the structure of the pension system. In 1989, a campaign by the Organizations of Pensioners and Retired, ratified with 80 percent general electoral approval, realized a reform by which pensions would be calculated as a function of the Median Salary Index adjusted with every salary increase of all public employees (Law 15.900). This reform was enshrined in the Constitution. By contrast, the amount of family allowances was adjusted on the basis of both the national minimum wage and the Consumer Price Index ± 20 percent, which constitutes a much less strict guarantee of the adequacy of family allowances.

The discrepancy in participation and representation between these two income transfer programs has had a direct impact on their quality—that is, on the effect they have on reducing poverty—which can be seen by the trend of high and increasing youth poverty as opposed to relatively lower poverty among seniors. Under the regular state family allowances program, families received a set sum—generally between 8 percent and 16 percent of the minimum wage. This resulted in income assistance that did not meet even the most basic needs of its beneficiaries, and surely did not promote social equity.[7] Under the pension program, however, the mechanism for calculating pensions (described above) has evolved to ensure the adequacy of pensions. The Plan for Social Equity has proposed an increase in the amount of household cash transfers and a differentiation of transfers according to the number and age of minors in the household. It also considers a system of regular reassessment of transfer amounts, although the method by which the amounts will be calculated is not codified as strictly as that of the pension system. Guaranteeing a means for continual revision of benefits is especially important in the case of social safety mechanisms because their relevance may change more frequently than do quality standards related to health, education, housing, or other services.

Redesigning the social contract with regard to income transfers would require a new fiscal pact within society as well. A combination of factors and instruments may be considered to finance long-term policies for poor and extremely poor citizens, while maintaining a viable pension system. Some options may include adjustments in the allocation of public revenues; a tax reform, as contemplated by the Plan for Social Equity; or the channeling of tax revenues from certain industries to specific social services, as Chile's Regime of Explicit Guarantees in Health has done with tobacco revenues.

Apart from increasing or reallocating resources, Uruguay's social spending could achieve a greater impact through reformulated entitlement structures. A fiscal pact generally is seen as a prerequisite for rights-based policies; however, a focus on rights in itself can facilitate the achievement of a fiscal pact. It may do so, first, by encouraging civil participation; second, by raising wider public debate on the importance of prioritizing equity and universal basic opportunities through social spending; and, finally, by creating channels for redress and ensuring that the state will be accountable for the quality impact of spent resources.

Lessons and Conclusion

Traditionally, social protection policies in Uruguay have been fragmented between a solid pension system, whose beneficiaries are strongly represented in policy decision making, and a system of family assistance that targets the most vulnerable groups but is not sufficient to alter substantially the structural factors that generate the circumstances in which they live. Since 2005, the government has adopted a new vision for social policy that reflects the new social risks and reality and attends to the needs of all citizens, regardless of their affiliation with the formal sector. The creation of the Ministry of Social Development, the National Social Emergency Program, and the Plan for Social Equity has been the main expression of this new vision. These entities progressively have introduced a more comprehensive approach to social protection, including services in multiple sectors and methods to widen their outreach to citizens in poverty.

Although this new vision for an integrated social policy notably has improved the structure of programs and benefits as well as the institutional framework to implement them, it still has not reached a sustainable fiscal agreement across social groups to consolidate the government's commitment to this new road for social policy. Establishing a fiscal pact to reflect the institutional and programmatic reforms in social protection in favor of the most vulnerable social groups, together with the appropriate legal arrangements, is one of the remaining challenges in consolidating the Plan for Social Equity.

The significance of political mobilization is well illustrated in the case of Uruguay's social protection sector. The historically well-organized pensioners' groups have managed to secure more adequate and sustainable benefits for their affiliates, while vulnerable groups of households (among whom resides a large part of Uruguay's youth) lack strong means of participating in and influencing policy. This discrepancy in participation and political influence between the two groups underlines the importance of realizing the subguarantee of participation at the national level so that social groups without strong representation in the formal political system can exert pressure for more equitable allocation of public resources.

On the one hand, it helps to identify concrete differences between the pension system and the social protection system for vulnerable groups. It helps to explain the different impact that each of the policies has had on the social and economic status of its targeted beneficiaries. These differences mostly are found in the areas of civil participation, quality, and redress. The more active representation of pension system beneficiaries in policy making has led to a more adequate structure of entitlements for them and, hence, a better quality of benefits and greater opportunity to claim and redress them. The family allowances system, traditionally designed with no civil participation, was less attuned to the needs of its beneficiaries, providing an inadequate amount of allowances and access limited to formal employees. The availability of redress mechanisms for families in poverty was irrelevant if it pertained only to entitlements not adequately structured from the beginning. In that light, the subguarantees analysis highlights more specific areas and challenges to be considered within the new Plan for Social Equity.

On the other hand, the social guarantees lens of analysis permits us to evaluate the progress and shortcomings of the already evolving social protection policy for vulnerable groups—from the old family allowances system, through PANES, to the Social Equity Plan. With their recent multisectoral focus, incorporation of more services and actors, and wider outreach to poor communities, the three policies progressively have improved quality and access to social benefits, with an overall positive impact on equity and inclusion.

Given the complex network of programs and responsible institutions in Uruguay's evolving social policy, the social guarantees analysis calls for stricter definitions of services and responsibilities in all aspects of the new and comprehensive social equity plan. In other words, it calls for an ability to translate social goals into a set of actionable mechanisms to uphold certain rights and entitlements. If such strict definition is not achieved, the citizens' awareness of existing opportunities and their access to benefits will be compromised. In addition, the analysis calls for a clear and operational monitoring and evaluation system with indicators that capture the objectives of the new plan—such as increasing the social network and productive capacities of poor people and increasing their monthly incomes. Without adequate indicators and monitoring, the quality and relevance of programs within the Plan for Social Equity cannot be guaranteed.

The Uruguayan government has taken timely measures to acknowledge the changing social reality in the country and to adapt its policies to respond to the emerging social risks. Instead of offering limited financial assistance to vulnerable groups, it has committed to a more sustainable and comprehensive social protection system that provides basic opportunities for all people who otherwise would not receive them. This universal and integrated approach has a clear objective: to help vulnerable groups exit poverty in the medium or long term. In this sense, Uruguay has advanced further than other countries in the region and the world that offer only limited income assistance that is not sufficient to transform, in a fundamental way, the life conditions of the poor. The facts that extreme poverty in Uruguay is very low (3.5 percent) and that poverty for a large proportion of households is transitional (60 percent of PANES beneficiaries held a formal sector job at some point in their lives) offer a great opportunity for social policies to help families overcome poverty and become fully integrated with the rest of society (World Bank 2008a:2). A regular assessment of the norms, institutional and programmatic mechanisms, financial sustainability, and monitoring of each program considered under the Plan for Social Equity will be essential to guarantee the long-term relevance of Uruguay's progressive social approach.

Notes

1. Statistics are from Index Mundial, http://www.indexmundi.com/uruguay/ethnic_groups.html (accessed March 18, 2009).
2. The first child welfare code in Uruguay was approved in 1934 (see Pilotti 1999).
3. It was limited to 8 percent of the minimum wage if the beneficiary's income was 6–10 times higher than the minimum salary. The allowance threshold was adjusted according to the number of dependents.
4. The analysis is based on the most current PANES evaluation and on the components and projected impact of the new Plan for Social Equity.
5. For more information, see http://www.presidencia.gub.uy/_web/noticias/2008/11/2008112804.htm.
6. The Social Observatory of Programs and Indicators is available on the Ministry of Social Development's Web site, http://mides.redirectme.net/mides/portalMides/portalMides/portal.php (accessed March 19, 2009).
7. Prior to 1970, allowances were determined on the basis of an estimate of the cost of children to the household.

References

Filgueira, Fernando, Sergio Lijtenstein, Denisse Gelber, Ruben Kaztman, Claudia Rafaniello, and Federico Rodriguez. 2007. "Una mirada desde los derechos a las políticas sociales en Uruguay." Unpublished manuscript, World Bank, Washington, DC.

IMF (International Monetary Fund). 2005. *Uruguay: Request for Stand-by Arrangement—Staff Report; Staff Supplements; Press Release on the Executive Board Discussion; and Statement by the Executive Director for Uruguay.* Country Report 05/235. Washington, DC: International Monetary Fund.

Pilotti, Francisco J. 1999. "The Historical Development of the Child Welfare System in Latin America: An Overview." *Childhood: A Global Journal of Child Research* 6 (4): 408–22.

Reuben, William, Marisa Miodosky, and Eri Watanabe. 2008. "Building on Experience: Improving Social Protection in Uruguay and the Plan for Social Equity." *En Breve* 132 (July). World Bank, Washington, DC.

Rofman, Rafael. 2007. *Las políticas de transferencia de ingresos en Uruguay: Cerrando las brechas de cobertura para ampliar el bienestar.* Montevideo, Uruguay: World Bank.

World Bank. 2008a. "*Del PANES al Plan de Equidad. Nota Técnica.*" World Bank, Washington, DC.

———. 2008b. *Realizing Rights through Social Guarantees: An Analysis of New Approaches to Social Policy in Latin America and South Africa.* Report 40047-GLB. Washington, DC: World Bank.

CHAPTER 10

A Bridge to Peace through Citizenship Building: Guaranteeing Health and Education Rights in Colombia

Flávia Carbonari and Jorge E. Vargas

Governance issues, poverty and inequality, volatile political systems, and social exclusion are general features that could be used to describe most of the countries in Latin America. In the case of Colombia, however, another key element must be added to that list: violence brought on by conflict. For almost 50 years, the country has suffered the consequences of an internal armed conflict that directly has hindered the realization of human rights and indirectly has shaped the way specific social needs are addressed.[1] This conflict, the longest in the region, has had far-reaching effects on all aspects of society. It has determined the formulation of the country's political system; influenced policy making in every sector and sphere; informed the development and growth of civil society; and exacted immeasurable economic, social, and cultural costs.

Just as conflict sets Colombia apart from its Latin American neighbors, so too do the persistence and continuity of its procedural democratic systems.[2] Key examples of this continuity include the country's maintenance of regular elections at all levels of government; its clear division of public powers; and its enactment of a new Constitution in 1991 that acknowledged the state's responsibility to provide social, cultural, economic, and political rights to its citizens. These basic forms and processes of a procedural democracy have coexisted with widespread deficits in the fulfillment of all dimensions of human rights (political, civil, economic, social, and

---

Rachel Nadelman provided significant editorial support for this chapter.

cultural) and with breaches of international humanitarian law. According to the 2006 report of the United Nations Office of the High Commissioner for Human Rights (OHCHR 2006:10), in Colombia there have been "numerous and frequent violations of the rights to life and personal integrity, freedom and security, and the right to due process and judicial guarantees." Regarding the protection and fulfillment of economic and social rights and realization of inclusive citizenship, significant disparities continue to exist in the population's income, education, and health. More than four decades of conflict and a severe internal displacement (the second largest in the world, after Sudan) have affected social investments and have led to urban influxes that severely tax education, health, sanitation, and other services. Therefore, in Colombia today there is a considerable gap between the obligations pledged by Colombia's formal democracy and the way in which these systems are put into effect for its citizenry.

Paradoxically, even when civil and political rights have been curtailed, a strong, resilient civil society has been able to flourish in Colombia. This resilience may be explained partially by the existence and expansion of formal democratic structures that have provided spaces for participation in different political spheres. In addition, the conflict itself has impelled civil society to become more vocal and active, both to support the struggle to achieve peace and to support citizens in claiming their rights where they have been stymied continually. Colombian nonprofit organizations and private foundations work across a variety of issues—from civic engagement to microenterprise and entrepreneurial development—providing technical and financial support to local communities and local and regional authorities in a search for peace, even in the midst of conflict. In this regard, it is important to highlight first the role of Colombian civil society organizations in developing peace initiatives and in strengthening democracy, diversity, and pluralism. Networks of civil society organizations, such as the Network of Initiatives for Peace and against War that spearheaded civil mobilizations for peace, provided an important platform for the development of nongovernmental organizations (NGOs) who work to transform the structural causes of conflict. Similarly, church-related NGOs—such as those linked to the Magdalena Medio Project, the Foundation Network for Development and Peace in Montes de Maria, or Caritas—have contributed to the development of strong community-based organizations and diverse alliances actively involved in the search for peace and the promotion of social and economic well-being. At the same time, many civil society organizations and private foundations are engaged in improving the economic conditions of the most vulnerable and poor sectors of society, thereby advancing the concept of respect for human dignity that enables the simultaneous integration of peace and development.

In this challenging context, it must be recognized that the country has made increasing progress in providing access to public social services to excluded segments of the population. These segments include the demobilized and the internally displaced, both direct victims of the conflict, who became vulnerable groups facing specific challenges to their incorporation into society and their receipt of rights.[3] The country has also been progressively creating and strengthening legal and administrative mechanisms that determine specific entitlements of and obligations to citizens on the part of the state. Other cultural and social rights (for example, regarding Afro-Colombian and indigenous populations) have been incorporated in legislation, policy strategies, and specific targeted programs. Improvements in civil society participation and an incipient implementation of quality standards in selected sectors may also be seen. These examples demonstrate that a rights-based approach could be applicable—and appropriate—in Colombia. Nevertheless, the context of violence, budgetary and institutional constraints, and political will poses significant challenges to the assimilation of rights principles as the basis of social policy making.

The social guarantees approach (as described in chapter 2 of this volume) seeks to define basic universal entitlements, rights, and standards and to ensure equal access to them for all citizens. That approach could provide a framework to address this fissure between formally guaranteed rights and their realization more extensively. Using the subdimensions of social guarantees previously discussed in this book, this chapter illustrates the extent to which rights-based norms and procedures have been integrated into the delivery of education and health services in Colombia. It highlights ways in which a social guarantees framework could contribute to the improvement of service delivery and the monitoring of social programs in the two sectors, exploring potential areas in which the framework could be helpful in bridging the gaps between declared universal rights and their effective implementation.

Poverty and Inequality in Colombia

High indexes of poverty and inequality often are correlated with social conflict and certainly play a key role in this case. Current estimates indicate that poverty reaches 45 percent of Colombians and extreme poverty reaches 12 percent of the population, despite significant economic growth

(World Bank 2008:7). Rural areas are the most vulnerable, with poverty at 68 percent (in 2006), compared with 42 percent in urban areas (World Bank 2008:7). There also are overwhelming disparities based on ethnic and gender differences, with Afro-Colombians (10.5 percent of the population), indigenous peoples (3.4 percent), and female-headed households disproportionately experiencing poverty. Colombia's Gini coefficient (0.57) shows that inequality within its society is even greater than the already high regional average (0.49),[4] with the poorest 20 percent of the population receiving only 3 percent of the national income. Colombia's human development index is 0.791, which situates the country in 75th place among 177 countries with data (UNDP 2007). These disparities are not properly addressed in the design of social policies.

Colombia's armed conflict is distinctive. Unlike many other internal armed struggles, it is not based on national, religious, or ethnic grievances. Its multidimensional character rests heavily on economics and power-driven issues related to social standing and ideology, as well as on control over illegal sources of wealth. Hence, although no single explanation can address fully the deep roots of the conflict, social inequities undeniably are among the key factors behind it. In this respect, guaranteeing equitable delivery of social rights, entitlements, and standards for all Colombians has the potential not only to improve delivery and monitoring of social programs, but also to benefit the country in channeling its most urgent and long-standing harm—the armed conflict. This chapter discusses the Colombian experience in that regard. It shows how participatory and accountable processes to make improvements in social policy can contribute to creating an enabling environment for dialogue among different stakeholders. By tackling some ways through which Colombia can address a few of its social problems, this discussion also suggests that progress on this front can affect some of the conflict's deep roots.

A Snapshot of Recent Social Policy

The evolution of social policy in Colombia over the past two decades illustrates a progressive movement toward the definition of fundamental rights and entitlements. The century's old Constitution—replaced in 1991—encouraged decentralization and guaranteed to everyone different levels of access to public services, such as education and health. The new political charter signaled a determined effort to find political solutions for the armed conflict through explicit objectives, such as increasing social expenditure. Article 350 of the 1991 Constitution states that public social spending has priority over any other spending. The new legislation also gave Colombia a pioneer position within Latin America, making it the country where citizen participation in government procedures and decision-making processes, beyond voting, was regulated at the national level. With the reformed regulations, citizen participation stopped being an option in local government, and municipalities no longer were able simply to choose either to disregard or to uphold the recommendations formulated by citizens present at annual meetings.

The new Constitution marked the beginning of a decade of transformations in the country. The 1990s actually may be viewed as a period that combined measures to modernize the economy and to ensure that social services would reach a larger portion of the population (Ocampo 2005). Social spending rose from 8.2 percent of gross domestic product (GDP) in 1990 to 14.4 percent in 1998. This increase was one of the steepest in Latin America, although it has not grown since that time. In 2004–05, for instance, public social expenditure represented 13.4 percent of GDP (ECLAC 2007:197).

The increase in social spending in the 1990s achieved the objective of broadening service coverage. Under the social security system, educational coverage rose from 48 percent in 1993 to 61 percent in 1997, and health coverage expanded from 23.9 percent to 57.1 percent. This process coincided with a phase of economic growth, and the human development index improved considerably—from 0.774 in 1991 to 0.811 in 1997 (Ocampo 2005:132). The 1990s were marked by an attempt to reconcile modernization with social equity and democracy.

The expansion of social expenditures in that period was accompanied by an improvement in targeting for the poorest segments of the population as a result of the concentration of spending increases in redistributive items, the allocation of transfers to municipalities where the proportion of unmet needs was the greatest, and the implementation of the Social Service Beneficiaries' Identification System (SISBEN). The system was designed in 1994, partially as a result of the decentralization of the social sectors effort that followed the constitutional reform of 1991. SISBEN's overall objective was to obtain consistent socioeconomic information on the most vulnerable groups so as to support local governments in targeting social programs and increasing their cost effectiveness. Targeted and conditional cash transfer programs were starting to become popular in Latin America at that time, and Colombia followed suit.

The expansion in coverage, however, was not enough to fill the gap left by the significant widening of the urban and rural divide, the uneven progress in modernizing urban areas, and the economic crisis that began in 1998. That crisis led to cutbacks in social public spending. Those cutbacks, coupled with the growing needs of the population, brought the expansion in coverage to a stop.

The administration of Alvaro Uribe undertook important reforms that contributed to the redesign of major social programs, reflecting a burgeoning culture of monitoring, evaluation, and control.[5] At the same time, the macroeconomic environment contributed to overall growth of the economy, and unemployment went from 15.6 percent in 2002 to 11.8 percent in 2005. In the same period, the percentage of the population living below the poverty line fell from 57 percent to 49 percent. In those three years, 8 million people were added to the subsidized system of health insurance, and education was expanded to cover 1 million new primary school students and 200,000 new secondary students (World Bank 2008:83). Significant advances were made in public safety, particularly in urban areas, and there was a significant return of some communities forcefully displaced by the conflict. The democratic security policy of Uribe's administration, geared to expanding the armed forces and state presence throughout the Colombian territory, yielded impressive results in terms of lowering indexes of violence virtually across the board.

Although national average indicators, such as those mentioned above, and targets can be helpful in guiding public policy planning and management, they do not offer a comprehensive picture of the processes of implementing social policies. Underlying aspects of these processes can affect the effectiveness and sustainability of social programs. Taking that analytical gap into consideration, the next section of this chapter explores current education and health programs in Colombia, focusing on barriers to access, quality standards, financial protection, monitoring and evaluation, redress and enforcement, and participation—all key subdimensions of the social guarantees framework.

Legal Guarantees

The social guarantees approach holds that rights and entitlements to basic public services should be defined clearly in the country's legal and institutional frameworks. Since the promulgation of the 1991 Constitution,

Colombia increasingly has been acknowledging citizens' social, cultural, and economic rights through legislation. The Constitution articulated fundamental reforms in the social sectors. It established proposals for a more inclusive and better-qualified educational system, ensuring its citizens 10 years of free and mandatory education, and declared social security a public right.

The Constitution states that the right to education needs to be guaranteed in any case, even when a child at the age of graduation from the elementary cycle has not attended school. Since 1994, other legal, institutional, instrumental, and financial mechanisms have been introduced to actualize the education guarantee. Law 115 of 1994, for instance, set the regulatory framework for the public education system, and Law 175 of 2001 defined the responsibilities and resources for the sector. Nonetheless, the legislation left space for governments to regulate public school fees, enabling them to charge those who "are able to pay." As a result, families even in the public system need to contribute with fees, tuition, and supplies, which makes primary education not free in practice.

In the health sector, the legal scenario is somewhat different. Although the Colombian Constitution does not guarantee the right to health services for all its citizens, it asserts social security as a public service and as an essential right, prescribing mandatory participation in the General System of Social Security in Health (SGSSS), created in 1993. Thus, health services are not seen as rights per se, but as free public services. According to the law, the SGSSS should regulate the basic public health services and create the conditions for the entire population to have access to a comprehensive variety of health services. The state should ensure the mandatory character of the SGSSS. The system is directed and regulated by the Ministry of Social Protection and the National Council for Social Security in Health. Other entities are in charge of vigilance and control (National Superintendence of Health), financial issues (Solidarity and Grarantee Fund), and service provision (Institutions of Health Services Provision).

Similar to the Chilean model prior to the health reform that led to implementation of the Regime of Explicit Health Guarantees,[6] the SGSSS formally is divided into two regimes, contributive and subsidized. In the former, every employer has the obligation to affiliate his or her workers with the system; in the latter, the state should facilitate the affiliation of those who are not employed or who are not able to contribute because they lack sufficient income. In 2006, according to the Ministry of Social Protection, 15.5 million people (the equivalent of 36 percent of the Colombian population) were affiliated through the contributive regime (Vargas 2007b:3). The number of people under the subsidized system is controversial. The Ministry of Social Protection estimates that 18.6 million (42 percent of the population, 63 percent of the most poor and vulnerable people) were affiliated through the subsidized regime in 2006 (Vargas 2007b:4). However, data from the National Demographics and Health Survey from 2005 (ENDS, in its Spanish acronym) show that only 12.8 million people (30 percent of the population) were affiliated through that system in 2006. This difference could be explained in part by cases of fictitious, duplicated, or noncommunicated beneficiary affiliations (Vargas 2007b:4).

In addition, there is a significant portion of the population that is not formally included in either regime of the system. During the transition process from the old system to the SGSSS, the government stated that people who were not affiliated would be assisted temporarily through the preexisting mechanism. These nonaffiliated citizens were called *vinculados* (linked). The government expected that their integration into the new system would be fast and that virtually all Colombians would be affiliated by 2000. Nevertheless, to this day a number of people—20 percent, according to the Ministry of Social Protection, and 32 percent according to ENDS—remain *vinculados,* and it is common to hear about a "*vinculado* system." There are no available data on how many of these people have actual access to health services or how many are excluded partially or completely (Vargas 2007b:4).

Finally, there is also a small segment of the population (3 percent) affiliated through special regimes that have been maintained as exceptions to the SGSSS for historical and political reasons (military forces and police, workers from the national oil company, and former employees of the extinct state company of ports, for example). Thus, despite the normative guarantee secured by the law that created the SGSSS, universal coverage does not exist in practice. Instead, four different types of rights regarding social security in health coexist: those of the contributors, those of the subsidized, those of the linked, and those of the people affiliated with special systems.

In sum, the discussion of education and health in Colombia from a sub-guarantees perspective shows that the country is well advanced in the legal domain: rights and entitlements generally are defined clearly. Minimums of access are regulated and well established in specific laws and norms that guarantee universal, equitable, and nondiscriminatory provision. In practice, however, several institutional, instrumental, and financial gaps remain, preventing all citizens from gaining access to good-quality social services in an equal manner. Some of these gaps will be discussed in detail below.

Opportunities and Barriers

Another fundamental principle of the social guarantees framework is that rights, entitlements, and standards should be delivered equitably and on a universal basis. Normative advances in the education sector in Colombia have been progressive in that respect. They have set administrative procedures, enhanced the attention to certain social groups, and created minimums of coverage and quality. Enrollment in public primary and secondary schools increased from 7.8 million students in 2002 to 9.2 million in 2006. Nearly one-third of the new students came from lower-income groups. As a result, literacy rates improved significantly, reaching 93 percent of the population in 2006 (Vargas 2007a:4).[7]

However, universal access to these minimums has yet to be realized fully. Twenty-two percent of children ages 5–6, 8 percent of those ages 7–11, and 15 percent of those ages 12–15 were not attending school in 2005 (Vargas 2007a:4). This means that 1.2 million children did not have access to the mandatory elementary and primary education guaranteed by law. Thus, in practice, the 10 years of mandatory education enshrined in the Constitution are not realized fully for everyone. Insufficient educational supply (that is, number of schools, teaching resources, and teachers), lack of resources to afford services, and social factors such as internal displacement and child labor somewhat explain this gap. Administrative conditions are also a key factor. In several municipalities, complex processes of registration and enrollment, long waiting lists, and the requirement of civil registration operate as significant barriers to access.

The most prominent barrier to access to primary and secondary education in Colombia is financial. Sixty percent of the poor are younger than age 18 and, therefore, are entitled to coverage in the system. However, many children are not able to attend school because of their families' economic situations and inability to afford such costs as transportation, school supplies, and uniforms. Others need to start working early in life to help with the family income. Some estimates show that almost 1.5 million children ages 7–17 work in Colombia, 90 percent of them in the informal sector (Vargas 2007a:14). Those identified as poor through SISBEN are eligible to receive subsidies to help cover monthly school fees, tuition, and supplies. But citizens are not well informed of this mechanism for financial protection. Scholarships also exist, but they are based on merit and usually exclude the most economically vulnerable students.

The necessary resources to realize the aforementioned guarantees in education are formalized by law. The national Constitution created a General System of Shares that concentrates the resources the central government transfers to states and municipalities to finance social services. This system declares that 58.5 percent of the resources should be directed to education. With a constitutional reform approved in 2007, the Constitution now states that the amount of funds dedicated to education, health, and basic sewerage coming from the General System of Shares should be increased annually according to the inflation rate for that year plus 4.0 percentage points in 2008, 3.5 points in 2010, and 3.0 points each year between 2011 and 2016. Between 1993 and 2001, total public expenditures for education increased from 2.8 percent to 4.5 percent of GDP. According to a decennial plan for education, this proportion should have been raised to 6.5 percent of GDP in 2005, but that goal has not been achieved to this point. In addition, the allocation of resources to education is misbalanced geographically, discriminating against some regions (Vargas 2007a:49).

In terms of institutional design, there is no unified and overarching educational system that could coordinate both public and private providers to guarantee universal provision of the mandatory education. Not having such a coordinating entity generates significant disparities between the public and private systems with regard to most subguarantees, especially access and quality. In general, the private educational system is used by people with higher and middle-level incomes, and the public system is used by lower-income groups. When the poorest families in major cities do not find schools in the public system, they send their children to private schools that generally are informal and characterized by having low fees and the lowest quality levels. Education authorities have distinct relationships (orientation, financing, supervision, vigilance, and so forth) with institutions and representatives of the public and private systems. Quality of service provision differs significantly as well, as demonstrated by the results of examinations taken by children in these different schools. Furthermore, not all schools in the public system and the low-level private system meet the standards of infrastructure, personnel, and management set by the Minister of Education.

Disparities in access to education based on other factors, such as area of residency and ethnicity, also exist. There is a clear difference between continued school attendance in urban areas and in rural areas. Most Afro-Colombians and indigenous populations inhabit regions where poverty and economic exclusion are more entrenched. Illiteracy in these two groups is estimated to be twice as high as the national average (World Bank 2008). Some of the barriers to access to school in rural areas are an insufficient number of services available, the government's lack of cultural adaptation to the specific needs and environments in the rural area, the presence of armed conflict, high poverty rates, and generally lower wealth and economic activity. To deal with this problem, Colombia has created the Rural Education Program to target this segment of the population. The program has reached 27 states and 115 municipalities so far. It is based on an approach that creates incentives for local communities to design their own educational projects with pedagogic models that respond to the particularities of their environment. The program therefore exemplifies an approach that can be implemented to address problems of access and quality in areas with special circumstances.

In the health sector, access to health services varies significantly, according to different plans. The SGSSS has two plans of complementary protection: (1) the Basic Care Plan and (2) the Obligatory Health Plan. The basic plan should promote health and prevent diseases through interventions directed to the entire population—for example, through vaccinations campaigns. It also should be universal, and its services should be free. However, indicators show some problems with access to the benefits provided by the basic plan (Vargas 2007b). For example, the number of deaths resulting from malaria and dengue is still high in Colombia. Some of the issues are related to a lack of information. The obligatory plan, based on individual contributions to the SGSSS, includes full maternity health care; provision of essential medications; and disease diagnosis, treatment, and rehabilitation. Its coverage is different for the contributive regime and for the subsidized regime. Those people who are affiliated with the subsidized system have access to half of the coverage provided by the plan to those affiliated with the contributive system. That fact reveals a significant disparity in access to health services. According to the 1993 law that created the SGSSS, every citizen should have been covered by the obligatory plan by 2001. To date, that has not occurred. In 2008, the Colombian Constitutional Court ordered that the benefits of both the contributive and the subsidized regimes be unified by January 2010. The Ministry of Social Security is studying the basis of this new benefits plan.

There are also an Emergency Care Plan, an Expanded Immunization Plan, and medical attention for those not affiliated with the system. Unlike the obligatory plan, the Emergency Care Plan covers all citizens in all public and private health institutions, regardless of their ability to pay. The costs of these services are shared among several entities, and that often leads to confusion. As a result, it is common that patients seeking care are rejected or that emergency care is delayed. In the case of emergency care, the law is not sufficient to guarantee universal provision.

Medical care for people who are not affiliated with the SGSSS is provided by public health institutions or by private entities that have service contracts with the government. There is no registry that could provide information about how many of the nonaffiliated people actually have access to these services, so there are no clear guarantees or standards for this segment of the population.

The budget of the SGSSS is protected by the law, which ensures the financial dimension of the health care guarantees (if such are to be established). The Constitution declares (1) that 46.5 percent of the taxes collected in the country should be directed to education, health, and basic sewerage; and (2) that the states, districts, and municipalities should manage these expenditures. As mentioned earlier, the constitutional reform approved in 2007 established new targets for the amount of resources dedicated to these sectors and coming from the General System of Shares. Relative to GDP, the percentage directed to health and social security increased from 7.5 percent to 10.3 percent between 1994 and 1997. Since 1997, it has fluctuated around 9 percent.

Notwithstanding advances in transfers of resources that should be directed to the health sector, there are several disparities in their distribution. The division of funds allocated in each department through the General System of Shares shows that the poor population in some states receives only half the amount of transfer per capita that people in other states receive. In addition, despite the normative guarantees of the laws that regulate the SGSSS, few people benefit from the financial protection they are supposed to have under this system. According to a national poll conducted in 2005, at least 20 percent of the people who became ill looked for solutions outside the SGSSS. More than 50 percent of those who did not receive medical care stated that their reasons for not receiving it were lack of money and problems with the provider (Vargas 2007b:25). The relationship of costs borne by the people and those carried by the SGSSS is 1 to 3. Hence, as in the case of education, financial conditions work as an access barrier to health services. Even though the law states that the system will provide the institutions and resources necessary to guarantee health allowances for all citizens, the extent of the guarantee is limited in practice by families' ability to pay and by the financial solvency of the system.

As a key prerequisite for any successful social policy based on the social guarantees approach, service quality needs to be legally, institutionally, and instrumentally ensured. Standards must be defined clearly, programs evaluated constantly, and both standards and results communicated effectively to the public. With regard to this subguarantee, increasing efforts to establish standards can be seen as a promising avenue toward the fulfillment of a rights-based approach in Colombia. To guarantee and monitor the quality of education, the government created a national system of evaluation in 1998 that periodically examines learning results and determines if students are achieving the established levels of competency. These standards are measured by two examinations (known as *SABER*) taken by every student during the last year of primary education and in the middle of secondary school. In the last grade of secondary school, there is a universal state examination, conducted by the Colombian Institute for Higher Education. Despite the limited capacity of the state to design policies and strategies to improve quality based on the results of these examinations, an increasing number of schools have started to formulate institutional projects and plans to improve their services on the basis of their students' scores. The state examinations also serve the purpose of monitoring disparities in the educational system. Wealthier children, who usually attend high-level private schools, tend to get higher scores, thus reaffirming that education has not been accomplishing its role of correcting inequalities and leveling opportunities for all.

Regarding standardization of the training and technical skills requirements for professionals in the education sector, there are no formal minimum standards that would guarantee the quality of education across different types of educational establishments. The majority of nonprofessional teachers are in preschools and elementary schools. There is no connection between the policies for teachers' professionalization and preparation and the evaluation of professors or the achievements of schools and students. Nevertheless, teachers' professionalism has progressed substantially, with an increase of 376 percent in the number of teachers holding a bachelor's degree in education between 1997 and 2002

(Vargas 2007a:8). This improvement was furthered by the creation of communities and networks of teachers, as well as by the educational portal Colombia Aprende[8] and the initiative Pedagogic Expedition. In the latter of those efforts, hundreds of teachers traveled around the country to identify different teaching practices, stimulate the academic debate, and exchange knowledge and experiences. The initiative resulted in an Atlas of the Colombian Pedagogy, which provides information and classifications for the different teaching practices, according to their geographic location.

Another advance in the subguarantee of quality is the country's participation in international evaluations, which has allowed the use of another set of standards for comparison. Furthermore, each school is required to produce an annual review of its infrastructure, personnel, and pedagogic resources; and teachers are evaluated by the state every 6 years. Prizes awarded for quality and improvement also have been inducing educational institutions to pursue improvement plans. Notwithstanding the challenges that remain to be overcome in other subguarantee levels, Colombia presents an illustrative case of instrumental policies adopted to advance the quality of the guarantee of education rights.

Attempts to decrease problems in quality by establishing standards for health services, however, have not been successful. The law that created the SGSSS in 1993 established mechanisms of control to supervise the provision of services and to guarantee quality. Nonetheless, those mechanisms have been very deficient. For example, the Obligatory System of Health Quality Guarantees was created only in 2006, and its implementation is very slow. There is no system to serve as an incentive for institutions to implement the process adequately. The first reports on this health quality guarantee system have administrative value, but have not been communicated efficiently to the public or relevant civil society groups.

The law that created the SGSSS also declares that the Ministry of Social Protection should define quality and user satisfaction norms. In addition, a decree of 1997 established that indicators of quality in the provision of health services should be defined and applied. However, that has not occurred; standards, indicators, or controls related to these issues have not been clarified to date. Thus, it is not possible to know if services have been improving or to evaluate the progress of users' satisfaction with SGSSS services. Citizens are also not informed about their rights to quality health services or about mechanisms by which to claim these rights.

Furthermore, as in the case of the education sector, the Colombian health system is very unequal in terms of quality of services received, presenting significant disparities based on whether citizens are affiliated with the contributive or the subsidized system or are not affiliated at all. Large insurance companies with high liability and investment rates and a large number of affiliates, all of which help them mitigate risks, assist the contributive regime. Small service providers—with weak structures, low solvency, and few affiliates—assist the subsidized system. As a consequence, the two regimes offer different guarantees to citizens, and quality disparities abound. This situation exposes the limitations of a system that has been conceived as a mandatory service, not as an essential right. The government had proposed to equalize the benefit plans of both regimes by 2019, but in 2008, the Constitutional Court ordered that the unification should be concluded by 2010.

This section has demonstrated that progress has been made in expanding access to services and in establishing quality standards in the education sector, but not so much in health. In both sectors, financial protection of these services is not fully realized, and disparities in access and quality among different segments of the population still exist, despite strong legislative frameworks guaranteeing universal and equal provision of services.

Challenges of Building Citizenship in a Context of Conflict

A rights-based approach to social policy is ultimately a means of building inclusive citizenship. It requires creating a social pact that, in short, is the understanding between state and citizens of the mutual rights and obligations of each in relation to the delivery of social policy. Reaching such an agreement can be especially challenging in Colombia where conflict has hindered the establishment of a dialogue between sectors of society. Hence, building inclusive citizenship through a social pact becomes very important. It serves as a window of opportunity to construct a balanced dialogue between the different actors involved in or victimized by the armed conflict, contributing to the construction of a sustainable peace. Participation, continuous revision, and redress are channels that can help guide policies toward establishing a new social pact.

The subguarantee of continuous revision and participation ensures that services are up-to-date—reflecting available resources, changing risks, advancing technology, and quality standards. It requires that citizens participate actively in the design and revision of policies, contributing to transparency, accountability, and better governance.

A system of social guarantees that can be actualized must include the participation of rightsholders in the design, implementation, and evaluation of the social guarantees and their associated entitlements. As in other countries in the region, Colombia has experienced a boom in institutions and mechanisms for citizen participation. These are important mechanisms that open channels for dialogue and feedback between public services users and providers. The increasing interest of civil society in participating in the educational process can be seen at every level. Beneficiaries can play a role at different institutional stages—from parents' associations to formal positions on school councils. The types and systems of participation established by the law enable citizens to oversee public management in its different administrative capacities. Citizens also have prompted important forms of mobilization, such as education forums. A national consultation on the new education decennial plan has been held and resulted in the mobilizing of several social actors who formulated more than 300,000 proposals. Such examples help explain Colombia's significant improvement in the Worldwide Governance Indicators' Voice and Accountability Index between 2000 and 2007—from −0.59 to −0.28, respectively (Kaufmann, Kraay, and Mastruzzi 2008).[9] Nonetheless, the country still falls short in this area when compared with the other countries in the region.

In the health sector, progress in citizen participation has been much slower. Such involvement in implementing and making decisions for health programs is not actively encouraged. There are no systematic records of participatory civil organizations or of their actions, which could be seen as evidence of their lack of importance within the SGSSS. In some municipalities and states, however, civic organizations have received ample support from citizens and local authorities. Through their negotiating capacity, they have the potential to contribute to the protection of rights and to the community participation of SGSSS affiliates.

Continuous revision, which can be enabled by monitoring and evaluation systems, is also important for strengthening governance and improving public service delivery. It has the potential to increase transparency, strengthen accountability relationships, and build a performance culture within governments that contributes to better policy making. Apart from its help with the design of new social policies, a monitoring system based on the five subguarantees can be used to evaluate and strengthen existing programs and regulations in social, legal, and political arenas. Colombia has progressed in this area mainly through the establishment of a monitoring and evaluation system called SINERGIA, which is considered one of the strongest such systems in Latin America in terms of its overall credibility and utilization. The system is used to support the government's accountability to ordinary citizens and to the Congress, and includes an ambitious agenda of evaluations for the coming years. However, it still requires greater clarity and focus of its monitoring and evaluation objectives and roles, responsibilities, and accountability. In the education sector, for example, monitoring is focused on processes and results, but not on access.

Although spaces for citizen participation have expanded in the country and mechanisms for continuous revision, such as monitoring and evaluation systems, have been gaining support, Colombia has few mechanisms for redressing unequal provision of entitlements. This lack of legal and effective means for citizens to claim their rights is one of the greatest challenges to establishing an accountable government. The state's responsibility in the matter is diluted into so many levels of institutional power that it is hard to define the responsible institution that should respond to claims of education rights violations or negligence. For instance, there is no record of sanctions applied to educational authorities who failed to guarantee minimums of coverage and quality. Without coherent supportive legislation establishing in detail the division of responsibilities for social services provision, citizens are unable to seek accountability from the appropriate institution when they think their rights are not being respected. Moreover, this legislative gap also prevents the different stakeholders (public, private, and civil and community institutions) from being aware of and prepared to deal with their own responsibilities.

The Colombian Constitution does declare that educational institutions and the Ombudsman should be responsible for promoting human rights, including the right to education. However, those agencies do not work as mechanisms for redress, but as tools for enforcement and information. The Ombudsman is responsible for educating citizens about their rights and for giving guidance on how to claim them. Upto this point in time, that entity has not managed to put a discussion about economic, social, and cultural rights into the political agenda.

The Colombian health system also has problems regarding revision and redress mechanisms. The inspection, vigilance, and control of SGSSS are focused on services (mechanisms and provision), not on rights (exercise of entitlement). For this reason, citizens usually appeal to the judicial system to claim their rights. In practice, these mechanisms of control are very deficient because the responsibilities are divided among a number of agencies and levels of power, making it hard for citizens to know which institution to approach. Furthermore, functions of vigilance and control very frequently are not separated from those of operation. Control is usually legal, financial, and operational rather than concerned with service coverage or quality.

An example of the lack of control over affiliation coverage is the fact that most Colombian municipalities do not know how many people need to be in the subsidized system and how many of them are not affiliated with the SGSSS. Also unknown is the number of people who have the ability to contribute to the system but prefer to stay out and use private health care. There are also no systematic investigations of bad practices. In addition, even though the National Superintendence of Health has powers to investigate and punish, there are no previous records of sanctions. The Ministry of Social Security has found serious deficiencies in the SGSSS information system since 2008, including a large percentage of the population in the subsidized system with no legal affiliation.

Information about the evolution of the SGSSS is minimal—published only under pressure by the authorities—and, thus, does not contribute significantly to the transparency or accountability of the system. Generally, service providers decide what kinds of information they want to make available to the public. For example, information on registered sanctions or statistics on intrahospital mortality rates are not available to the public. There are also no direct mechanisms for redressing inadequacies within the system.

In short, continuous revision and participation, which could contribute to forming a new social pact within Colombian society, have been enhanced at least in the education sector. In that area, participatory spaces have been opened, some practices have been institutionalized, and civil participation has advanced. However, citizens still need access to adequate information if a balanced dialogue is to be reached. A culture of monitoring and evaluation is developing, although systems need to be better structured. Finally, mechanisms of redress are missing, and it is very difficult to demand rights and services in both education and health.

On the basis of the concept of social guarantees adopted in this book, table 10.1 summarizes this chapter's discussion. Through answers to basic questions, it reveals whether and where Colombia currently has instruments to address the key aspects (subguarantees) of educational and health services delivery: access, quality, financial protection (affordability), mechanisms of redress and enforcement, and continuous revision and civil participation.

Table 10.1. The Social Guarantees Matrix for Health Care and Education in Colombia

Subguarantees	Basic health care	Social security in health	Education provision
Access			
Are the beneficiaries and services clearly defined?	Yes	Yes	Yes
Are there institutional procedures for monitoring access?	Yes; procedures exist for monitoring vaccination services, epidemiologic vigilance, and emergency cases; there is only partial monitoring of basic service provision of the public health.	There is incipient monitoring of service coverage and quality.	No
Are there legal or institutional mechanisms that ensure nondiscrimination in access to services?	No	No	Yes
Are services guaranteed for the amount of time needed?	Yes	Yes	No
Is there a maximum waiting period for receiving a service?	There is no period in promotion and prevention, but it exists in some emergencies and in vaccination.	Yes; there is a period in some services, but it is not monitored.	The right to education needs to be guaranteed in any case, even when a child at the age of graduation from the elementary cycle has not attended school.
If the service is unavailable within the prescribed waiting period, what is a guaranteed alternative (in the same time period)?	No	No	No

(continued)

Table 10.1. The Social Guarantees Matrix for Health Care and Education in Colombia (*continued*)

Subguarantees	Basic health care	Social security in health	Education provision
Quality			
Are there clear quality standards?	There are none for promotion and prevention; to a certain extent, there are clear standards for emergency services; vaccination service quality standards are clear.	Yes	Yes
Are programs being evaluated on a regular basis?	Services of prevention and promotion have a weak evaluation system; vaccination services respond to international standards; emergency services are autoevaluated by the service provider itself.	Yes	Programs are not evaluated, but there are biennial standardized tests to measure academic achievement. In addition, teachers and institutions are evaluated on a regular basis.
Are standards and evaluation results communicated effectively to the public?	No	No; minimal information is available on the Web, but is not widely accessed by beneficiaries.	Yes; but information is difficult to understand and, therefore, not widely consumed by citizens.
Financial protection			
Do beneficiaries need to contribute to the cost of service?	No	Yes	Yes
Are services accessible to beneficiaries who cannot contribute to the cost?	Yes	Yes	Yes; there are partial subsidies for poor populations. Scholarships also are available on a merit basis.
Is this information communicated effectively to the public?	Yes	Yes; there is effective communication in the contributive system; but not in the subsidized system	Yes

Redress and enforcement

Are there mechanisms allowing citizens to claim adequate provision of the services guaranteed?	No	No	No

Continuous revision and participation

Are there mechanisms that allow for continuous improvement of services	Dissemination campaigns abut health care programs and plans are revised periodically; vaccination follows international standards; emergency health care is subject to national quality controls.	Services are not monitored, but administrative procedures are revised continuously. Periodically, the mandatory health plans are revised to include new and additional services.	Yes, but they hardly ever work. The national government determines quality improvement plans and strategies that are seldom applied at the local level because of a lack of incentives.
Do civil, parent, or community organizations have a concrete role in the design, implementation, and monitoring of the program?	No	Yes	Yes
Which law or institution guarantees citizens' involvement?	Law 100 of 1993	Law 100 of 1993	Law 115 of 1994 and Law 175 of 2001

Sources: Vargas 2007a:56–58; 2007b:56–60.

Conclusion

The examination of the education and health sectors in Colombia suggests that there is institutional potential and an appropriate context for implementing rights-based policies. In the legal domain, the country is well advanced. Rights and entitlements are defined clearly, and they emphasize universality and equality in social services provision. There have been significant improvements in the establishment of quality standards in education, and the results have been quite positive. Civil society has grown stronger, and participation has expanded in the design and monitoring of social programs in the area of education. There is also an incipient monitoring of coverage and quality of services in the health sector.

Nonetheless, the analysis of these two social sectors from a subguarantees perspective shows that, beyond recent improvements in national average indicators, Colombia still has several limitations to its implementation of a social policy that fulfills fundamental social and economic rights. This process becomes even more challenging in the context of conflict. Realizing social rights is mostly at a "preguarantee" stage. In the education sector, universal access to free and mandatory services, as declared by law, is limited by the lack of effective financial protection, and is influenced by weak and unclear mechanisms for redressing inadequacies within the system. Few of the existing laws stipulate in detail the institutional responsibilities and procedures for each stage of social program development. In the health sector, disparities exist in access to and quality of services. Colombians' capacity to claim improvements in quality is restricted by weak mechanisms of redress and enforcement, and citizens usually turn to the courts to claim their rights. Unlike the educational system, there are almost no mechanisms or incentives for citizen participation in the design, monitoring, or implementation of health sector policies. Thus, reducing inequalities and promoting the social and economic inclusion of vulnerable groups remain two of the country's most critical unmet challenges.

Adopting an integrated approach to social policy through a social guarantees framework has the potential to address these issues in a profound manner. First, the framework supports the building of citizenship by turning beneficiaries into citizens with rights and responsibilities who should participate in the processes of public policy design and monitoring. Adopting such an approach seems adequate in the Latin American and Caribbean region, which has been characterized as having "weak social contracts between government and citizens and little societal consensus on and enforcement of the principles of fairness and solidarity" (Glassman and Handa 2005:56), and even more so in a country such as Colombia, where the lack of dialogue among different sectors has helped perpetuate the long-standing armed conflict. Pursuing a guarantees approach to social services delivery would contribute to building peace because it requires a solid and balanced dialogue among different sectors of society.

Second, civil society is essential for the implementation of a social guarantees system. Building citizenship requires clear mechanisms for civil society participation and accountability. Colombia has made considerable advances in that respect. Strong citizenship can contribute to the sustainability of good social policies over time by enforcing both the demand for (citizens requesting) and the supply of (government complying) accountability. In Colombia, strengthening civil society participation is crucial. Pearce (2007) argues that civil participation can interrupt the intergenerational cycles of violence that are characteristic of "chronic violence" contexts, such as Colombia.[10] Contexts of chronic violence place particular constraints on citizenship, both in state-citizen relationships and in relationships between citizens. Building citizenship by establishing a social contract within society—a prerequisite for successfully applying the social guarantees framework—may help embed rights in social consciousness and practice, thereby breaking this cycle and promoting the effective (rather than the formal) exercise of voice.

Finally, the social guarantees framework assists in bridging social inequalities and ensures that the poorest and most vulnerable people have access to public services. To ensure such access, society must have in place the institutional and financial mechanisms needed to include these people in the system. Access must be of equal quality also, and the system requests mechanisms to ensure that there are no significant disparities in the quality of the services to which different groups have access. In that respect, adopting a social guarantees framework could benefit the country by pushing for clearer legal and administrative mechanisms of enforcement and redress to ensure the fulfillment of those obligations.

An analysis of formally protected social services and their functioning, according to a subguarantees framework, could be deepened and used by civil society groups and policy makers to diagnose areas that prevent social programs from fulfilling their objectives adequately and universally. Colombia could build on its general progress in the legal domain, citizen participation, implementation of educational quality standards, and expansion of coverage to include various mechanisms for monitoring access and quality, enforcing financial protection, and designing accessible channels for claiming entitlements. Improvements in these spheres would not only help the state increase accountability in its legal obligations, but also help the country move toward the fulfillment of social, economic, and cultural rights as stipulated in national and international legal commitments—and help Colombia achieve sustainable peace.

Notes

1. The beginning of the ongoing armed conflict in Colombia is associated commonly with the 1960s emergence of leftist guerrillas, the Revolutionary Armed Forced of Colombia (FARC) and the less-known Army of National Liberation (ELN). The two organizations initially pushed the government toward agrarian reform and economic and political change for the benefit of the poor and marginal sectors of the population. Throughout the years, however, both organizations evolved into military groups engaged in criminal activities, and they started resorting to force to gain territory and political power. The conflict worsened with the creation of right-wing paramilitary units—particularly, the Self-Defense Units of Colombia (AUC) —which became large, brutal, and powerful counterinsurgency forces that also indulged in human rights violations, massacres, and forced displacement of peasants they designated as subversives. The AUC fully demobilized in 2006, but remnant combatants still operate in newly organized small and regional groups under new names. Drug trafficking helped sustain both sides of the conflict. For a deeper understanding of the origins of the conflict, see Chernick (2007).

2. In an empirical investigation into the effects of political regimes, constitutional changes, quality of institutions, and social conflict on governance and on the economies of the Andean countries, Solimano (2005) finds that Colombia had the lowest frequency of new constitutions in the 20th century (just one, approved in 1991), compared with other Andean nations. According to the same study, the country had the lowest number of presidential crises in the 1950–2003 period: two crises, compared with 17 in Bolivia, 10 in Ecuador, six in Peru, and four in the República Bolivariana de Venezuela. Solimano defines "presidential crisis" as a "situation in which a head of state (the president) does not complete his/her constitutional term for various reasons: forced removals by a coup d'état, resignation, and so on" (2005:2). Moreover, during the 20th century, Colombia was governed by a military regime only once, whereas its Andean neighbors had several military governments.

3. The vast internal displacement that resulted from the armed conflict has affected severely the fulfillment of a number of human rights for this vulnerable group,

including the rights to education and health services. The consequences of the violence are so intense that the Constitutional Court has established that expenditures on displaced people should be considered more urgent than public social expenditures. Estimates are that between 1.8 and 3.4 million people have been displaced internally in the past 10 years, and more than half of this total is younger than 18 years of age (Vargas 2007a). Aside from the post-trauma syndromes, children involved in the armed conflict face problems of maladjustment, discrimination, and stigmatizing in schools. In addition, they rarely can afford education expenses, such as enrollment fees, uniforms, and school supplies. Their physical and nutritional conditions are critical, with one in every four displaced children suffering from malnutrition (World Food Programme 2003). Several international organizations, NGOs, and public institutions give support to displaced families, emphasizing the reestablishment of the right to education. Some specific initiatives have been undertaken to guarantee their access to school. In the country's capital, Bogotá, for example, displaced children do not have any costs during their first year in school. But displaced children have not been relieved formally from all education costs in most of the country.

4. A Gini index of 0 represents perfect equality, and an index of 1 implies perfect inequality.

5. Uribe was elected first in 2002 and then reelected in 2006. His first development strategy had four main pillars, among them the construction of an equitable society with a focus on improving quality, efficiency, and access to education, health, and social security.

6. The Regime of Explicit Health Guarantees became effective in Chile in 2004. It stands out in the region as one of the few practical experiences conceived and implemented within a social guarantees framework. The regime outlines concrete administrative steps to ensure access, quality, financial protection, and opportunity for redress regarding a set of 56 medical conditions that have been established as epidemiologic priorities in the country. For more information on the Chilean case, please refer to chapter 5 of this book.

7. The Latin American and Caribbean average literacy rate was 90 percent in the same period (World Bank 2008).

8. Colombia Aprende (http://www.colombiaaprende.edu.co) is the educational portal of the Ministry of Education. It was created in 2004 as part of the sector's strategic plan for 2002–06.

9. The index measures, among other things, the level of citizen participation in a certain country.

10. Pearce (2007) defines "vicious cycles of violence" as those in which violence has become embedded in several socialization spaces. Chronic violence is characterized as a context in which acts of violence recur in different spaces and over time.

References

Chernick, Marc. 2007. "FARC-EP: From Liberal Guerrillas to Marxist Rebels to Post-Cold War Insurgents." In *Terror, Insurgency, and the State: Ending Protracted Conflicts,* ed. Marianne Heiberg, Brendan O'Leary, and John Tirman, 51–82. Philadelphia: University of Pennsylvania Press.

ECLAC (Economic Commission for Latin America and the Caribbean). 2007. *Panorama Social de América Latina 2007.* Santiago, Chile: ECLAC.

Glassman, Amanda, and Sudhanshu Handa. 2005. "Poverty, Inequality and Public Policy in the Andean Region: A Comparative Perspective." In *Political Crises, Social Conflict and Economic Development: The Political Economy of the Andean Region,* ed. Andrés Solimano, 45–72. Northampton, U.K.: Edward Elgar.

Kaufmann, Daniel, Aart Kraay, and Massimo Mastruzzi. 2008. "Governance Matters VII: Aggregate and Individual Governance Indicators, 1996–2007." Policy Research Working Paper 4654, World Bank, Washington, DC. http://papers.ssrn.com/sol3/papers.cfm?abstract_id=1148386 (accessed March 21, 2009).

Ocampo, José Antonio. 2005. "The Economy, Conflict and Governance in Colombia." In *Political Crises, Social Conflict and Economic Development: The Political Economy of the Andean Region,* ed. Andrés Solimano, 115–55. Northampton, U.K.: Edward Elgar.

OHCHR (United Nations Office of the High Commissioner for Human Rights). 2006. "Report of the United Nations High Commissioner for Human Rights on the Situation of Human Rights in Colombia." United Nations, New York.

Pearce, Jenny. 2007. "Violence, Power Sharing and Participation: Building Citizenship in Contexts of Chronic Violence." Working Paper 274, Institute of Development Studies, Brighton, U.K.

Solimano, Andrés. 2005. "Political Instability, Institutional Quality and Social Conflict in the Andes." In *Political Crises, Social Conflict and Economic Development: The Political Economy of the Andean Region,* ed. Andrés Solimano. Northampton, U.K.: Edward Elgar.

UNDP (United Nations Development Programme). 2007. *Human Development Report 2007/2008: Fighting Climate Change: Human Solidarity in a Divided World.* New York: UNDP. http://hdr.undp.org/en/media/HDR_20072008_EN_Complete.pdf (accessed March 11, 2009).

Vargas, Jorge E. 2007a. "Colombia: La educación desde la perspectiva de los derechos humanos." Unpublished manuscript, World Bank, Washington, DC.

———. 2007b. "Colombia: La salud y la seguridad social en salud desde la perspectiva de los derechos humanos." Unpublished manuscript, World Bank, Washington, DC.

World Bank. 2008. "Country Partnership Strategy for the Republic of Colombia for the Period FY2008–2011." World Bank, Washington, DC.

World Food Programme. 2003. *Vulnerabilidad a la inseguridad alimentaria de la población desplazada por la violencia en Colombia*. Bogotá, Colombia: World Food Programme. http://documents.wfp.org/stellent/groups/public/documents/ena/wfp036410.pdf (accessed March 20, 2009).

Boxes, figures, notes, and tables are indicated by b, f, n, and t respectively.

ECO-AUDIT
Environmental Benefits Statement

The World Bank is committed to preserving endangered forests and natural resources. The Office of the Publisher has chosen to print ***Building Equality and Opportunity Through Social Guarantees*** on recycled paper with 30 percent postconsumer fiber in accordance with the recommended standards for paper usage set by the Green Press Initiative, a nonprofit program supporting publishers in using fiber that is not sourced from endangered forests. For more information, visit www.greenpressinitiative.org.

Saved:
- 5 trees
- 2 million British thermal units of total energy
- 34 pounds of net greenhouse gases
- 2,132 gallons of waste water
- 72 pounds of solid waste